Training the Protector: Green Beret Instructor's Guide For Armed Professionals

"Elevating Armed Professionals to Peak Performance and Beyond"

Kyle A. Barrington

USArmy Special Forces (Ret)

Kyle "Panda" Barrington
US Army Special Forces (Retired)
Owner: Modern American Combative Arts LLC
Disabled Veteran Owned Small Business

All Rights Reserved

Copyright © 2025 by Kyle A. Barrington

This book is protected by the laws of the United States of America. Any reproduction or other unauthorized use of this material or artwork herein is prohibited without written permission of the author.

This is a book that covers aspects of training for pistol shooting, which is by definition inherently a dangerous endeavor. Never try anything presented in the guide without full knowledge and acceptance of the risk associated with that activity.

Always follow the rules of gun safety. These are including but not limited to:

- Always treat a firearms as if it is loaded, until you are positive that it is not.
- Always keep the gun pointed in a safe direction and never point it at anything you are not willing to injure or destroy.
- Always keep your finger off the trigger until you have made a conscious decision to shoot.
- Always know your target and backstop. Know what is in front of, behind and to the sides of your intended target.

An accident that takes place is the responsibility of the shooter. This book covers drills and exercises in live-fire and dry-fire settings.

Never have live ammunition near your dry-fire training area and always ensure that your firearm has been inspected and that it is unloaded why performing any dry-fire exercises.

The reader of this book acknowledges and accepts all risks associated with the live-fire and dry-fire activities and herby accepts all risks associated with any and all shooting and related activities.

Why I Do What I Do

Every book I write is more than a project—it is a journey of remembrance. With each page, I rediscover lessons I once lived, revisit memories long buried, and confront truths I cannot ignore. Writing has become my therapy. It allows me to process, to teach, and to honor those who walked beside me.

I carry with me the weight of friends laid to rest in the hallowed grounds of Arlington—far too many, more than I wish to count. For me, serving in Special Forces was never about dying for my country. It was about living for my brothers, my mission, and the families we all left behind. I never hesitated when it came to taking life in defense of my country, but I often prayed—silently, humbly—that if my time came, I would die well. Twice, when the risk was high and the outcome uncertain, I whispered to God, *"If today is the day You call me home, let me die well."*

I have faced death both in uniform and in my private life. I have looked into the eyes of true evil and felt the presence of demons. I believe, more than once, that my Guardian Angel interceded on my behalf. When I was diagnosed with cancer, my first thoughts were not for myself, but for my wife—how to solve problems quickly, how to ensure she would be cared for, how to prepare without knowing the time I had left. That mindset, forged in war and refined in crisis, shapes everything I teach today.

Armed professionals live a life most will never understand. Every day, law enforcement officers, soldiers, and guardians step forward, not knowing what awaits. Many say a quiet prayer before the shift begins: *"Lord, watch over my family. And if today is my end of watch, please watch over them in my place."* Before deployments, we wrote letters to loved ones—letters that might outlive us—telling them of our love, reminding them to take care of one another. These rituals remind us that while we may face the worst of humanity, our purpose is rooted in love, duty, and sacrifice.

This is why I do what I do. As an instructor, I owe my students everything I have—my knowledge, my skill, my experience. Too many instructors blame a student's failure on the student. I reject that. If a student falls short, it is my responsibility to search deeper, adapt, and find the way to reach them. I pray every day that my students never need to use the skills I teach. But if the day comes, I must know—deep in my soul—that their success or survival will not be limited by what I failed to give them.

That is my calling. That is why I write, why I teach, and why I strive to pass on every lesson I can. This guide is not about me—it is about you, the instructor, and the professionals you train. It is about ensuring that those who stand guard over our families, our communities, and our nation are ready.

I do this so that when the moment comes—when life and death hang in the balance—our students will not falter. They will prevail.

 In Memory of Our Fallen Brothers
"Greater love hath no man than this, that he lay down his life for his friends."

Acknowledgements:

I do need to thank all the true "Pipe Hitters" that I had the honor of working beside in the United States Army Special Forces. I know that our past does not define us, but mine did lay a very solid foundation.

To all the Instructors that I worked beside in the 3rd Special Forces Group (Airborne) Advanced Urban Combat Course. Thank you MSG Steve Park and MSG Mike Stack for allowing to me teach.

Thank you "Super" Dave Harrington for always sharing your knowledge from the Special Operations Techniques (SOT) and Special Forces Advanced Reconnaissance, Target Analysis and Exploitation Techniques Course (SFARTAETC), and for the friendship.

Thank you to the members of the 3rd Special Forces Group (Airborne) that allowed me to walk beside them into combat and continue to foster the bond that only those that have walked into the fire and returned truly understand. De Oppresso Libre , Nous Defions

Thank you to Northrop Grumman for hiring me after the US Army to teach CQB and Nuclear Warhead recovery operations.

Thank you to Adam Painchaud for trusting me to be a Master Instructor and Adjunct Instructor for the Sig Sauer Academy.

Thank you Sheriff Jeff Brown for deputizing me so that I could see behind that fence.

I want to extend my thanks to the staff of the Firearms Division at the Federal Law Enforcement Training Center. To those who shared their knowledge openly, who had the confidence in their own skill to debate ideas—and, when necessary, step onto the range to prove what truly worked—you challenged me, sharpened my thinking, and pushed me to raise my game. To those who lacked the ability or the courage and chose instead to hide behind students, you also made me stronger. You reinforced my conviction in my own ideals, methods, and skills. Every one of you, in your own way, helped forge me into a more capable instructor and a more resilient professional.

Thank you to the Federal Agents, Officers, and United States Marshals who sought me out and placed their trust in me to teach their students and future peers. Your confidence was an honor I never took lightly. Being entrusted to provide a standard for others to strive toward was both humbling and deeply motivating, and it pushed me to give my very best every single time.

I pray each day that none of my students will ever face a moment where they must use the skills I have taught them. But if that moment comes, I pray they will not falter because of any weakness in my ability or instruction. I have given them everything I have—my full skillset and my heart—so they are prepared to solve complex problems under extreme duress. They are ready, because I taught them the right way.

Most of all, I need to acknowledge and thank my better half—my wife, Cindy. For more than forty years, she has loved me with patience and fortitude, enduring my stubbornness and my BS with grace. She has been my sounding board not only for this book, but for my life. As a retired English teacher, she has also been pulled into my writing adventures, and she will be the first to attest that I am not always as articulate, patient, or concise as I should be. Yet through it all, her love and support have been unwavering, and for that I am deeply grateful.

TABLE of Contents

Adult Learning Firearms Instruction	31
Hicks Law	67
EDIP-T	71
ADDIE	77
EDIP-T vs ADDIE	81
This Illusion of Proficiency	84
Principles over Techniques	89
Inductive Fire Lessons from a Green Beret	102
Comparative Principles	106
Mind Visualization	113
The Human Response	117
Understanding the Human Body	121
Attack Indicators and Decisions	131
Proprioception	140
Proprioception Drills	141
Repetitions	149
Live Fire Standard	153
Barrington Survival Formula	161
The Principles of Combat	163
The Trinity	178
Vision	179
Instructor Knowledge	189
Visual Confirmations Levels	199
Standard Comparable Systems	203
Color Confirmation in Predictive Shooting	210
Clean Sight Package in Reactive Shooting	215
Grip Instructor View Point	220
Grip	221
Trigger Control	237
Symbiotic Relationship between Grip and Trigger	244
Pistol Presentation Index Points	252
Draw-stroke	256
Shooter Performance Objective	291
Shooting Structure Anatomical	313
Building Structure	338
Weapon Reloads	347
The 3 Ps of Pistol Presentation	368
Holding, Aiming, Firing and Timing	380
Armed Professional wears Body Armor	390
Aggressive Shooting	404

The B-8 Speed Bull Standard	408
No Light	410
The importance of Dry Fire	429
Anticipation in Shooting	446
Every Round Counts	453
Calling Your Shot	458
Distance Exposes Limitations	466
Cycle of Operations	470
Ballistics	477
The Mathematics of Designing a Shooting Drill	479
Team Room Wall	482
Finial Reflection	483

Romans 13:4
For he is GOD's servant to do you good. But if you do wrong, be afraid, for he does not bare the sword for nothing. He is GOD's servant, an agent of wrath to bring punishment on the wrongdoer.

Finial Thoughts provided by some very good professional firearms instructors and friends of mine-

"High Performance exists in a calm mind and a relaxed body". - Alan Grey

"Do the right thing, at the right time, every time." - Super Dave Harrington

Bear Bryant once said, *"No coach ever won a game by what he knows, it is what his players know that counts."* I have lived this truth in the firearms world. From thatched huts in Central and South America, to tin-roofed shacks in Africa, to tents in the Middle East and Afghanistan—on Law Enforcement and Military ranges and in shoot houses across the United States, including the Federal Law Enforcement Training Center—I have seen firsthand that it's not about what I know, but about what my students can learn, retain, and apply under pressure.

As instructors, we owe it to our students to give them everything they can absorb, to push them past comfort into growth, and to always explain the *why* behind the *how*. Excellence is not optional—it is the standard. Our students deserve nothing less, and we must demand nothing less of ourselves as their teachers.

Preface: A Professional Instructor's Statement

Over the past three decades, I have devoted my career to the study, practice, and instruction of firearms proficiency. My journey has encompassed coaching novice shooters as well as developing and mentoring elite military and federal law enforcement professionals. Each phase has enriched my comprehension not only of shooting fundamentals but also of effective instructional methodologies. Consequently, while this book is crafted for the Professional Instructor, it is rooted in the principles of advanced instruction, incorporating lesson cues, training philosophies, and insights derived from practical applications that will benefit any Armed Professional or true student of the "Art of the Gun"

The Modern American Combative Arts Creed

This book is written for the armed professional. Its purpose is not entertainment. It exists to **distill and deliver the lessons of three decades spent shooting, teaching, fighting, and surviving.** These lessons were not found in theory. They were **forged in training, tested in combat, and validated in blood.**

At Modern American Combative Arts, we hold one standard: **fundamentals are survival.** There are no advanced techniques—only fundamentals executed with precision, under pressure, and on demand. The professional who masters them lives. The one who does not, fails.

I have trained with world-class shooters, studied under legendary instructors, and fought alongside warriors who demanded absolute competence. The most profound lessons did not come from books or classrooms. They came in moments when hesitation was fatal, when decision had to be immediate, and when failure carried a price no man can afford. They came later, in reflection, when the truth cut through illusion and only performance remained.

This book is not opinion. It is not suggestion. It is a framework of **proven principles**—principles that will prepare you to train with discipline, fight with clarity, and prevail when survival is on the line.

This is not casual knowledge.
This is not optional.
This is the standard.

This volume is not an introductory manual. Instead, it serves as a professional reference for readers who already command a firm foundation in pistol marksmanship and firearms safety. Expanding upon the content of my prior works—***Responsible Citizens Seeking Responsible Training* (ISBN 9780692114452)** and *A Green Beret's Guide to Enhanced Pistol Skills* **(ISBN 9798218640354)** and **Green Beret Instructor's Guide to Everyday Carry (ISBN 979-8-218-78586-4)** this book elevates the discourse with broadened instruction, deeper contextual analysis, and refined methodologies suited for dedicated armed professional and instructors aiming to amplify their efficacy.

Within these pages, you will encounter drills, techniques, and pedagogical frameworks that I employ in my personal and professional endeavors. These approaches have been tempered in the fires of combat, honed through decades of experience, and articulated with the precision expected of a seasoned instructor. My objective is to furnish resources that bolster both formalized training settings and individual advancement. The stratified instructional structure ensures accessibility for learners while compelling instructors to refine their expertise.

As professionals, we are obligated to perpetually assess our performance, interrogate our presuppositions, and pursue ongoing development. Complacency undermines mastery. I exhort every shooter—particularly instructors—to venture beyond familiar territories in training. Explore diverse disciplines: glean from competitive marksmen, long-range specialists, and combatives authorities. Even when their emphases diverge from yours, their insights often prove unexpectedly pertinent. From competition, I acquired lessons in speed and mechanical precision; from long-range pistolcraft, I derived strategies for accuracy and error mitigation. Every field yields valuable contributions.

Instruction must be anchored in reality. As a lifelong proponent of the Second Amendment, I maintain that training should mirror potential real-world encounters.

Genuine threats transcend static range exercises. Success amid duress hinges not merely on knowledge but on what has been ingrained through realistic, pressurized rehearsals.

One of the most potent instruments for cultivating such skills is dry-fire practice. I have championed dry-fire since my early days in Special Forces. During the Special Operations Techniques (SOT) and Advanced Reconnaissance, Target Analysis, and Exploitation Techniques Course (SFARTAETC), we dedicated two hours nightly to dry-fire, following eight hours of live-fire sessions. Dry-fire was mandatory, not elective. Repetition fosters consistency, and consistency underpins excellence.

My own path recently veered dramatically when I was diagnosed with Stage III throat and tongue cancer. Compelled to reconstruct my physique after shedding over 100 pounds and substantial muscle mass, I scrutinized every motion and technique accumulated over decades. What persisted were the essential fundamentals: principles grounded in biomechanics rather than raw power. These enduring verities form the crux of this book, techniques resilient to stress, exhaustion, and hardship.

My instructional odyssey commenced as a young Green Beret in SOT and SFARTAETC. I subsequently advanced to Special Forces Advanced Urban Combat (SFAUC) Instructor and undertook multiple combat deployments. Post-Army retirement, I trained Air Force nuclear security units via Northrop Grumman. Later, at the Federal Law Enforcement Training Center (FLETC), I held the position of Senior Firearms Instructor for the Survival Shooting Training Program (SSTP) and Reactive Shooting Instructor Training Program (RSITP), contributing to their evolution into the Advanced Pistol Training Program (APTP) and Advanced Pistol Instructor Training Program (APITP).

Furthermore, I established Modern American Combative Arts, served as an adjunct instructor at Sig Sauer Academy, and functioned as a certified NRA Training Counselor, equipping hundreds of NRA instructors. Throughout, my ethos has endured:

disseminating lessons steeped in operational veracity, substantiated by rigorous training, and conveyed with pedagogical exactitude.

This is no treatise on abstract theory; it is a compendium of applied proficiency. Whether addressing grip, sight alignment, or trigger manipulation, the principles expounded here are universal and vetted in battle, validated in educational arenas, and polished across a lifetime of pedagogy. Though nomenclature may shift, the fundamentals abide eternally, resonating with historical lineages of combat shooting, such as the Japanese *Ho-Jutsu*, the "Art of the Gun."

This book delineates a layered, principled trajectory toward mastery. Whether you are an armed professional, armed citizen, a veteran instructor, or a practitioner charged with educating others, I implore you to engage this material with humility, inquisitiveness, and discerning analysis. We owe our pupils nothing short of excellence, and ourselves the rigor to evolve unceasingly. Let us commence.

9/11 Reflection

As I was finishing the final edits of this book, the anniversary of September 11th came around again. My memories of that day are not like most. They are not of watching the news in shock, or wondering what might happen next—they are of immediate action, of knowing without question that our world had just changed, and that our time had come.

The morning the first plane struck the North Tower, a teammate and I were walking out the door headed for the SFAUC range and bunkers. It was supposed to be just another day of instructor training. By the time the second plane hit, the phone rang with orders—Fort Bragg was locked down. Support Company was rolling out to secure our ammunition and explosives, and it was our job to escort them back to Group.

We knew exactly what this meant. It was game time. All the years of sweat, blood, and training—it was no longer just preparation. The war had come to us, and now we would carry it back to them.

As we rolled out with several truckloads of gear, we were flagged down on Chicken Road by a lone MP. His mission was to stop traffic. Our mission was clear. We were heavily armed, stacked and ready for anything, and when we stopped to talk, he admitted something that struck me to my core—he had a pistol but no ammunition. He was standing alone, on American soil, against an enemy we hadn't even fully seen yet, and he was empty-handed.

I pulled three prepared magazines from my kit and pressed them into his hand. I explained our orders, he nodded, and there was no doubt in his eyes about who we were or what we were about to do. His last words to us, words I will never forget, were simple and sharp: *"Good hunting."*

That night, I sat down at my desk and wrote my last will. I wrote letters to my wife and my children. And in doing so, I made peace with the warrior's philosophy that had always been whispered to us but now rang true in my heart—to live as though you are already dead. Accept your fate, sharpen your will, and walk into battle without hesitation.

I knew then, and I know now, that I was surrounded by the finest men this nation has ever produced. Honorable men. True pipehitters. Warriors who lived the motto *Nous Defions*—"We Defy." I vowed that I would never falter, that I would never let them down, no matter what came.

The training cycles began. The missions came. And the war did not disappoint. But when I look back on that day—on the chaos, the fear, the uncertainty—I don't remember despair. I remember resolve. I remember brotherhood. I remember that we stood ready when America needed us most.

Nous Defions, my brothers. I sleep well knowing I kept my vow. I did not let you down.

Philosophy of Training: Modern American Combative Arts

Listen up. Firearms training for armed professionals isn't a hobby, a sport, or a casual pursuit. It's survival. It's duty. It's the bedrock of public trust. You carry a firearm and the authority to wield it in defense of innocents. That demands more than bare-minimum skills—it requires unyielding judgment, ironclad confidence, and flawless performance under chaos where failure means death. Mediocrity? Unacceptable. Your training philosophy must demand discipline, accountability, and brutal real-world relevance. Fall short, and you betray your students, your team, and the citizens you protect.

Demonstrate or Step Aside

As instructors, you owe it to your students: prove what you preach. Words are worthless without action. Live-fire demonstration isn't optional—it's your obligation. In Special Forces, trust came from leaders who performed under fire. The same holds here. Show your students you can execute the drills you demand—accurately, efficiently, under pressure. Build their confidence. Validate your methods. Set the bar high. If you can't perform, you erode the entire program's credibility. Step up or step out.

The Trinity of Marksmanship: Your Unbreakable Foundation

Mastery starts here, with the three pillars that never waver:

- **Vision**: Process your sight picture, target, and surroundings with laser focus.
- **Structure**: Lock in physical stability to conquer recoil and deliver consistency.
- **Trigger**: Control the mechanism with discipline, no disruption, no excuses.

Teach this Trinity relentlessly. Explain it clearly. Demonstrate it precisely. Guide imitation. Drill until it's automatic. This isn't theory—it's the cycle that forges competence. But don't stop at basics. Test them under fire, with standards that crush weakness.

Enforce Rigid Standards and Inject Stress

Training without standards is just noise. Demand measurable excellence: accuracy, speed, consistency. No bending, no excuses. But standards alone won't cut it. Hammer in stress—timers, decisions, movement, consequences. Inoculate against panic. Expose flaws. Forge resilience. You must condition professionals to thrive when adrenaline surges, fatigue hits, and doubt creeps in. Reality doesn't forgive. Your training must mirror it, or you're setting them up for failure.

Drive Inductive Learning for Subconscious Mastery

In the fight, there's no time to think. Mechanics must be subconscious, freeing your mind for tactics. Achieve this through inductive learning: hands-on reps in realistic scenarios. Repeat until the gun is an extension of you—not a distraction. Shift focus outward to threats and decisions. That's where victory lives. Earn it through sweat, not shortcuts.

The Layered Learning Model: Build Them Step by Step

Tailor your approach. Not every student starts equal, so layer it:

- **Beginner**: Hammer safety, basics, and the Trinity. Explain, demonstrate, imitate, and practice.
- **Intermediate**: Ramp up pressure—time, movement, simple stress. Demand efficiency.
- **Advanced**: Throw scenarios that force adaptation, decisions, and problem-solving. Make the gun a tool for chaos.
- **Instructor**: Shift to leadership. Perform on command, diagnose flaws, adapt to all. Raise others while proving your worth.

This model scales, progresses, and demands accountability at every level.

Duty as Instructor

You carry weight heavier than your students'. Teach practical, battle-tested skills. Demonstrate under scrutiny. Demand excellence in safety, precision, professionalism. Fail here, and you jeopardize lives. Own it.

At Modern American Combative Arts, fundamentals aren't optional—they're survival. Master them or perish. No "advanced techniques" exist; only flawless execution of basics under duress. The elite shooter isn't flashy—they're reliable, predictable, and automatic. Train until wrong is impossible.

Growth spirals: revisit grip, stance, vision, and trigger. Each cycle deepens the imprint. Forge neurological reflexes through reps, stress, and adversity.

Center on the Combat Triad:

1. **Marksmanship**: Hit precisely, repeatedly—no misses.
2. **Gun-Handling**: Operate smoothly, safely, efficiently—every time.
3. **Mindset**: Decide fast under pressure, with unbreakable resolve.

Ingrain this triad until mind and body fuse. Perform at combat speed: see, move, manipulate, and engage seamlessly. Earn it rep by rep—no simulations, no cheats.

Seasoned pros get it: humility drives you back to basics. Skills fade; ego blinds. Re-center relentlessly.

This philosophy distills three decades of soldiering, instructing, combat. Lessons from violence, not books. From teammates who demanded perfection because failure killed.

Tools evolve—optics, calibers—but principles endure: vision, structure, trigger, mindset, composure.

The pistol? It's martial art incarnate—an extension of your will to project force, deter, defend with precision.

Competence: Your Non-Negotiable Obligation

Your Obligations are Non-Negotiable
Competence Is Duty
The Stakes Demand Nothing Less

Humility drives you back to the basics

For you—armed professionals and instructors—competence is duty. To self, team, public. Forge it through fundamentals, standards, stress, and progression.

This isn't theory. It's proven. Adopt it, adapt it, live it. Stakes demand nothing less. Get to work.

Instructor Truths: Addressing Deficiencies in Instructor Knowledge

In the firearms industry, a myriad of beliefs and methodologies abound. I readily concede that any instructor proclaiming "this is the only way" is likely mistaken.

Many instructors derive their doctrines and qualification standards from their personal capabilities—or, more accurately, their limitations.

If an instructor asserts that "all gunfights occur within 21 feet, rendering training beyond 7 yards unnecessary," one might reasonably infer that they themselves struggle to meet standards at greater distances.

Distance reveals shortcomings, and most instructors hesitate to expose their vulnerabilities to students. At the 7-yard line, anyone can appear competent. Yet, it is essential to recognize that errors persist, even if the target appears acceptable, a dangerously flawed assumption for any competent instructor.

Studies indicate that elite Special Operations personnel experience a 30% to 50% performance degradation in actual kinetic encounters compared to their peak range performance. This effectively halves engagement distances, even for operators firing 2,000 rounds weekly. Average law enforcement officers suffer a 70% to 85% decline, reducing viable hits to roughly 3 feet. Factoring in scoring zones, impacts often fall outside effective areas.

Dismissing training beyond 21 feet fosters a perilous, potentially lethal mindset.

Another common instructor limitation involves advocating a slow, deliberate trigger press: taking up slack, reaching the wall, and gradually building pressure until the shot breaks.

This approach persists among instructors with rudimentary skills. If it dominates your methodology, your students and you will remain at a journeyman level.

Under stress, the human body instinctively squares to the threat, keeps both eyes open, focuses on the target, and rapidly actuates the trigger until the slide locks back, this is a fundamental physiological response.

Students must eventually confront real-world conditions and learn to operate effectively therein.

I maintain that only instructors proficient at speed from the 25-yard line, and capable of imparting those skills, fulfill their responsibilities.

What constitutes effectiveness at distance with speed? I delve into speed bulls and the 300-point aggregate later in this book, but these form the foundation of my philosophy.

I was taught and firmly believe, that a proficient shooter should draw and hit an A/C-zone target (approximately 11 by 24 inches, akin to the "bottle" on standard qualification silhouettes) in 2.5 seconds at any distance with any handgun.

FBI statistics suggest most gunfights last three seconds and involve three rounds; thus, a 2.5-second single-shot draw enables three rounds in three seconds.

For instance, online videos demonstrate my drawing a SIG P365 subcompact with iron sights and hitting an A/C-zone target at 50 yards in under 2.5 seconds a basic competency, not an extraordinary feat. With any full-size pistol I own, I achieve the same at 100 yards. This should be the instructional standard.

Distance exposes limitations; speed reveals inefficiencies. Combining both unveils all shooter and instructor deficiencies.

I employ the speed bull as my baseline: 10 rounds in 10 seconds from the 25-yard line on a B-8 bullseye target. Instructor proficiency requires 90 or better; basic competency, 70 or above.

This standard demonstrates mastery of visual cues, sight picture and alignment, trigger control and reset, and recoil management. It also illustrates that the trigger is not manipulated slowly and deliberately.

A student scoring 70 or better possesses foundational understanding and application of shooting fundamentals.

Never allow instructor Limitations to Compromise student Learning

Instructors must Self assess, avoiding Complacency

Instructors who deem this unnecessary likely lack the requisite knowledge and skills. I challenge them to refute that it exemplifies high proficiency.

Even the straightforward Vickers 10-10-10 drill—10 rounds from the holster in 10 seconds at the 10-yard line, all within a 10-inch circle, eludes most shooters.

Having trained tens of thousands in military and law enforcement shooters, I use the Vickers drill as an eye-opener. In follow-on sessions for FLETC graduates who passed qualifications, most full-time officers and agents fail initially.

The same holds in advanced pistol instructor classes: many fail to fire all rounds or keep them centered.

This underpins my methodologies. No excuse exists for armed professionals or instructors unable to perform it, a clear indicator of deficient foundational principles.

I often hear dismissals of "competition stuff." Though not a competitor, I collaborate with exceptional ones and engage in informed discussions. Not all competition techniques transfer to everyday carry (EDC) or law enforcement, but gun handling does.

Drawing from personal experience grants insight into diverse disciplines. Instructors must explore other shooting branches for self-improvement.

Bullseye shooters impart sights and trigger mastery; at 50 yards, nuances emerge. You must then integrate speed.

A USPSA Grand Master teaches velocity and efficiency; faster handling, reloads. Movements may be abrupt and prolonged beyond tactical "up-seen-down" timing, but adaptation yields EDC applicability.

Instructors must self-assess, avoiding complacency in "good enough" or student superiority. Qualifying at 300 with ample time does not mirror real-world demands. Seek evaluators and trainers for growth.

As a professional instructor, I train across disciplines due to broad understanding, but I refer students to experts when needed. For example, teaching a "Girls & Guns" class in Florida, a participant queried shotgun competition: shooting, reloading while moving to positions, timed. She over-verified shots, inefficiently positioned the shotgun, and halted for dropped shells. I advised rolling the shotgun onto her shoulder (loading port up) while moving immediately post-shot, unfixable errors demand progression. Hold two rounds per load; avoid stops. Efficient handling and movement boosted her scores dramatically.

Readers should grasp the "why" behind my book's tenets. Rooted in Special Forces, they encompass diverse disciplines. As my prior books note, I am a martial artist viewing pistol shooting similarly: proficiency levels vary, styles differ, but skilled practitioners perpetually improve.

I pray daily that students avoid lethal kinetic encounters, but if compelled, ensure my knowledge and demonstrable skills prevent their failure.

Never permit your instructor limitations to compromise your students.

Good Instructors Never Stop being Students

Be Adaptive
Observent and
Humble
Always Learn

I once taught a two-day class at NRA Headquarters in Virginia through a SIG Sauer program for NFL players. Most were from Washington or Baltimore, with a few from Miami and Denver. Incredible athletes. One long snapper, in the league for ten years, had never shot a pistol. We outfitted them with SIG 226 X5s for their large hands. I asked how he picked it up so quickly. He said, "I'm a professional athlete. I'm used to being coached and following the process." I learned that if I explained in detail, demonstrated to standard, let them imitate, and then practice, the results could be extraordinary.

At FLETC, I have seen thousands of students. With experience, I can diagnose most shooting issues in seconds. But even after decades, students still surprise me. I have unloaded a Remington 870 with every shell loaded backwards including one chambered through sheer effort. I have seen a pistol loaded with 9mm ammunition on qualification day when the issued caliber was .40, and been told, "I knew it was different, but it still fit."

An instructor must read people. Each student requires a unique approach. Recently, a young woman broke down in tears during on the firing line. She was a Division One college rugby player with a 4.0 GPA, training for a Federal agent position. She was tense in the shoulders, causing unnecessary gun movement. Her tears came from frustration, this was the first skill she couldn't master instantly. One hundred rounds later, with calm coaching and a detailed breakdown of cause and effect, she was calling her shots. Days later, she qualified in the high 90 percentile.

Adapting Your Style

Teaching 18-year-old warriors is easy. The challenge lies in modifying your style for children, seniors, or women. Differences in age, sex, and background create barriers that require adaptation. I have learned the most from teaching people unlike me.

Teaching Green Berets in the Special Forces Advanced Urban Combat course was straightforward, we shared a common reference. Teaching women has been my greatest challenge and my greatest learning experience. Women often require a better answer than men, they want the "why" and the "how," and they are not afraid to ask questions. Many men would rather figure it out alone.

I once taught a "Girls with Guns" class in Florida. I was confident the students were learning, judging by their targets. Later, the range owner told me that one student, Crystal, nearly quit because my delivery was too intense. That was early in my relationship with A Girl & a Gun. My wife began attending these classes, sitting quietly in the back to provide feedback during the drive home. That female perspective changed how I taught younger women at FLETC.

Physical Challenges

Age and physical condition also influence instruction. I taught a woman in her mid-80s with severe arthritis who lived alone and insisted on self-sufficiency. She couldn't rack her pistol, so we developed a method using an empty magazine to lock the slide to the rear, then inserting a loaded magazine. I would never have taught this technique under normal circumstances, but necessity drove innovation.

An 87-year-old man in New Hampshire impressed me by moving slowly to the line with a cane, then sheathing it to draw a 1911 and shoot dime-sized groups. His cane was an ASP-style defensive tool, another lesson in adaptive equipment.

In South Carolina, I met an older man who carried cross-draw. When I asked why, he said his first carjacking taught him that a seat belt made strong-side carry inaccessible. His second carjacking proved that practice still mattered. By the third, with cross-draw, he successfully defended himself. Lesson learned.

Diagnosing Before Adjusting

Many instructors want to "call for fire" and adjust after each shot in an initial assessment. The problem is that one shot tells you little. At FLETC, our ten-round assessment is a grouping exercise. I encourage letting all ten rounds go, then analyzing the group. Ben Stoeger reinforced this in his Doubles Diagnostic, groups tell the real story, fliers included.

Learning From Others

I had the privilege of co-teaching with Ken Hackathorn. Rather than ask questions, I would state my diagnosis of a student's issue and wait to see if he agreed. I didn't want to influence his analysis, a reaffirming approach.

I have also trained under "Super" Dave Harrington, later assisting in his classes. During a class in Savannah, Dave invited me to shoot the Speed Bull Drill beside him. That day, I scored a 96 with my SIG 226; he scored a 94 with his Glock 19. He simply said, "That was a nice piece of work." A very fond memory and shooting reaffirmation!

Final Lesson

Instructing firearms for 35 years has taught me that the best instructors never stop being students. Take classes, teach everyone from children to the elderly and embrace every opportunity to adapt. The next lesson that changes your teaching might come from the most unexpected place.

Methodology, Adult Learning, and the Context of Firearms Instruction

With over three decades of professional experience as a firearms instructor, I have forged a philosophy and methodology shaped by thousands of hours on the range, in combat zones, and in classrooms. My approach is rooted in **inductive learning**—the belief that true proficiency is not achieved by rote memorization but developed through experience. Skills are strengthened when shooters work through repetitions, make mistakes, adapt, and ultimately succeed under controlled conditions. Errors on the range become lessons that, if properly cultivated, may one day save a life.

At the center of this methodology stands the **EDIP-T model—Explain, Demonstrate, Imitate, Practice, and Test**. This sequence provides a clear framework for teaching high-stakes kinesthetic skills. First, I explain the concept and its purpose. Then I demonstrate the task, showing the standard with precision. The student imitates under direct supervision, internalizing the physical process. Through practice, they reinforce skill until it becomes second nature. Finally, testing validates that the student can perform under pressure, not just once, but consistently.

The EDIP-T model works because it unites the **body and the mind**. Yet no single method is universal. Every student brings different experiences, temperaments, and learning preferences to the range. The skilled instructor must recognize these variables and adapt methods accordingly. Instruction is not about the instructor—it is about the student's ability to absorb, retain, and perform. A professional instructor therefore becomes a craftsman, adjusting tools and techniques to fit the mission and the learner.

The Role of Adult Learning Theory

In the domain of **armed professionals—law enforcement officers, military personnel, and protective security specialists—errors carry catastrophic consequences.** It is not enough for instructors to know how to shoot. They must also understand **adult learning theory, or andragogy.** Adult learners differ from children in critical ways: they arrive with habits, biases, prior training, and deeply ingrained experiences. They demand relevance, they expect to understand why they are being taught something, and they retain knowledge best when training is practical and directly tied to their real-world responsibilities.

Failure to respect these principles leads to predictable outcomes: poor comprehension, shallow skill retention, and unnecessary risk in the field. Conversely, when instructors deliberately address the needs of adult learners, training becomes not just effective, but transformative. Students learn to handle firearms responsibly, apply skills with discipline, and retain proficiency over the long term.

To meet these challenges, the professional instructor must deliberately employ several frameworks:

- **Keirsey's Four Temperaments** (Rationals, Guardians, Idealists, Artisans) to account for differences in personality and approach to learning.
- **The Three Primary Modalities** (visual, auditory, kinesthetic) to ensure instruction resonates with every type of learner.
- **Inductive Learning** to empower students to discover, adapt, and own the skill for themselves rather than relying solely on top-down instruction.

When these elements are integrated into the EDIP-T framework, the result is instruction that connects with the learner, sustains proficiency, and ultimately saves lives.

Distinctions Across Professional Contexts

Not all armed professionals share the same mission, and therefore, not all should be trained in the same way. **Context dictates application, and application dictates methodology.**

- **Military**: Military personnel must achieve proficiency in lethal application of force, often at distance, under extreme stress, and within team-based environments. Training emphasizes combat marksmanship, small-unit tactics, and survivability under fire. The standard is uncompromising: in combat, failure is not an option.
- **Law Enforcement**: Officers operate in civilian environments where every round fired carries immense legal, moral, and tactical weight. Training must therefore stress threat recognition, escalation and de-escalation, and precision shooting in close proximity to innocent bystanders. Officers must be able to transition instantly from restraint to lethal force, and their decisions will be judged under both law and public scrutiny.
- **Protective Security**: The protector's role is fundamentally defensive. The mission is to **avoid, deter, and prevent threats** while shielding the principal. Firearms are a tool of last resort. Training emphasizes situational awareness, early threat recognition, and controlled, surgical responses in crowded or confined spaces. Accuracy and discretion are paramount.
- **Church Security**: This environment is unique. The mission is defense within a sanctuary—a place filled with families, children, and noncombatants. Training must therefore prioritize rapid threat identification, absolute fire discipline, and decisive but restrained action. The church security professional must balance vigilance with compassion, recognizing that their role is not just to protect life but to preserve the sanctity of the environment itself.

The Instructor's Responsibility

The common denominator across all these domains is the **responsibility of the instructor**. A true firearms instructor does not rely on a single formula. They refine, adapt, and demand accountability—of themselves and their students. Training a Special Forces operator, a patrol officer, a protective agent, or a church security volunteer requires not only technical expertise but also mastery of adult learning principles and contextual nuance.

The stakes are too high for complacency. In firearms instruction, the cost of ignorance is measured in lives. An instructor who fails to understand adult learning, ignores the distinctions of mission context, or neglects the value of inductive learning is not just ineffective—they are dangerous. Excellence in instruction is not optional. It is a professional duty and a moral obligation.

Adult Learning Theory (Andragogy)

Malcolm Knowles' Andragogy framework highlights that adult learners are self-directed, experience-driven, and motivated by immediate relevance. Key principles include:

- **Experience as a Foundation**: Adults learn best when new knowledge builds on prior experiences, allowing them to connect abstract concepts to tangible, lived realities.
- **Relevance**: Training must connect to real-world applications or personal goals, ensuring learners see the direct impact on their safety, proficiency, or decision-making.
- **Readiness**: Adults are motivated to learn when they see immediate value in the material, such as how it enhances survival in high-threat situations.

- **Self-Direction**: Adults prefer self-directed learning and problem-solving over rote memorization, fostering ownership and intrinsic motivation.
- **Diverse Learning Styles**: Adults favor visual, auditory, or kinesthetic methods based on their dominant learning style, requiring instructors to adapt dynamically.

Firearms instructors must design training that is engaging, practical, and relevant to learners' goals, aligning with these principles. Central to this is the integration of inductive learning, a process where learners derive general principles from specific observations and experiences. Unlike deductive learning, which starts with rules and applies them to examples, inductive learning encourages adults to explore patterns through trial and error, experimentation, and reflection. This is particularly vital in firearms training because it mirrors real-world unpredictability—learners might observe multiple shooting scenarios to generalize about optimal grip under stress, building adaptive skills rather than rigid adherence to theory. Inductive approaches enhance critical thinking and retention by making learning active and discovery-based, reducing the likelihood of mechanical errors in life-or-death situations.

Moreover, repetitions, self-learning, and experiences are necessary components that reinforce Andragogy. Repetitions solidify muscle memory through consistent practice, transforming conscious effort into automatic responses; without them, skills degrade under pressure, increasing accident risks. Self-learning empowers adults to explore at their own pace, reflecting on mistakes and successes to internalize knowledge deeply—essential for building confidence and autonomy in solo practice sessions. Experiences, both prior and newly acquired, serve as the bedrock, allowing learners to contextualize new information; neglecting this can lead to superficial understanding, where trainees fail to apply skills beyond controlled environments. Together, these elements ensure training is not just informative but transformative, equipping adults with resilient, adaptable expertise.

Learning Modalities

- **Visual Learners**: Prefer step-by-step demonstrations, diagrams, and videos, benefiting from observing clear examples to visualize techniques like sight alignment.
- **Auditory Learners**: Excel with verbal explanations, discussions, and sound cues, thriving in interactive lecture settings where instructors describe recoil anticipation.
- **Kinesthetic Learners**: Learn best through hands-on practice and physical repetition to build muscle memory, such as repeatedly dry-firing to ingrain trigger control.

Incorporating all three modalities creates a versatile learning environment that addresses diverse learner needs. **Inductive learning** amplifies this by encouraging learners to experiment across modalities—e.g., kinesthetic learners might induce principles of stance stability through repeated physical trials, while visual learners derive patterns from video replays of their own performances. Repetitions are crucial here, as they allow for iterative refinement; without sufficient repeats, kinesthetic learners may not achieve the neural pathways needed for instinctive actions. Self-learning integrates by letting individuals revisit modalities independently, such as reviewing personal videos or practicing solos, while experiences provide the raw data for induction, turning past mishaps into future safeguards.

Keirsey's Temperament-Based Learning Styles

David Keirsey's temperament theory identifies four learning styles that align with adult learner preferences in firearms training:

- **Rationals (NT)**:
    - **Traits**: Analytical, logical, enjoy problem-solving and critical thinking.
    - **Learning Preference**: Structured, theory-driven training with lectures, handouts, and data analysis.
    - **Firearms Application**: Excel in understanding ballistics, safety protocols, or technical aspects (e.g., explaining bullet drop physics or recoil management). For Rationals, inductive learning is key as it allows them to hypothesize from data points, like analyzing shot groupings to induce trajectory principles.
- **Guardians (SJ)**:
    - **Traits**: Practical, dependable, prefer structure and tangible outcomes.
    - **Learning Preference**: Hands-on activities, clear rules, and real-world examples.
    - **Firearms Application**: Thrive in disciplined settings with clear objectives, such as range drills or safety procedures. Repetitions build their reliability, ensuring procedural adherence through habitual practice.
- **Idealists (NF)**:
    - **Traits**: Creative, intuitive, value relationships and abstract thinking.
    - **Learning Preference**: Discussions, exploration of theories, and collaborative problem-solving.
    - **Firearms Application**: Enjoy analyzing tactical scenarios or ethical considerations in use-of-force situations. Self-learning suits them by

enabling reflective journaling on experiences, inducing ethical frameworks from personal narratives.

- **Artisans (SP)**:
    - **Traits**: Hands-on, experimental, thrive on immediate feedback and tangible results.
    - **Learning Preference**: Practical exercises, teamwork, and creative problem-solving.
    - **Firearms Application**: Excel in scenario-based training, live-fire drills, or competitive exercises. Experiences are vital, as Artisans induce skills from immersive trials, with repetitions honing their improvisational edge.

Inductive learning is indispensable across temperaments because it promotes generalization from specifics, fostering adaptability crucial when theoretical knowledge meets chaotic realities. Repetitions ensure procedural fluency, self-learning encourages personalization, and experiences ground induction in authenticity, preventing over-reliance on untested assumptions.

Applying Learning Styles to Firearms Instruction

To optimize training, instructors should align methods with learners' temperaments:

- **Rationals**: Provide logic-based training focusing on safety and precision, incorporating inductive exercises like data-driven shot analysis.
- **Guardians**: Incorporate structured, practical exercises with clear objectives, emphasizing repetitions for mastery.
- **Idealists**: Foster creative discussions and collaborative problem-solving, using self-learning to explore ethical inductions.
- **Artisans**: Emphasize hands-on practice with immediate feedback, leveraging experiences for inductive skill-building.

This approach ensures engagement and effective skill acquisition across diverse learners, with inductive processes enhancing transferability by letting learners form their own rules from repeated, self-directed experiences.

Instructional Methodologies in Firearms Training

Firearms instructors can employ various methodologies, each suited to different learner types and training goals, while integrating inductive elements, repetitions, self-learning, and experiences for holistic development:

1. **Authoritative/Drill Instructor Style**:
    - **Description**: A structured, command-driven approach where instructors lead with authority and expect precise execution.
    - **Pros**:
        - Ensures safety and discipline.
        - Effective in high-pressure environments (e.g., law enforcement or military training).
        - Builds confidence through repetition, allowing inductive pattern recognition over time.
    - **Cons**:
        - May intimidate or demotivate some learners.
        - Limits creativity and autonomy, potentially hindering self-learning.
    - **Firearms Application**: Ideal for beginners to instill safety and fundamentals through repetition and immediate correction (e.g., proper trigger discipline in a basic handgun class), with experiences accumulating to induce broader principles.

2. **Facilitator/Coaching Style**:
   - **Description**: A guiding approach where instructors provide feedback, ask questions, and encourage self-discovery.
   - **Pros**:
     - Promotes autonomy and critical thinking via inductive questioning.
     - Engages learners and builds confidence through self-directed exploration.
     - Effective for intermediate to advanced students, incorporating personal experiences.
   - **Cons**:
     - May require more time for beginners to grasp fundamentals.
     - Less effective in high-pressure settings requiring quick compliance.
   - **Firearms Application**: Suited for refining skills in concealed carry classes, encouraging problem-solving in scenario-based exercises where repetitions reinforce induced strategies.
3. **Task-Oriented/Scenario-Based Training**:
   - **Description**: Training centers on realistic tasks or threat scenarios, with instructors guiding the process.
   - **Pros**:
     - Directly applicable to real-world situations, facilitating inductive learning from simulations.
     - Enhances practical problem-solving and situational awareness through experiential immersion.
     - Highly engaging and relevant, with repetitions building resilience.

- **Cons**:
  - Can overwhelm beginners without foundational knowledge.
  - Requires skilled facilitation to avoid resistance and promote self-learning.
- **Firearms Application**: Common in defensive shooting, such as home defense or active shooter drills, where experiences drive inductive generalizations about threats.

4. **Demonstration-Heavy/Modeling Approach**:
   - **Description**: Instructors model skills, and students replicate them, often with live-fire practice.
   - **Pros**:
     - Builds trust and confidence through clear demonstrations, setting the stage for inductive imitation.
     - Effective for teaching technical skills with repetitions for muscle memory.
   - **Cons**:
     - Can become repetitive if overused, stifling self-learning.
     - Limits student autonomy unless paired with experiential reflection.
   - **Firearms Application**: Used in introductory classes to demonstrate techniques like grip, stance, or trigger control, allowing learners to induce refinements from practice.

5. **Lecture-Based/Didactic Teaching**:
   - **Description**: Traditional lecture-style teaching with minimal student interaction.
   - **Pros**:
     - Efficient for delivering foundational knowledge, which can spark inductive curiosity.

- Covers material quickly, leaving room for self-directed application.
        - **Cons**:
            - Less engaging for some learners, ignoring kinesthetic repetitions.
            - May not address diverse learning styles effectively without experiential ties.
        - **Firearms Application**: Used in classroom settings to cover theory and safety basics, enhanced by encouraging learners to induce applications from their experiences.
6. **Peer-to-Peer/Group Learning**:
    - **Description**: Students work in pairs or groups, reviewing performance or solving problems collaboratively.
    - **Pros**:
        - Promotes teamwork and engagement through shared inductive discussions.
        - Allows practical application with instructor supervision, incorporating diverse experiences.
    - **Cons**:
        - Challenging to manage without clear guidance.
        - May not suit highly independent learners who prefer solo repetitions.
    - **Firearms Application**: Effective in competitive shooting, where students learn from peers' techniques, using self-learning to refine induced insights.

Inductive learning elevates these methodologies by shifting from passive reception to active pattern-forming, making training more resilient. Repetitions are essential for embedding skills neurologically, self-learning for personalization and motivation, and experiences for grounding induction in reality—without them, methodologies risk producing rote performers ill-equipped for variables.

Comparison of Methodologies

Methodology	Description	Adult Learning Fit	Firearms Example
Authoritative/Drill Instructor	Strict, command-driven; expects precise execution.	Best for Guardians; limits autonomy for self-directed learners, but supports repetitions.	Demonstrating trigger discipline with immediate correction and inductive pattern spotting.
Facilitator/Coaching	Guides students, encourages self-discovery and problem-solving.	Supports self-directed learning; ideal for Rationals and Idealists, emphasizing experiences.	Guiding concealed carry scenarios, fostering decision-making through self-learning.
Task-Oriented/Scenario-Based	Realistic tasks/scenarios with guided practice.	Engages Artisans and Idealists; may overwhelm beginners, but builds via induction.	Practicing home defense drills with real-world scenarios and repetitions.
Demonstration-Heavy/Modeling	Instructors model skills; students replicate.	Suits visual and kinesthetic learners; less effective for autonomous learners without self-reflection.	Modeling proper stance and grip in introductory classes, inducing from demos.

Methodology	Description	Adult Learning Fit	Firearms Example
Lecture-Based/Didactic	Traditional lectures with minimal interaction.	Efficient for Rationals; less engaging for kinesthetic learners, enhanced by experiential ties.	Delivering safety and theory basics in a classroom setting, sparking induction.
Peer-to-Peer/Group Learning	Collaborative learning in pairs or groups.	Promotes Idealist collaboration; requires strong instructor oversight for repetitions.	Peer review of techniques in competitive shooting drills, drawing on shared experiences.
EDIP+T Model	Combines explanation, demonstration, imitation, practice, and testing.	Balances all learning styles; aligns with Andragogy's self-directed principles, incorporating all elements.	Teaching handgun grip through structured progression with feedback, testing, and induction.

Every firearms instructor must command a thorough mastery of adult learning principles, including Andragogy, diverse learning modalities, and Keirsey's temperament styles, alongside proven methodologies like the EDIP+T model—there is no room for compromise in this arena where lives hang in the balance. The inclusion of **inductive learning,** repetitions, self-learning, and experiences elevates this mastery, ensuring trainees not only absorb information but actively construct knowledge that withstands real-world chaos. Failure to internalize and apply this knowledge invites disaster: preventable accidents, ineffective training, and eroded public trust in responsible firearm use. It is your imperative duty to integrate these elements rigorously, ensuring that every session produces competent, safety-conscious individuals equipped for real-world demands; anything less is unacceptable and endangers us all.

Instructor Note: After more than three decades as a professional firearms instructor, my philosophy and methods have been honed through relentless trial and error on the range, embodying the inductive learning process where shooters forge genuine mastery via experiential discovery rather than mechanical repetition. The EDIP-T model—Explain, Demonstrate, Imitate, Practice, and Test—remains a cornerstone for imparting kinesthetic skills, harmonizing cognitive understanding with physical execution. However, true instructional excellence demands a deep grasp of adult learning theories, such as andragogy's emphasis on self-directed growth; diverse learning modalities, including

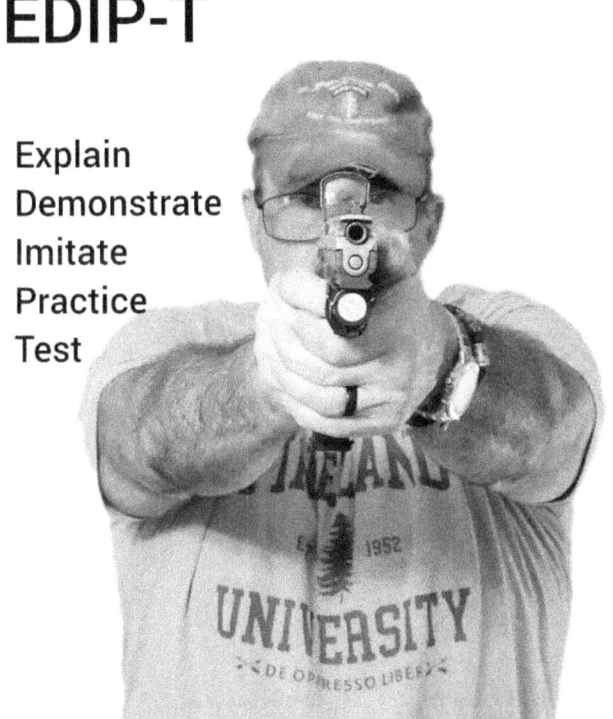

visual, auditory, and kinesthetic approaches; and individual learning styles, like experiential or reflective preferences, to tailor content effectively. As instructors, we must actively seek and integrate the methodologies that resonate most with our own expertise while optimizing outcomes for our students, ensuring safety, proficiency, and empowerment in every session

The EDIP+T Model: A Comprehensive Framework for Armed Professional Firearms Training

The EDIP+T model—**Explain, Demonstrate, Imitate, Practice, Test**—is a structured, military-derived instructional framework designed to ensure effective skill transfer under stress. It integrates authoritative instruction, facilitative learning, and demonstrative modeling, making it highly effective for teaching firearms skills to armed professionals. By aligning with adult learning principles, EDIP+T builds confidence, reinforces safety, and develops reliable performance through repetition, guided feedback, and progressive autonomy.

1. Explain

Purpose: Establish mental clarity before physical execution.

The instructor begins by clearly defining the skill, its purpose, and its operational relevance. Learners are given context on **what the skill is, why it matters, when it is applied, and how it integrates into the larger shooting process.** This ensures students understand not only the mechanics but also the tactical decision-making behind the action.

Firearms Example: Before teaching an emergency reload, the instructor explains the difference between an emergency and tactical reload, why speed is critical in a fight, and how the technique preserves combat effectiveness.

Best Practices:

- Use precise terminology (grip, sight alignment, and follow-through).
- Break the technique into clear, digestible steps.
- Anticipate common errors and misconceptions.

- Always integrate **safety language**—safe direction, trigger finger discipline, muzzle awareness.

2. Demonstrate

Purpose: Provide an exact visual model for replication.

The instructor performs the skill smoothly and correctly, showing it both in real time and in slow motion. Demonstrations should be performed from multiple perspectives so students can fully grasp the movement. Armed professionals copy not only the technique, but also **efficiency of motion and adherence to safety protocols.**

Firearms Example: Demonstrating a draw from concealment with proper grip, sight picture, and smooth presentation.

Best Practices:

- Maintain flawless safety habits—every movement you model will be copied.
- Emphasize economy of motion—students replicate inefficiencies as readily as correct movements.
- Use deliberate, deliberate slow-motion breakdowns for complex techniques (malfunction clearance, strong-hand only shooting).

3. Imitate

Purpose: Transition from observation to supervised execution.

Students replicate the skill under close instructor supervision. This stage moves knowledge from visual input to kinesthetic performance. Immediate feedback prevents bad habits from forming and accelerates learning.

Firearms Example: Students dry-fire a reload exactly as demonstrated, pausing mid-action when the instructor calls "freeze" to correct hand placement or body mechanics.

Best Practices:

- Start with **dry-fire repetitions** before progressing to live-fire.
- Keep drills short and focused to prevent fatigue-induced errors.
- Use corrective feedback in the moment—address errors immediately, not later.
- Encourage students to **verbalize the sequence** as they move; this reinforces mental mapping.

4. Practice

Purpose: Build automaticity through structured repetition.

Students perform multiple repetitions under varying conditions, refining their skill through feedback and self-adjustment. Practice begins slow and deliberate, then builds to speed and stress. Armed professionals must train until execution becomes **unconscious competence.**

Firearms Example: Repetitive failure-to-fire clearance drills, progressing from controlled dry-fire to live-fire at full speed under time constraints.

Best Practices:

- Progress from isolated skills to integrated drills (e.g., reloads into transitions and movement).
- Introduce variable conditions—different distances, lighting, time pressure—to replicate operational stress.

- Track performance with **objective metrics** (time, accuracy) and introduce corrective drills when plateaus occur.

5. Test

Purpose: Confirm skill transfer and performance under realistic conditions. Testing verifies that the skill is not only retained but repeatable under stress. This stage closes the loop, giving both the student and instructor an objective measure of proficiency.

Firearms Example: Running a timed El Presidente drill to evaluate transitions, reloads, and accuracy under pressure. Scenario-based training—low-light, multiple targets, decision-making—ensures the skill holds in operational environments.

Best Practices:

- Conduct timed and scored evaluations to quantify performance.
- Incorporate stressors—physical exertion, time pressure, complex decision-making.
- Require students to self-diagnose errors, reinforcing critical thinking and self-correction.
- Provide both **objective scoring** and **subjective feedback** to encourage continued progression.

Why EDIP+T Works for Armed Professionals

- **Safety First:** Structured explanation and demonstration reinforce proper handling before students touch a firearm.
- **Progressive Learning:** Each step builds upon the last, preventing overwhelm and ensuring comprehension.

- **Error Control:** Mistakes are identified and corrected early, preventing reinforcement of poor habits.
- **Retention Under Stress:** Testing ensures that skills survive the transition from the training environment to real-world defensive encounters.
- **Adult Learning Alignment:** The model respects learner autonomy, balances authoritative instruction with self-discovery, and incorporates visual, auditory, and kinesthetic elements.

Step	Purpose	Instructor Actions	Firearms Example	Key Notes
Explain	Build mental clarity before action.	Define skill, purpose, context. Use precise terms.	Emergency reload—explain need for speed.	Always stress safety language.
Demonstrate	Provide accurate model for replication.	Show in real time and slow motion, multiple angles.	Draw from concealment with perfect grip.	Students copy efficiency and safety.
Imitate	Transition to supervised execution.	Guide step-by-step, freeze errors, correct instantly.	Dry-fire reload under supervision.	Keep reps short; reinforce mental mapping.
Practice	Build muscle memory through repetition.	Start slow, progress to live-fire, vary conditions.	Failure-to-fire clearances under time.	Track accuracy and speed; break plateaus.
Test	Confirm retention under stress.	Run timed/scenario drills; provide feedback.	El Presidente drill under time pressure.	Simulate real-world conditions.

This refined framework presents EDIP+T not only as an instructional tool, but as a professional standard for firearms training that ensures safety, skill mastery, and performance under stress.

The EDIP+T Model: A Comprehensive Instructional Framework for Armed Professional Firearms Training

The EDIP+T model—**Explain, Demonstrate, Imitate, Practice, Test**—provides a structured, military-derived instructional approach designed to ensure the effective transfer of firearms skills to armed professionals. This article examines its relevance to firearms instruction, its grounding in adult learning principles, and its application to law enforcement and military contexts. By integrating authoritative direction, demonstrative modeling, facilitative feedback, and iterative assessment, EDIP+T ensures that skills are taught, reinforced, and validated in a manner that supports safe, reliable, and mission-relevant performance.

Instruction in firearms skills differs fundamentally from recreational shooting or competitive marksmanship. For armed professionals, training is not merely technical—it is ethical, legal, and life-preserving. Instructional frameworks must therefore emphasize clarity, safety, and retention under stress. The EDIP+T model, originally derived from military pedagogy, is particularly suited to this task. It provides instructors with a step-by-step methodology that aligns with adult learning theory (Knowles, 1984), principles of motor skill acquisition (Schmidt & Lee, 2011), and operational requirements of law enforcement and military service.

The EDIP+T Framework

1. Explain

The instructor provides a clear, detailed explanation of the technique, emphasizing its **purpose, execution, and tactical relevance.** This stage establishes mental clarity prior to physical execution and anchors new information to learners' prior experiences.

- **Objective:** Build conceptual understanding.

- **Firearms Example:** Before teaching an emergency reload, the instructor explains the difference between emergency and tactical reloads, when each applies, and how reloads affect survival in armed encounters.

Instructional Consideration: Explanations must integrate **safety language**—safe direction, trigger discipline, and muzzle awareness—into every phase.

2. Demonstrate

The instructor provides an **accurate visual model** of the skill. Demonstrations should be performed smoothly, correctly, and from multiple perspectives. For complex actions, deliberate slow-motion demonstration clarifies sequencing and reinforces economy of motion.

- **Objective:** Provide a precise performance template for visual learning.
- **Firearms Example:** Drawing from concealment with correct grip, sight alignment, and presentation, modeled with strict adherence to safety protocols.

Instructional Consideration: Learners will unconsciously copy inefficiencies as readily as correct behaviors; therefore, every demonstration must be flawless.

3. Imitate

Students replicate the skill under direct supervision. This stage shifts knowledge from **visual observation to kinesthetic performance.** Immediate correction is critical, as poor habits can become ingrained after only a few repetitions.

- **Objective:** Transition from cognitive understanding to initial physical execution.
- **Firearms Example:** Students conduct dry-fire reloads step-by-step under supervision, with instructors calling "freeze" to adjust hand placement or body mechanics.

Instructional Consideration: Encourage students to **verbalize procedural steps** during imitation; verbal reinforcement strengthens cognitive mapping.

4. Practice

Students engage in **deliberate, repeated practice** to build neural pathways and muscle memory. Practice begins slowly and deliberately, then progresses to live-fire under varied conditions and stressors.

- **Objective:** Achieve automaticity and integrate the skill into broader task sets.
- **Firearms Example:** Repeated malfunction clearance drills, progressing from controlled dry-fire to timed live-fire scenarios.

Instructional Consideration: Metrics such as time, accuracy, and decision-making must be tracked. Corrective drills should be introduced when students plateau in performance.

5. Test

The instructor formally evaluates the learner's ability to perform the skill reliably under realistic stress conditions. Testing ensures skills survive the transition from training to operational use.

- **Objective:** Confirm retention, adaptability, and operational readiness.
- **Firearms Example:** Running a timed El Presidente drill or conducting low-light, scenario-based training requiring target discrimination and reloads.

Instructional Consideration: Testing must include **objective scoring** (time, accuracy) and **subjective feedback** (economy of motion, decision-making, safety adherence).

Alignment with Adult Learning Principles

The EDIP+T model naturally aligns with Malcolm Knowles' andragogy framework (1984), which emphasizes self-directed learning, experiential grounding, and immediate applicability. Specifically:

- **Explain** provides relevance by linking new skills to operational needs.
- **Demonstrate** leverages visual and observational learning preferences.
- **Imitate** creates a guided bridge from theory to practice.
- **Practice** reinforces through repetition and self-adjustment.
- **Test** validates learning while promoting reflective self-diagnosis.

Additionally, the progression from structured instruction to independent testing supports **inductive learning**, wherein learners generalize proficiency from specific demonstrations and experiences.

Application of Firearms Instruction Across Domains

Military Firearms Instruction

The military environment demands a very specific kind of firearms training—one centered on lethality, adaptability, and survivability under the harshest conditions. Soldiers are not trained for courtroom scrutiny or civilian security details. They are trained to fight, win, and endure in combat. This reality shapes not only what is taught, but how it must be taught.

Mission Context

The battlefield is unforgiving. Soldiers must perform under fatigue, chaos, and constant stress while functioning as part of a team. Every skill must support the mission—whether clearing a room, suppressing an enemy position, or covering a teammate's movement. Firearms proficiency is not an accessory; it is a survival skill and a mission enabler.

Training must therefore address:

- The fundamentals of combat marksmanship—speed, accuracy, and repeatability under stress.
- Team-based shooting and movement, ensuring soldiers can integrate into squads, platoons, or larger units.
- Adaptability to shifting environments—urban combat, open terrain, or close-quarters fighting.
- Resilience, both mental and physical, to keep fighting when exhausted, injured, or under fire.

Instructional Priorities

Military firearms instruction must prioritize **combat application over sterile marksmanship.** While tight shot groups are valuable, combat demands that soldiers place accurate fire on the enemy quickly, under pressure, and in coordination with others. Key priorities include:

- **Combat Marksmanship Fundamentals**: Grip, stance, sight alignment, trigger control, and recoil management adapted for combat speed.

- **Target Discrimination**: Identifying friend, foe, or civilian under stress.
- **Shooting While Moving**: Maintaining accuracy while advancing, retreating, or moving laterally.
- **Team Integration**: Firing in coordination with teammates, communicating effectively, and maintaining situational awareness.
- **Stress Inoculation**: Training under fatigue, low visibility, loud noise, and simulated chaos to harden soldiers against battlefield conditions.

Adult Learning in the Military Environment

Many military students are young adults, often with minimal firearms experience prior to enlistment. Their learning is heavily kinesthetic—they learn by doing, by feeling the rifle in their hands, by experiencing recoil and repetition.

Yet the military also values discipline and uniformity. Repetition and drilling instill baseline proficiency. However, to produce adaptable fighters, instructors must go beyond rote memorization and incorporate **inductive learning**. Soldiers must learn not just how to follow a procedure, but how to think and adapt when doctrine fails.

An instructor must therefore blend rigid discipline with controlled opportunities for problem-solving. For example, once the fundamentals are drilled, soldiers should be placed in scenarios where targets appear unexpectedly, where weapons malfunction, or where teammates go down. These repetitions build adaptability and initiative—critical survival skills in combat.

The Instructor's Imperative

Military instructors carry a heavy burden. They must balance precision with realism, discipline with adaptability. Soldiers who fail in training may one day fail in combat, with consequences measured in lives and missions lost.

The professional instructor must:

- Model competence, discipline, and composure under stress.
- Demand accountability from every soldier—no excuses, no shortcuts.
- Create training that is as realistic as possible without compromising safety.
- Instill not only technical skill but also confidence, initiative, and resilience.

The bottom line is simple: in the military, firearms training is not about sport, recreation, or qualification scores. It is about preparing men and women to survive and prevail in the most dangerous environment on earth. The instructor's role is to ensure they are ready—every time, without exception.

Law Enforcement Firearms Instruction

Law enforcement officers operate in a vastly different environment than soldiers. Their battlefield is the street, the traffic stop, the domestic disturbance, or the active shooter. Their decisions carry not only life-or-death consequences but also legal, ethical, and societal scrutiny. This context demands a unique approach to firearms training.

Mission Context

Police officers must be ready to act instantly, transitioning from verbal commands to lethal force in the blink of an eye. Unlike the soldier, who engages a designated enemy, the officer must identify threats in crowded environments, often within arm's reach of innocent civilians. Every trigger press must be legally defensible and tactically sound.

Training must therefore emphasize:

- **Threat identification and discrimination.**
- **Escalation and de-escalation of force.**
- **Precision shooting in close quarters.**
- **Integrating firearms with communication, tactics, and decision-making.**

Instructional Priorities

The law enforcement officer's firearm is a tool of last resort, but when deployed, it must be used with speed and precision. Instruction must prioritize:

- **Precision Marksmanship at Close Distances**: The majority of law enforcement shootings occur within a few yards. Training must reflect this reality.
- **Shoot/No-Shoot Scenarios**: Incorporating realistic role players, decision-making, and legal review into training.
- **Stress Exposure**: Officers must perform under flashing lights, loud noises, and chaotic scenes.
- **Integration with Defensive Tactics**: Firearms must not be taught in isolation; they must be part of a continuum of force options.

Adult Learning in the Law Enforcement Environment

Unlike many soldiers, law enforcement officers often come into training with prior firearms experience—sometimes from recreational shooting, sometimes from previous training. This can be a double-edged sword. On one hand, familiarity helps. On the other, ingrained habits may conflict with best practices.

Instructors must therefore be deliberate in connecting new skills to officers' daily duties. Adults learn best when training is relevant, and nothing is more relevant to an officer than the possibility of surviving a deadly encounter on patrol. Scenario-based training is invaluable, as it bridges classroom lessons with real-world decision-making.

The Instructor's Imperative

For the firearms instructor training law enforcement, the standard must be uncompromising. The goal is not just to produce accurate shooters, but to develop officers who can make rapid, legally defensible, and tactically sound decisions under stress.

The professional instructor must:

- Teach precision, judgment, and restraint.
- Instill confidence without arrogance.
- Hold officers accountable to a higher standard than mere qualification scores.

In law enforcement, success is measured not by the number of rounds fired, but by the preservation of innocent life—including the officer's own. The instructor's duty is to ensure officers leave training not just more accurate, but more disciplined, more prepared, and more capable of protecting their communities.

Protective Security Firearms Instruction

Protective security professionals operate in a world where success is defined not by the ability to engage threats, but by the ability to prevent them. The protector's firearm is a last resort, not a first response. Their mission is to **avoid, deter, and defend**—always keeping the principal safe, unharmed, and out of danger.

Mission Context

The protector's task is unique. They must operate in urban environments, crowded spaces, and fluid situations where discretion is critical. Unlike soldiers or police, the protector's job is not to confront threats, but to shield the principal from them and extract them to safety.

This context demands training that emphasizes:

- **Early threat recognition and avoidance.**
- **Movement and protective formations.**
- **Close-quarters precision shooting.**
- **Evacuation and disengagement techniques.**

Instructional Priorities

Firearms training for protective security is about precision, restraint, and professionalism. Key priorities include:

- **Situational Awareness**: Recognizing threats before they materialize.
- **Protective Formations and Movements**: Using the body, the environment, and positioning to shield the principal.
- **Surgical Marksmanship**: Being able to stop a threat instantly without collateral damage, often in dense crowds.
- **Extraction Under Fire**: Shooting only to create space and time to move the principal to safety.

Adult Learning in the Protective Security Environment

Protectors often come from diverse backgrounds—some from the military, some from law enforcement, some from civilian sectors. Their training must therefore bridge varied levels of experience and mindset.

The instructor must emphasize **restraint and discretion.** Many protectors arrive with a "fighter's mindset," but in protective work, success means never needing to fire a shot. The firearm is simply a tool for the worst-case scenario.

The Instructor's Imperative

For the protective security instructor, the mission is clear: train protectors to ensure the safety of the principal above all else.

The professional instructor must:

- Teach that avoidance is preferable to engagement.
- Build precision and restraint into every repetition.
- Reinforce the mindset that the mission is protection, not combat.

In protective security, success is measured not by neutralizing threats, but by ensuring the principal remains unharmed. The protector lives in the shadows, unseen and unnoticed, but always ready. The firearms instructor must instill this quiet professionalism into every student.

Church Security Firearms Instruction

Church security is perhaps the most delicate and unique firearms training environment. Here, the mission is not only protection but also the preservation of peace in a sacred place. The sanctuary is filled with families, children, and worshippers who expect safety, not the presence of violence.

Mission Context

Church security teams operate in a world of extremes. Threats are rare, but when they appear, they materialize instantly and violently. Team members must transition from a posture of watchful peace to decisive action in seconds.

The environment itself adds complexity:

- High-density gatherings with no safe backstops.
- Plainclothes operation, blending in with congregants.
- Volunteers of varying skill levels working as a team.

Instructional Priorities

Training church security teams requires a unique emphasis on:

- **Rapid Threat Recognition**: Distinguishing between genuine threats and non-threats in crowded environments.
- **Extreme Fire Discipline**: Every shot must be precise, as missed rounds endanger innocents.
- **Plainclothes Operations**: Drawing, moving, and shooting without the benefit of uniforms or overt gear.
- **Team Coordination**: Volunteers must learn to communicate and act as a cohesive unit despite varied backgrounds.

Adult Learning in the Church Security Environment

Unlike soldiers or police officers, church security teams are often composed of volunteers—businessmen, teachers, veterans, or retirees. Their firearms experience may range from none to advanced. Instructors must therefore tailor methods to mixed groups while still holding every member accountable to professional standards.

Inductive learning plays a vital role here. Volunteers must be given opportunities to learn through repetitions, drills, and scenarios that replicate the confusion and chaos of an actual threat. These experiences build confidence and competence under stress.

The Instructor's Imperative

For the church security instructor, the mission is dual: to train protectors who can act decisively when required, while ensuring they embody restraint and discernment at all times.

The professional instructor must:

- Demand precision above all.
- Teach restraint as the first instinct, not the last.
- Reinforce that every decision carries consequences not only for safety, but for the sanctity of the church environment.

In church security, hesitation can be deadly, but overreaction can be catastrophic. The instructor's duty is to prepare volunteers to navigate this razor-thin margin with clarity, confidence, and discipline.

The Instructor's Responsibility Across Contexts

While the missions of the soldier, the police officer, the protector, and the church security volunteer differ, one truth unites them: **the responsibility of the instructor.**

Unifying Principles

Across all domains, the professional instructor must:

- Apply adult learning theory to connect with each student.
- Use the EDIP-T model to build proficiency step by step.
- Incorporate inductive learning to build ownership, adaptability, and confidence.
- Tailor methods to the mission context, never defaulting to a one-size-fits-all approach.

The Instructor's Burden

Firearms instruction is not about checking a box or passing a qualification. It is about preparing men and women for life-and-death encounters where failure is not an option. The instructor's burden is heavy, because the consequences of failure fall not on them, but on their students in the field.

The true firearms instructor must:

- Refine their craft continually.
- Demand accountability from every student.
- Instill judgment, discipline, and restraint alongside technical skill.
- Recognize that the ultimate goal is not shooting proficiency alone, but survivability, mission success, and the preservation of life.

Explain- Provides Relevance
Demonstrate-Leverages Learning
Imitate-From Theory to Practice
Practice-Reinforcement
Test- Validation

Develops Reliable Proformance

Excellence in instruction is not optional. It is a professional duty and a moral obligation. Those who take on the mantle of instructor must understand that they are not merely teaching skills—they are shaping the judgment and survivability of the armed professionals who protect our communities, our leaders, our soldiers, and our sanctuaries.

The EDIP+T model remains one of the most effective instructional frameworks for firearms training. Its structured progression from explanation through testing ensures that learners move beyond rote mechanical execution to operational competence under stress. By combining authoritative guidance with opportunities for experiential learning and self-reflection, EDIP+T equips armed professionals with the confidence, discipline, and reliability demanded in high-stakes environments.

Application to Armed Professional Training

For law enforcement officers, military personnel, and security professionals, the EDIP+T model is especially valuable because it:

- Ensures **safety-first instruction** through deliberate, progressive exposure.

- Builds **confidence and competence** in a structured sequence.
- Controls errors by catching and correcting mistakes early.
- Validates retention under **operational stress conditions.**

When properly implemented, EDIP+T provides a scalable framework that works for both novice shooters developing foundational safety skills and advanced professionals refining mission-critical techniques.

Hick's Law: Understanding Decision-Making Under Stress

Definition

Hick's Law, named after British psychologist William Edmund Hick, and describes the relationship between the number of choices presented to an individual and the time it takes them to make a decision. In its most basic form, the law states:

"Decision time increases logarithmically as the number of choices increases."

In simple terms, the more options a person has, the longer it takes them to choose one.

The Core Concept

- With **two choices**, decision time is short.
- With **multiple choices**, the brain must sort, compare, and evaluate, which slows reaction time.
- The relationship is not linear. Doubling the choices does not exactly double the decision time—it increases disproportionately because the brain processes options through a comparative evaluation model.

Hick's Law is often expressed in the formula:

RT = a + b · log$_2$(n + 1)

Where:

- **RT** = reaction time
- **a** = baseline reaction time with a single option
- **b** = added time for each additional option
- **n** = number of choices

Application in Training and Performance

1. **Firearms and Defensive Shooting**
   - **Too many options** in grip variations, draw methods, or reload techniques can cause hesitation under pressure.
   - **Streamlined decision-making**—such as training one consistent draw stroke, one reload method, or one malfunction clearance sequence—reduces the number of competing choices.
   - In a gunfight, the shooter who must decide *"Do I move, draw, shout, or disengage?"* under stress may hesitate, while the trained individual defaults to a simple, conditioned response.
2. **Military and Law Enforcement Operations**
   - Mission planning emphasizes **standard operating procedures (SOPs)** for this reason. Soldiers don't need to invent a response to every possible threat—they follow rehearsed protocols.
   - Fewer options = faster reaction = increased survivability.

3. **Everyday Civilian Application (Concealed Carry)**
   - A civilian with multiple holster positions (appendix, strong-side, small of back) or multiple carry pistols may slow their own response time in a crisis because the brain must recall *which pistol, where, and how.*
   - The principle: **Consistency builds speed.**
4. **Instructional Relevance**
   - Instructors must recognize when they overload students with too many techniques at once.
   - A layered approach—introducing only one or two valid options at a time—ensures students can internalize actions into **muscle memory**, bypassing conscious choice in favor of conditioned response.

Hick's Law vs. Experience

It's important to note that while Hick's Law applies broadly, training and repetition mitigate its effect. When responses are **overlearned and automated**, the brain no longer actively chooses; it executes.

- **Novice shooters** face longer decision times because each action is conscious.
- **Experienced shooters** reduce decision time because repeated practice collapses multiple possible actions into one dominant motor program.

This is why elite performers—whether athletes, musicians, or warriors—seem "fast." They are not deciding; they are executing a trained pattern.

Key Takeaways

- Hick's Law highlights the cost of too many choices.
- Decision speed directly affects survival, safety, and performance.

- In training: **simplify, standardize, and repeat.**
- In real-world application: **consistency beats variety.**

As a firearms instructor, I believe that one must demonstrate multiple techniques for completing a task, such as reloading a pistol under stress or clearing a malfunction in low light. It is important to guide students to recognize that certain methods outperform others based on the weapon's design, ammunition type, or environmental factors like confined spaces or adverse weather. This approach builds versatility while emphasizing efficiency.

Hick's Law captures this dynamic: a student will face longer decision times as the number of choices grows, following a logarithmic curve. Put simply, you take more time to select an option when options multiply.

At its core:

- You decide quickly with just two options, as your brain processes them swiftly.
- You slow down with several options, because your brain actively sorts, compares, and evaluates each one against the others.

This relationship defies linearity—doubling your choices does not merely double your decision time. Instead, it escalates the delay disproportionately, as your brain engages in a deeper comparative analysis to identify the optimal path.

When designing your training sessions, apply Hick's Law actively: streamline choices during high-pressure drills to sharpen reaction times, then introduce variations progressively to teach adaptability without overwhelming students. The instructor must foster muscle memory for primary methods first, ensuring they execute efficiently in real-world scenarios, before layering in alternatives. This method equips shooters to adapt fluidly, minimizing hesitation when seconds count.

EDIP-T model (Explain – Demonstrate – Imitate – Practice – Test)

EDIP-T model (Explain – Demonstrate – Imitate – Practice – Test) is a structured, military-derived instructional framework that works extremely well for pistol shooting training because it combines clear communication, modeling, hands-on replication, repetition, and objective performance assessment. It ensures both new and experienced shooters receive information in a logical progression, and it gives the instructor a built-in feedback loop to confirm skill transfer.

1. Explain

The instructor **verbally introduces the concept, skill, or technique**.

- **Objective:** Build mental clarity before physical action.
- **Pistol application:** Before teaching a draw, reload, or trigger press, the instructor explains:
    - *What* the skill is.
    - *Why* it's important (context—defensive, competitive, tactical).
    - *When* to use it (operational decision points).
    - *How* it fits into the bigger shooting process.
- **Best practices:**
    - Use correct terminology (grip, sight alignment, follow-through).
    - Break the skill into small, digestible steps.
    - Anticipate student questions and misconceptions.

2. Demonstrate

The instructor **physically shows the skill** exactly as it should be performed.

- **Objective:** Provide a precise visual model for the student's brain to copy.

- **Pistol application:**
    - Show the entire movement smoothly and correctly (no shortcuts).
    - Demonstrate from both the shooter's and observer's perspective.
    - Use slow motion for complex actions (e.g., clearing a malfunction).
- **Best practices:**
    - Maintain perfect muzzle discipline and trigger finger discipline to model safe behavior.
    - Emphasize economy of motion—students tend to copy *everything* you do, including inefficiencies.

3. Imitate

The student **mimics the instructor's demonstration** under supervision.

- **Objective:** Transition knowledge from visual input to kinesthetic output.
- **Pistol application:**
    - Dry-fire repetitions before live-fire to reinforce movement and grip without recoil interference.
    - Correct errors immediately before bad habits take root.
    - Use "freeze" moments—stop the student mid-action to point out proper or improper form.
- **Best practices:**
    - Keep imitation drills short and focused.
    - Encourage students to verbalize key steps as they move (helps mental mapping).

4. Practice

The student **performs the skill repeatedly** to build neural pathways and muscle memory.

- **Objective:** Achieve *unconscious competence*—the skill becomes automatic.
- **Pistol application:**
    o   Begin with slow, deliberate dry-fire, then progress to live-fire.
    o   Start with single isolated skills (e.g., strong-hand only shooting), then integrate with others (e.g., transitions, movement).
    o   Vary conditions—different distances, lighting, time constraints—to stress-test the skill.
- **Best practices:**
    o   Use performance metrics (time, accuracy) to measure improvement.
    o   Introduce corrective drills if performance plateaus.

5. Test

The instructor **evaluates the student's performance** to ensure knowledge retention and operational capability.

- **Objective:** Verify the skill is repeatable under realistic conditions.
- **Pistol application:**
    o   Timed qualification drills.
    o   Scenario-based shooting (e.g., multiple threat engagements, low-light).
    o   Stress shooting (adding time pressure, physical exertion, or decision-making).
- **Best practices:**
    o   Provide objective scoring and subjective feedback.
    o   Identify strengths and areas for continued practice.

- Encourage self-diagnosis—students should be able to articulate what went wrong and how to fix it.

Why EDIP-T Works for Pistol Shooting

- **Safety first:** Students receive clear verbal and visual safety cues before handling firearms.
- **Structured learning:** Each step builds on the last, reducing overwhelm.
- **Error control:** Mistakes are caught early before they become ingrained habits.
- **Retention under stress:** Testing ensures skills survive the jump from the range to real-world defensive situation

EDIP-T Pistol Training Quick-Reference Chart

Step	Purpose	Instructor Actions	Pistol Example	Key Safety/Performance Notes
Explain	Build mental clarity before physical action.	- Clearly define the skill. - State its purpose, when to use it, and common pitfalls. - Break it into small steps using correct terminology.	Before teaching an emergency reload: Explain why speed is critical, when it's needed, and the difference from a tactical reload.	Always integrate **safe direction** and **trigger finger discipline** in verbal brief.

Step	Purpose	Instructor Actions	Pistol Example	Key Safety/Performance Notes
Demonstrate	Provide an accurate visual model for the student's brain to replicate.	- Show skill in real time, then slow motion. - Demonstrate from multiple angles. - Maintain perfect form and economy of motion.	Demonstrate drawing from concealment smoothly, with proper grip and sight alignment.	Every movement you make will be copied—remove inefficiencies.
Imitate	Transition from visual learning to physical execution under supervision.	- Have student mimic step-by-step. - Correct errors immediately. - Use "freeze" moments to point out key positions.	Student dry-fires reload technique exactly as shown.	Keep reps short to avoid fatigue-induced bad habits.
Practice	Reinforce correct performance through repetition and	- Start slow, build speed. - Progress from dry-fire to live-fire. - Integrate	Multiple repetitions of failure-to-fire clearance followed by	Track both **accuracy** and **time**; adjust drills for plateaus.

Step	Purpose	Instructor Actions	Pistol Example	Key Safety/Performance Notes
	varied conditions.	skills into larger drills.	immediate re-engagement.	
Test	Confirm skill retention and application under realistic pressure.	- Run timed or scenario-based evaluations. - Score objectively, give feedback. - Encourage student self-diagnosis.	Timed El Presidente drill to evaluate transitions, reloads, and accuracy.	Testing should simulate the environment where the skill will be used.

ADDIE training model (Analyze, Design, Develop, Implement, and Evaluate) specifically applied to **firearms training**, along with its **pros and cons**:

ADDIE in Firearms Training

1. Analyze

- Identify training goals, skill gaps, and student backgrounds (civilian, law enforcement, military, armed professional).
- Assess requirements: range facilities, safety standards, policy/legal considerations, and equipment needs.
- Define performance standards (accuracy, speed, judgment under stress).

2. Design

- Structure the course objectives, lesson plans, drills, and progression.
- Decide on teaching methodologies: classroom, dry-fire, live-fire, scenario-based training.
- Sequence skills: safety → fundamentals → manipulations → defensive application.

3. Develop

- Create actual materials: manuals, slides, qualification standards, targets, evaluation rubrics.
- Build-in safety protocols and contingency procedures.
- Incorporate layered instruction (basic to advanced, skill → application).

4. Implement

- Deliver training: live-fire instruction, drills, and simulations.
- Instructor demonstrations, guided practice, corrective coaching.
- Ensure safety, range management, and accountability.

5. Evaluate

- Test student performance through qualifications, scenario assessments, and stress drills.
- Gather student feedback.
- Review instructor performance and program effectiveness.
- Adjust curriculum for gaps (e.g., too much emphasis on marksmanship, not enough on judgment-based shooting).

Pros of ADDIE in Firearms Training

Structured process – Prevents "winging it" and ensures training is progressive and organized.

Safety-oriented – Analyzing risks and designing protocols before training increases safety on the range.

Accountability – Standards and evaluations provide measurable student performance benchmarks.

Scalable – Works for small classes, academies, or organizational training programs.

Customizable – Allows tailoring for different groups (civilian defensive shooting vs. law enforcement).

Feedback loop – The evaluation phase ensures continuous improvement in both student skills and training design.

Cons of ADDIE in Firearms Training

Time-consuming – The structured model can be slow to develop, especially if an agency needs rapid training deployment.

Rigid if misapplied – Real-world firearms encounters evolve; training needs flexibility, while ADDIE can become too procedural.

Resource-heavy – Requires instructors, facilities, safety officers, and evaluation tools—difficult for smaller organizations.

Overemphasis on process – If instructors focus too much on paperwork and design, live-fire demonstration and coaching may suffer.

May not address "human factors" fully – Stress inoculation, judgment under duress, and decision-making require scenario-based training beyond ADDIE's linear structure.

Evaluation challenges – In firearms training, metrics like accuracy and speed are easy to measure, but judgment, mindset, and real-world adaptability are harder to quantify.

In short: **ADDIE is excellent for building structured, safe, and scalable firearms training programs**, but instructors must guard against being overly rigid and ensure the model integrates **realism, adaptability, and stress-based training**.

As a long time firearms instructor and with this being an instructor guide it is important to understand instructional design models and how they are used. If you have read any of my other books, you know that I am an EDIP-T guy! While serving as a Special Forces Advanced Urban Combat Instructor I was expected to Explain and demonstrate everything that was presented. In my mind the Field Manual that covered the entirety of the Special Forces Urban Combat Course served as our ADDIE model. A strategic overlay that did not interfere with Tactical Planning or implementation.

While teaching for the Sig Sauer Academy I was required to Explain and demonstrate every drill, anything the students had not seen prior to the block of instruction. At that time we had no strategic overlay other than be professional and use Sig firearms to demonstrate the potential to students.

Of course, I adopted this philosophy when starting my own business, Modern American Combative Arts LLC. With the intent of teaching each class independently and to provide the classes that people wanted. As I progressed I did develop a 40 hour block taught in 4 hour blocks one Friday night a month for Harry Beckwith Guns and Range in Micanopy Florida, my Guardian Program.

The Federal Law Enforcement Training Center uses the ADDIE methodology to design complete programs lasting several months and then attempts to use the same model for induvial blocks within programs and classes in Firearms. I have found this to be very problematic at the Firearms instructor class level.

I wanted to ensure that this instructor guide presented information on designing programs and individual classes so that the Academy, school house or individual instructor good understand and decide what works best for their own needs,

Both **EDIP-T** and **ADDIE** are instructional models, but they serve different purposes and operate at different levels of training design. Let's compare and contrast them directly, especially in the **firearms training context**:

EDIP-T vs. ADDIE in Firearms Training

EDIP-T Model

Explain – Demonstrate – Imitate – Practice – Test
A **micro-level teaching model** designed for skill acquisition on the range or in drills.

- **Explain** – Instructor breaks down the skill verbally (safety, technique, why it matters).
- **Demonstrate** – Instructor performs the skill live (slow and fast demos).
- **Imitate** – Students attempt the skill under supervision, replicating the demonstration.
- **Practice** – Repetition with coaching, corrections, and reinforcement.
- **Test** – Evaluation of student performance against standards.

Strength in firearms training:

- Immediate, practical skill transfer.
- Works exceptionally well for motor skill-based tasks (draw, reload, malfunction clearance, target transitions).
- Reinforces **instructor credibility** through demonstration.
- Students see, do, refine, and prove competency in one session.

ADDIE Model

Analyze – Design – Develop – Implement – Evaluate

A **macro-level training development model** designed for entire programs or courses.

- **Analyze** – Identify training needs, skill gaps, requirements.
- **Design** – Structure curriculum, sequence lessons.
- **Develop** – Create training materials, drills, evaluations.
- **Implement** – Deliver instruction.
- **Evaluate** – Measure effectiveness, adjust program.

Strength in firearms training:

- Provides structured curriculum design.
- Ensures training meets organizational goals (qualification, policy compliance, performance standards).
- Focuses on long-term training systems, not just one drill.

Aspect	EDIP-T	ADDIE
Level	Micro (individual skill/drill delivery)	Macro (course/curriculum design)
Focus	Teaching and reinforcing a **specific skill**	Building and evaluating a **training program**
Timeframe	Immediate, on the range	Long-term planning and execution
Instructor Role	Hands-on, demonstrator, coach	Designer, planner, program manager

Aspect	EDIP-T	ADDIE
Student Role	Actively imitates, practices, tests	Receives structured training across phases
Strength	Efficient skill transfer and confidence building	Comprehensive, scalable, and accountable training system
Weakness	Not designed for long-term curriculum planning	Can be rigid, slow, and paperwork-heavy
Example	Teaching emergency reloads in one block of instruction	Designing a 40-hour pistol qualification program for a police academy

How They Work Together

- **ADDIE** builds the **program** (decides what skills must be trained, how they'll be sequenced, and how performance will be measured).
- **EDIP-T** is used within **ADDIE's Implement phase** to deliver individual lessons and ensure students acquire the required skills.
- In other words: **ADDIE is the blueprint; EDIP-T is the execution method.**

The Illusion of Proficiency

Armed professionals—and more importantly, those who train them—must accept an often uncomfortable truth: a high score on an agency qualification course does not equate to true proficiency. Most agency standards are designed to produce a 95% or higher pass rate. The reality is that the average journeyman shooter will land comfortably in the middle to upper curve of these qualifications without demonstrating the depth of skill required for real-world performance.

A qualification course measures the bare minimum. It does not measure readiness for lethal encounters.

Instructor Note: *Passing a qualification is not performance. Do not confuse the minimum standard with operational readiness.*

Agency Standards

Agency courses of fire are often structured for mass success, not for excellence. For example:

- **Customs and Border Protection (CBP):** 48 rounds on the DHS "coke bottle" target, one point per hit in the inner zone, with an 80% passing score.
- **Federal Law Enforcement Training Center (FLETC) – CITP:** Passing score of 210/300, or 70%.
- **Other Federal Agencies:** Some raise the bar slightly to 240/300, or 80%.
- **Firearms Instructor Training Program (FITP):** Sets the mark at 255/300 (85%) on the PPC course of fire—but that course remains forgiving, with generous time limits and static positions.

A competent instructor can often shoot side-by-side targets, maintain the same pace, and post passing scores on both. That reality reveals just how undemanding many standards truly are.

Instructor Note: *Standards are written for institutions, not for survival. Treat them as a floor, not a ceiling.*

Distance and Time Never Lie

Distance and time are the great truth-tellers of shooting. Stretching shooters to distance exposes mechanical flaws in grip, trigger control, and sight management. Cutting time forces efficiency in draw, presentation, and weapons handling. Combined, these two factors strip away illusions of competence and reveal the shooter's true performance level.

Instructor Note: *If you want to see a shooter's truth—push them back and speed them up.*

Raising the Bar

In the Advanced Pistol Instructor Training Program (APITP), I challenged students with standards drawn from my Special Forces background. The test was deceptively simple: three bullseyes at 25 yards.

- First shot with a **10-minute** time limit.
- Second shot within **one minute.**
- Third shot within **ten seconds.**

Aggregate score: 300. Instructor standard: 270/300 (90%).

Time and again, seasoned law enforcement instructors—experienced shooters from the field—failed to meet that mark. These were not novices. Yet the higher standard revealed the deficiencies that routine qualifications had concealed.

Instructor Note: *Simple tests with strict time or distance standards reveal more than complicated qualification ever will.*

The Instructor's Responsibility

Most law enforcement officers are at their absolute best on academy qualification day. From there, their skill typically degrades in the field. Only a small minority will compete in USPSA or IDPA. Fewer still will attend follow-on training at academies. An even smaller number will invest their own money in professional classes.

That reality places the responsibility squarely on the instructor's shoulders. Our role is not to simply prepare students to pass a test, but to prepare them to survive.

Instructor Note: *Your students will not maintain themselves. Their skill will fade unless you push them past minimums.*

Professional Growth

Professional instructor organizations mandate ongoing training for a reason. A true instructor invests in growth continuously. At a minimum, I attend one professionally run course every year. Often, I deliberately step outside my comfort zone:

- **Competition courses** to refine mechanics, speed, and movement.
- **Long-range pistol courses** to expose breakdowns in fundamentals.
- **Specialty classes** to explore new carry methods, structures, or teaching methodologies.

Every class sharpens my craft and expands my teaching perspective.

Instructor Note: *If you are not training yourself, you are unfit to train others.*

Demonstration and Credibility

When an instructor steps onto the line to demonstrate, credibility is on the line. Students must see that their instructor holds himself to the same—or higher—standards he demands of them. A competent instructor does not just pass qualifications; he demonstrates performance under pressure, at speed, and at distance.

Instructor Note: *Never ask students to do what you cannot demonstrate yourself.*

Test Yourself, Then Test Them

Never forget: your students' high scores on agency qualifications do not equal competence. And your own ability to shoot "Distinguished Expert" on a qualification means very little. These are baseline standards—nothing more.

True mastery begins when you push yourself into uncomfortable territory. Raise the bar beyond the minimums. Test yourself. Refine yourself. Then challenge your students to do the same.

Instructor Note: *The standard is not the standard. Survival is the standard.*

Closing Thoughts on this

A true instructor does not excuse student failure with phrases like, *"Look who the agency is hiring—it's not my fault."* In an academy setting, the reality is clear: not all students should pass. Some individuals are simply not equipped to serve as law enforcement officers. That is a hard truth, but it must be accepted. However, what must never be accepted is failure that results from the instructor's own shortcomings. If a student fails because you lacked the knowledge, skill, or ability to train them effectively, then you—not the student—are the problem. Professional instructors take full responsibility for their craft, refining their methods, sharpening their own skills, and exhausting every avenue to bring each student to their highest potential. Only then does failure rest where it belongs—on the student, not the instructor.

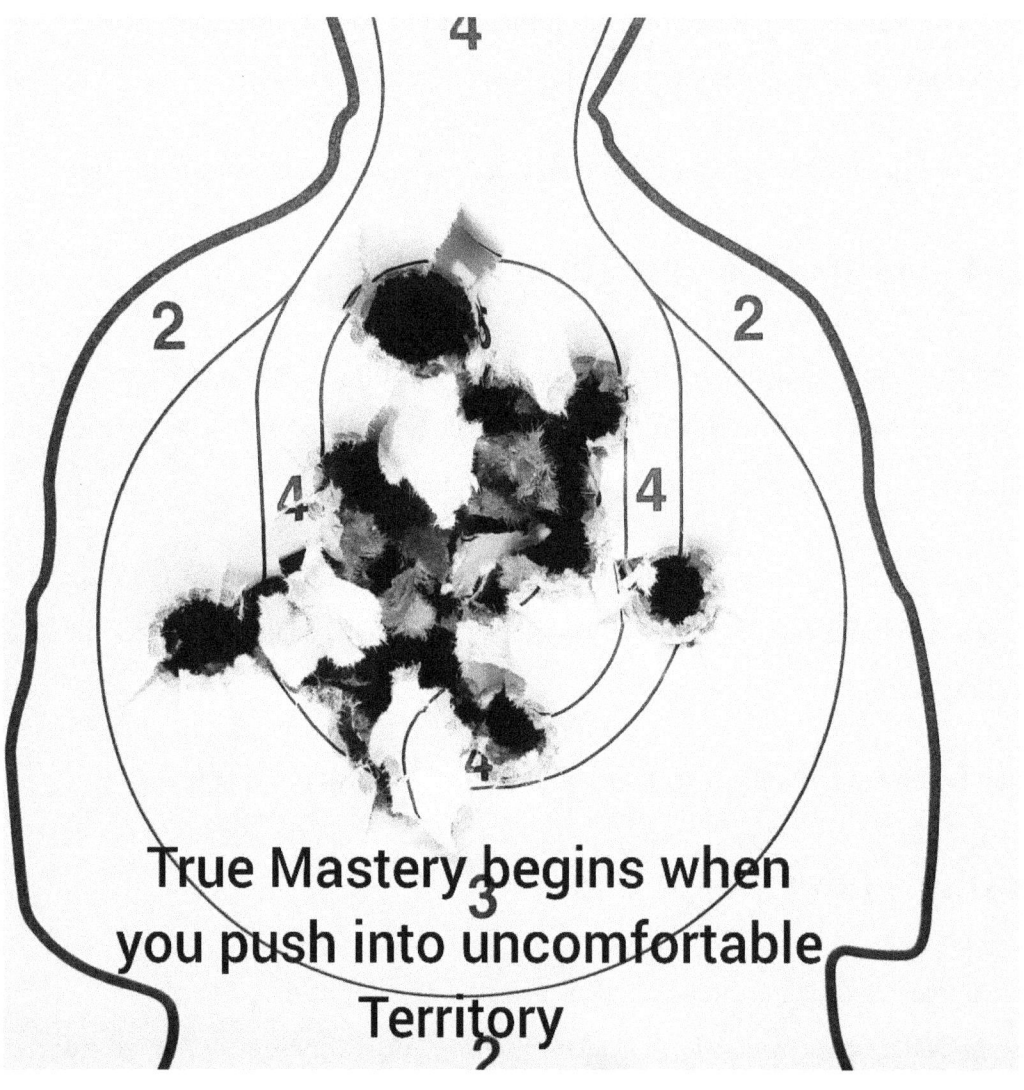

Principles Over Techniques

Instructional Philosophy: Principles Over Techniques

Professional Definition and Rationale

As a firearms instructor, your primary objective extends beyond teaching students to execute specific tasks; it is to arm them with the foundational "why", the guiding principles that underpin all effective actions under duress. Techniques represent mere applications of these principles, tailored to particular scenarios, body types, mission requirements, or environmental factors.

Why Principles Matter More Than Techniques

- Techniques are situational; principles are universal.
- Techniques falter when contexts shift; principles adapt seamlessly.
- Principles cultivate problem-solvers; techniques breed rote performers.
- Principles endure under stress; isolated techniques erode.

By emphasizing principles, instructors empower students to critically assess their actions, improvise in fluid situations, and transcend inflexible methodologies.

Core Firearms Principles (with Examples of Supporting Techniques)

Principle	Description	Techniques That Support It
Efficient Movement	Movement should minimize exposure while maximizing survivability.	- Slicing the pie - Lateral movement off the X - Bounding overwatch
Consistent Sight Alignment and Visual Control	The ability to align sights or dot predictably with the eyes, irrespective of position or pace.	- High-ready presentation - Compressed ready - Temple index for movement
Trigger Control Relative to Visual Confirmation	Precision in trigger manipulation must align with visual input and target size/distance.	- "Confirmation 1–2–3" model - Prep and press vs. fast slap reset shooting
Situational Awareness and Cognitive Processing	Shooters must detect threats, process data, and decide in real time.	- OODA loop-based drills - Reactive steel drills - Shoot/no-shoot scenario-based training
Balance of Speed and Precision	The shooter must discern when to accelerate or decelerate, harmonizing accuracy with exigency.	- Failure-to-stop drills - Bill drill vs. Dot Torture - Speed reload vs. retention reload decision-making

Example for Instructional Use: Drawing the Firearm Technique-Oriented Approach (Limiting)

"You must always draw from the 3 o'clock outside-the-waistband (OWB) holster using this exact step-by-step sequence: 1. Clear cover garment, 2. Establish master grip, 3. Lift and rotate, 4. Join hands, 5. Extend to target."

Principle-Oriented Approach (Flexible)

"The governing principle is an efficient, consistent draw that orients the muzzle toward the target and aligns the sights as swiftly as the situation demands. Techniques—whether from OWB, appendix inside-the-waistband (AIWB), or concealment—must accommodate your attire, holster configuration, and threat distance. While steps may vary subtly, the principle endures: clear, grip, draw, orient, engage."

Guidelines for Instructors

1. **Always Explain the Why Behind the How**
   Link every technique to its principle. For instance: "Why index this way? To maintain control and minimize profile."

2. **Present Multiple Valid Techniques When Possible**
   Provide options suited to diverse physiques, gear, or expertise levels. This enables students to tailor their approach while remaining anchored in principles.

3. **Use Failure Points to Reinforce Principles**
   When a technique falters, redirect to the principle. Example: "Your reload stalled due to lost visual control of the magwell—let's revisit the principle of visual indexing."

4. **Evaluate Progress by Principle Application, Not Mere Drill Performance**
   Probe: "Can they articulate why they selected this method?" or "Can they adapt amid evolving conditions?"

Summary Statement for Instructor Use

"Techniques are tools in the toolbox, but principles form the blueprint. My role isn't to stock your toolbox solely with my tools—it's to furnish the blueprint, enabling you to select the optimal tool for the moment."

A Deeper Dive into the Principles of Combat and Their Influence on Pistol Shooting

Combat—whether in military operations, law enforcement encounters, or personal defense—adheres to timeless principles that shape the deployment of tactics, techniques, and tools such as the pistol. Fundamentally, these principles revolve around securing and sustaining superiority in volatile, high-risk settings. This exploration is structured to facilitate instructor-level discourse, bridging conceptual divides for civilian and professional shooters alike.

I. Core Combat Principles (Strategic and Tactical)

1. **Violence of Action**
    - **Definition**: Swift, overpowering force to stun, disrupt, and overpower the adversary.
    - **Influence on Pistol Shooting**:
        - Rapid, resolute engagements.
        - Aggressive target transitions.
        - Unwavering commitment to each shot.
2. **Speed**
    - **Definition**: Achieving tempo superiority; outpacing the opponent's response.

- **Influence on Pistol Shooting**:
    - Prioritizes draw velocity, target acquisition, and firing rhythm.
    - Stresses streamlined manipulations: reloads, clearances, and movement.
    - Aligns with visual Confirmation Level 1 (high-speed shooting).

3. **Surprise**
   - **Definition**: Attacking in unanticipated ways to generate exploitable edges.
   - **Influence on Pistol Shooting**:
     - Exploitation of angles, motion, and timing.
     - Concealed carry strategies: masked draw strokes, misleading stances.
     - Firing from atypical positions or while in transit.

4. **Security / Force Protection**
   - **Definition**: Safeguarding one's operational capacity during engagement.
   - **Influence on Pistol Shooting**:
     - Utilization of cover and concealment.
     - Post-engagement assessments and vigilance.
     - One-handed techniques for injury or constrained scenarios.

5. **Offensive Action (Initiative)**
   - **Definition**: Proactively imposing one's intent to control engagement dynamics.
   - **Influence on Pistol Shooting**:
     - Preemptive preparedness (OODA cycle leverage).
     - Instant counteroffensive exercises.
     - Psychological ascendancy via posture and pace.

6. **Adaptability (Flexibility)**
   - **Definition**: Rapid recalibration to evolving battle elements—terrain, foe strategies, equipment issues.

- **Influence on Pistol Shooting**:
  - Seamless malfunction resolutions.
  - Effortless shifts between dominant and support-hand firing.
  - Agile cognitive handling amid duress (decision-making under fire).

7. **Economy of Force**
   - **Definition**: Deploying minimal essential power at pivotal junctures.
   - **Influence on Pistol Shooting**:
     - Ammunition conservation.
     - Prioritizing precision over barrage.
     - Measured application of burst fire or suppressive volleys.

II. Translating Combat Principles into Pistol Shooting Fundamentals

These combat tenets morph into the bedrock principles of proficient pistol handling. Instructors must convey that pistol shooting transcends mechanical proficiency—it embodies combat conduct, steeped in these immutable truths.

III. Pistol Shooting Principles Shaped by Combat Realities

Combat Principle	Pistol Shooting Translation	Instructional Focus
Violence of Action	Commit unequivocally to the shot. Eliminate hesitation. Bridge the mental divide.	Foster assurance via force-on-force simulations.
Speed	Attain swift sight pictures and controlled triggers.	Instruct on confirmation tiers and shot responsibility.

Combat Principle	Pistol Shooting Translation	Instructional Focus
Surprise	Employ concealment, misdirection, and novel draw paths.	Highlight mindset and tactical positioning.
Security	Maintain unwavering weapon command. Avoid outpacing your sights.	Incorporate compressed ready positions, retention firing, and single-hand proficiency.
Initiative	Position yourself as the aggressor, not merely the reactor.	Promote anticipatory choices and immersive scenarios.
Adaptability	Navigate, fire, and resolve issues with fluidity.	Prioritize kinetic range work and mental stress exercises.
Economy	Fire only as necessary. Ensure hits with every round.	Bolster accuracy, discipline, and resource stewardship.

IV. Layered Teaching Framework

Beginner Level

- Frame pistol mechanics as self-preservation tools.
- Concentrate on controlled fundamentals: stance, grip, sight alignment, trigger control.
- Introduce basic combat contexts (e.g., pressured draws from concealment).

Intermediate Level

- Integrate judgment calls and timed exercises.
- Advance to mobility, multi-target engagements, and malfunction handling.
- **Accentuate principles such as speed, initiative, and economy of force.**

Advanced Level

- Incorporate role-based simulations (force-on-force, shoot/no-shoot).
- Demand combat ethos amid exhaustion.
- Challenge against intricate principles like adaptability and surprise.

Instructor Level

- Train practitioners to reason in principles, eschewing rote techniques.
- Elucidate the stress-resilience of each principle.
- Tailor exercises to isolate targeted combat tenets.

V. Example Drill: Principle Integration

Drill Name: Combat Triad Engagement

- **Setup**: Three laterally spaced targets.
- **Purpose**: Fuse Violence of Action, Speed, and Economy of Force.
- **Sequence**:
    1. Draw and deliver two rounds to Target 1 (combat-effective accuracy).
    2. Swiftly shift to Target 2 with one precise round (economy emphasis).
    3. Relocate offline to cover while addressing Target 3 (adaptability and security).
- **Debrief**: Evaluate decisiveness, purposeful movement, and shot accountability.

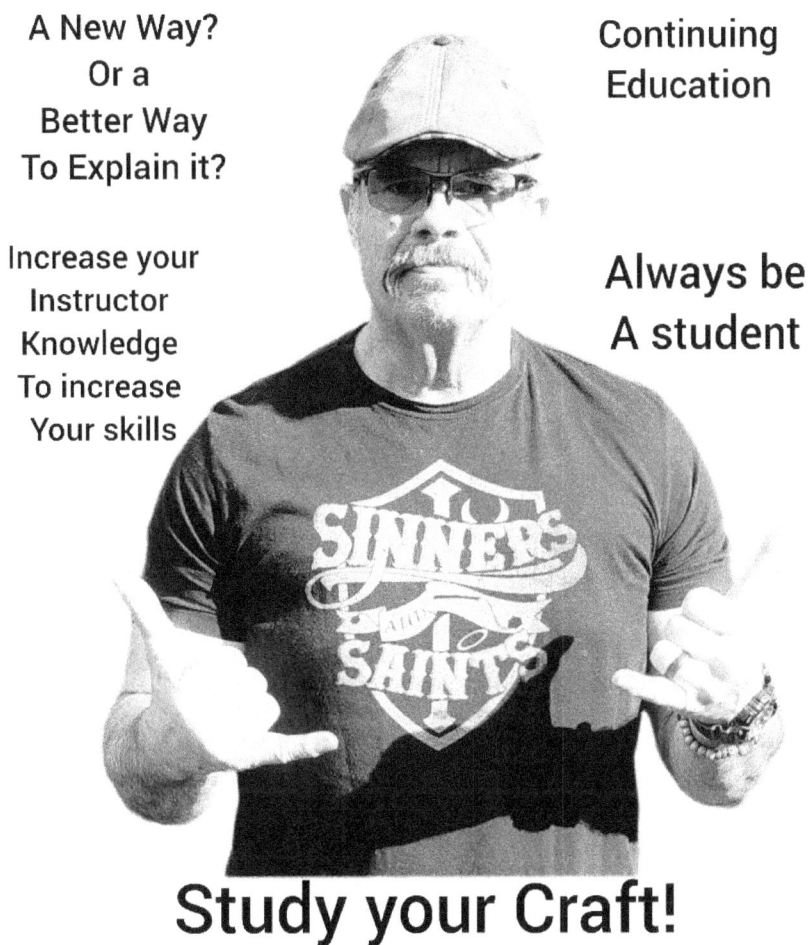

Teaching Combat Principles in Pistol Instruction

Remember that as firearms instructors, our responsibility transcends simply teaching students how to shoot a pistol. Our true mission is to instill the foundational "why" behind every action—equipping students with the combat principles that underpin effective decision-making and execution under pressure. Techniques are transient, tailored to specific scenarios, physiques, or environments, but principles are timeless and universal. Divorcing pistol instruction from these core combat principles is like teaching swimming in a desert—useless and disconnected from reality. This presentation outlines how to prioritize principles over techniques, ensuring students are prepared to triumph in adversity.

Core Objective: The Blueprint, Not the Tools

Our goal isn't to produce students who mindlessly replicate a set of prescribed techniques. Instead, we must provide them with the intellectual and practical framework—the blueprint—that governs all effective actions in combat. Techniques are merely tools in a toolbox, adapted to the moment's demands. Principles, however, are the bedrock that guides which tool to select and why. As instructors, we must:

- **Shift focus from rote memorization to understanding.** Teach students to internalize the reasoning behind their actions, not just the actions themselves.
- **Empower adaptability.** By grounding instruction in principles, we enable students to adjust techniques to fit unique scenarios, body types, or mission requirements.
- **Prepare for chaos.** Combat is unpredictable. Principles provide the clarity needed to make split-second decisions when plans fail.

Remember Why Principles Matter

Every discharge, maneuver, and choice in pistol employment must stem from a combat-honed perspective. Without principles, techniques lack context and purpose, leaving students vulnerable in high-stakes situations. Consider the following:

- **Combat is not a range.** Marksmanship excellence is a means, not the end. The ultimate aim is survival and victory under duress, not perfect groupings on paper.

- **Principles breed resilience.** When students understand *why* a technique works (e.g., economy of motion, situational awareness, or threat prioritization), they can adapt it to dynamic, real-world threats.
- **Techniques are fleeting.** A technique that works for one student in one scenario may fail for another in a different context. Principles, like maintaining control under stress or exploiting cover, remain constant.

Teaching the Blueprint

To effectively teach combat principles, we must reframe our approach as instructors. Here's how:

1. **Start with the "Why."**
    - Begin every lesson by explaining the combat principle behind the skill. For example, when teaching grip, emphasize how it enhances recoil management and weapon retention under stress, not just how to hold the pistol.
    - Use real-world scenarios to illustrate principles in action. Share examples of how situational awareness or movement saved lives in actual engagements.
2. **Deconstruct Techniques as Applications.**
    - Present techniques as flexible applications of principles, not rigid dogma. For instance, a Weaver stance may suit one student, while an isosceles stance may better serve another—both can align with the principle of stability under fire.
    - Encourage students to experiment and adapt techniques to their unique needs, guided by the underlying principle.

3. **Simulate Stress and Chaos.**
    - Incorporate stress-inducing drills (e.g., time pressure, physical exertion, or decision-making scenarios) to test how well students can apply principles under duress.
    - Use scenario-based training to reinforce principles like cover, movement, and threat assessment in dynamic environments.
4. **Foster Critical Thinking.**
    - Challenge students to justify their choices. Ask, "Why did you choose that grip?" or "Why did you move to that position?" This forces them to connect actions to principles.
    - Teach students to self-assess and adapt, ensuring they can select the right "tool" for the moment without relying on rote instruction.

Practical Framework: Key Combat Principles

Here are core principles to weave into pistol instruction, with examples of how they manifest:

- **Situational Awareness:** Always know your environment, threats, and resources. Example: Teach students to scan for exits and cover before engaging a target.
- **Economy of Motion:** Minimize unnecessary actions to maximize efficiency. Example: Streamline reloads to reduce time exposed to threats.
- **Control Under Stress:** Maintain composure to execute decisions effectively. Example: Use breathing techniques to steady aim during high-pressure drills.
- **Threat Prioritization:** Address the most immediate danger first. Example: Train students to engage the closest or most lethal threat before others.
- **Adaptability:** Adjust to changing conditions. Example: Practice shooting from unconventional positions to prepare for real-world variables.

Instructor Mindset: Be the Architect

As instructors, we're not here to stock students' toolboxes with our favorite gadgets. Our role is to be architects, providing the blueprint that empowers students to build their own solutions. This means:

- **Avoid dogma.** Don't push one technique as the "only way." Show students how to align techniques with principles.
- **Embrace discomfort.** Teach students to thrive in uncertainty, not just succeed in controlled environments.
- **Model the principles.** Demonstrate combat principles in your own actions—show situational awareness, decisiveness, and adaptability in your teaching.

My finial thoughts

It is our duty as firearms instructors is to forge students who can think, adapt, and prevail in the crucible of combat. By prioritizing principles over techniques, we equip them with the mental and practical tools to navigate any scenario. Techniques will evolve, but principles endure. Let's commit to teaching the blueprint, not just the tools, and prepare our students to triumph in adversity.

Inductive Fire: Lessons from a Green Beret on Training Armed Professionals

I've spent more than 30 years teaching men and women who carry guns for a living. My classroom has ranged from dusty village ranges in Central America to state-of-the-art facilities here in the U.S. As a U.S. Army Special Forces soldier, I cut my teeth on Foreign Internal Defense missions—training local forces in the Caribbean, Central and South America, Africa, and the Middle East. Many of those missions were linked to counter-drug operations and paired us with host-nation law enforcement.

One lesson became clear early: the gap between military and law enforcement training isn't about motivation. It's about mindset and resources.

In Special Forces, the Army has no qualms about pouring time and ammunition into building competence. During the opening days of our own SOT pipeline, we burned through 1,000 rounds a day for 10 straight days—inductive learning at its finest. You learned by doing, until the gun felt like an extension of your body. Only then did we move into two more weeks of close-quarters battle.

It was the same story later in my career. At SFARTEAC and then as a Special Forces Advanced Urban Combat instructor for 3rd Group, the curriculum followed a familiar rhythm: high-volume shooting first, then the live-fire CQB that separates good shooters from effective assault force members. Watching a Commander's In-Extremis Force element—or three ODAs running their final SFAUC hit—clear a target complex is like watching a symphony. Precision, violence of action, and complete mastery of the fundamentals under pressure.

Contrast that with the average law enforcement program. On overseas FID missions, our host-nation students would get a week with us, 500 rounds a day. Back home, working with state, local, and federal agencies, we were lucky to get two or three days. Even when training "top-tier" hostage rescue teams, their reputations sometimes outpaced their skill sets. That's not a dig; it's reality. They simply don't get the same depth of reps.

Later, I spent over 15 years as a full-time firearms instructor at the Federal Law Enforcement Training Center. Most academy students only had two-hour range blocks. By graduation, their skills were journeyman level at best. In our advanced programs—Survival Shooting, Reactive Shooting Instructor, Advanced Pistol, and Advanced Pistol Instructor—we ran five-day courses with 500–700 rounds a day. The first two days were usually spent just getting students to a baseline so real learning could begin.

Here's the rub: many of those advanced classes were canceled for lack of students. It wasn't because officers didn't want the training; it was because agency culture made it hard to attend. The military sends soldiers away to learn, expecting them to return as force multipliers. Law enforcement officers often have to fight their own administration to get the same opportunity.

The officers who truly want to get better usually do it on their own time and dime. They seek out reputable classes, or they compete in USPSA or IDPA to pressure-test themselves. Those are the folks who understand what's at stake.

If there's a takeaway here for instructors, it's this: know your audience. Understand the institutional limits they operate under, set realistic expectations, and then build a program that wrings every ounce of value from the time and ammo you have. Don't compare cops to Green Berets. Don't compare a two-day class to a month-long pipeline. Build training that fits the reality, while still holding the line on safety and performance.

In the end, whether you wear a uniform or a badge, the mission is the same: win the fight and go home alive. The paths to that goal are different. The job of a good instructor is to meet students where they are and take them as far as you can—round by round, rep by rep.

Instructors matter as much as or more than the students! Encourage your organization to seek out those that have that special skillset because it does matter. As a firearms instructor who has worked both in Special Forces and at the Federal Law Enforcement Training Center, I'm blunt: how an organization chooses and develops its trainers determines how well it will perform under stress. In Special Forces we pursued excellence by seeking the best outside instruction—Shaw and Rogers taught us advanced marksmanship on different systems, Gracie and Thompson taught us how to fight, Scott Racing taught us to drive—and then we elevated the best students into instructor roles and sent them back through courses repeatedly until the nuance became second nature. That hunger for continuous education never allowed us to settle for "good enough." FLETC, by contrast, too-often hires inside its own bubble: former law-enforcement for law-enforcement instruction, with preference for federal agents and only reluctantly pulling from state, local, or military police when forced. That incestuous hiring model creates a self-reinforcing illusion of superiority and discourages the very cross-pollination that builds real skill and adaptability. Continuing education is the rule in virtually every profession—my wife, a teacher, has 40 hours yearly—and firearms instruction should be no different. Shooting is a perishable skill: most shooters shoot their absolute best on qualification day, then erode from that level unless they deliberately train. Simple diagnostic drills—Ken Hackathorn's Wizard and the Vickers 10–10–10—take 15 rounds and will humble anyone who earned "expert" on paper but hasn't maintained the craft. It is unacceptable for instructors to avoid live-fire demonstration, to refuse personal investment in training, or for organizations to place bureaucratic barriers between instructors and the classes that will improve them. You choose what kind of instructor you will be: complacent and insulated, or relentless and accountable. If you want your organization to perform when it matters, stop protecting the status quo—hire, fund, and require continual, external competency development, and hold instructors to the same standards you expect from frontline operators.

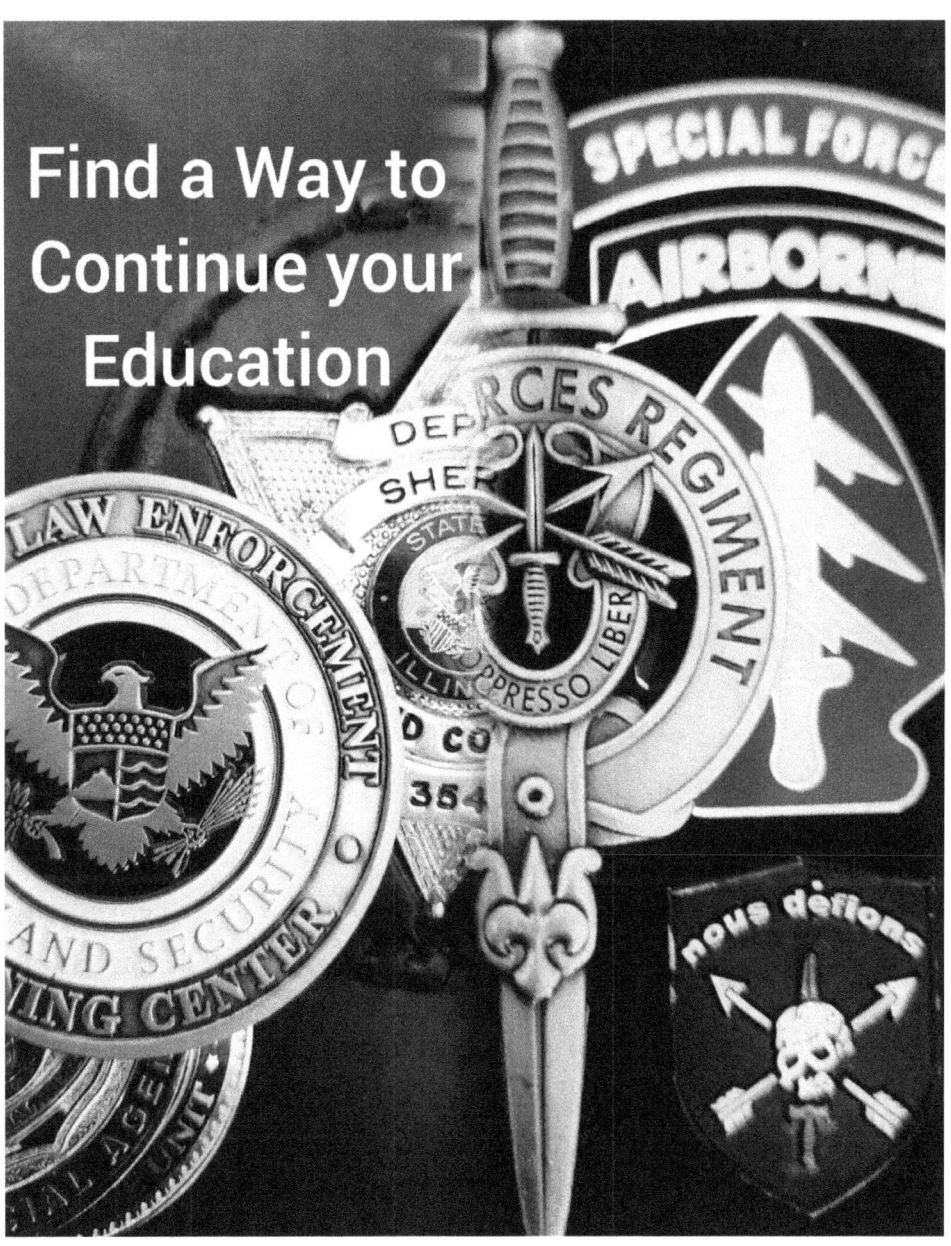

Comparative Principles: Military vs. Law Enforcement Engagement

While both military personnel and law enforcement officers operate in environments where the use of lethal force may be necessary, the context, constraints, and expectations differ significantly. Understanding these distinctions is critical for professional training, operational planning, and legal accountability.

1. Purpose of Engagement

Military: Engagements are typically mission-driven, focused on neutralizing hostile threats to accomplish operational objectives. The emphasis is on **lethal effectiveness, target prioritization, and mission success**. Every round must serve a tactical purpose, conserving ammunition while ensuring the enemy is decisively engaged.

Law Enforcement: Engagements are primarily defensive, aimed at protecting life—both the officer's and civilians'. Use-of-force decisions are heavily influenced by legal and ethical standards. Here, the emphasis is on **threat mitigation, precision, and minimizing collateral damage**, with each shot subject to post-engagement legal scrutiny.

2. Weapon Employment

Military: Pistols are generally secondary weapons, deployed when rifles are impractical or unavailable. Operations may involve confined spaces, CQB (close-quarters battle), or rapid weapon transitions. Training emphasizes **controlled, accurate fire under stress**, combined with situational awareness and operational tempo.

Law Enforcement: Pistols are often the primary weapon for patrol or off-duty encounters. Officers train for rapid deployment, accuracy under physiological stress, and safe engagement in complex civilian environments. Every trigger press must be **legally defensible and tactically justified**.

3. Ammunition Management

Military: Ammunition is finite in extended operations, particularly for special operations teams operating deep behind enemy lines. This drives a **conservation-focused mindset**: deliberate, precise fire and minimal wastage are essential to maintaining operational capability.

Law Enforcement: While ammunition is generally more abundant, officers still must recognize that missed rounds increase risk—to themselves, bystanders, and fellow officers. **Controlled, accurate fire** is critical to reduce liability and maximize threat neutralization.

4. Training Philosophies

Military: Emphasis is on **stress inoculation, weapon transitions, mission-driven engagement**, and precision under dynamic conditions. Training scenarios replicate operational complexity, including confined spaces, limited visibility, and high-threat environments.

Law Enforcement: Training focuses on **decision-making under pressure, target discrimination, legal defensibility, and threat mitigation**. Stress inoculation is paired with real-world scenario training to simulate patrol encounters, ambushes, and active-shooter situations.

5. Shared Principles

Despite differences in context, military and law enforcement professionals share several core principles:

- Every round counts; indiscriminate fire is unacceptable.
- Controlled, precise engagement is superior to volume-based tactics.
- Situational awareness, target selection, and threat assessment are essential.
- Training must replicate the stress and unpredictability of real encounters.

This comparison provides both **operational clarity** and a framework for designing training programs that respect the distinct missions of military and law enforcement while reinforcing shared principles of firearms discipline and accountability.

Every Round Counts: Principles of Precision and Accountability in Lethal Kinetic Engagements

Introduction

Whether on the streets or the battlefield, every round fired carries consequences—tactical, operational, and legal. Officers and military personnel alike must internalize that indiscriminate or uncontrolled fire is rarely acceptable. Controlled, precise engagement is not optional; it is a professional imperative. This module presents a unified framework for understanding the **legal, operational, and training considerations** governing the use of firearms in both law enforcement and military contexts.

Section 1 – For Law Enforcement Officers

Legal Accountability

Every trigger press carries legal and ethical weight. Discharged rounds are subject to investigation, and officers may face civil or criminal scrutiny if shots miss, strike unintended targets, or fail to neutralize the threat. Officers must view each engagement as both a tactical and legal act.

Performance under Stress

Human physiology under high-stress conditions—elevated heart rate, tunnel vision, auditory exclusion, and degraded fine motor control—reduces accuracy. Training must prepare officers to overcome these limitations and maintain effective engagement under real-world pressures.

Controlled Engagement

Missed rounds increase risk to bystanders, fellow officers, and the shooter's legal standing. Each shot must be deliberate, defensible, and mission-relevant. Officers must prioritize **target identification, threat neutralization, and ammunition discipline**.

Training Recommendations

- Realistic scenario-based drills
- Stress inoculation exercises
- Decision-making under time pressure
- Controlled, deliberate fire with target discrimination

Section 2 – For Military Personnel (Infantry & Special Operations)

Tactical Imperatives

Military warriors operate in mission-driven environments where indiscriminate fire is rarely tolerated. Success requires **precision, target prioritization, and ammunition conservation**. Pistols are secondary weapons, employed when rifles are unavailable or in confined spaces.

Operational Scenarios

- **Weapon Transitions:** Rapid shifts from primary to secondary weapons while maintaining threat suppression.
- **Confined Areas:** Engagements in close-quarters environments, vehicles, or urban structures where rifles are impractical.

- **Ammunition Management:** Finite rounds necessitate disciplined, deliberate engagement.

Training Philosophies

- Stress inoculation and dynamic, mission-relevant scenarios
- Integration of precision, speed, and controlled aggression
- Target selection and threat discrimination under operational stress
- Emphasis on every round's contribution to mission success

Section 3 – For Instructors and Leadership

Law Enforcement Perspective

Leaders must ensure officers understand that missed rounds carry **tactical and legal consequences**. Training programs should integrate stress, decision-making, and scenario-based engagements to prepare officers for real-world encounters.

Military Perspective

Instructors must design programs reflecting operational realities: weapon transitions, limited ammunition, and confined-space engagements. Training should simulate **combat stress, mission complexity, and decision-making under pressure**.

Shared Instructional Principles

- Every round counts; uncontrolled fire is unacceptable
- Accuracy, control, and threat discrimination are paramount
- Scenario-based stress training enhances decision-making
- After-action reviews should analyze performance, misses, and lessons learned

Section 4 – Comparative Analysis

Principle	Military	Law Enforcement	Shared
Purpose	Mission success, neutralize hostile threats	Protect life, mitigate threats	Controlled, precise engagement
Weapon Use	Secondary weapon in transitions or CQB	Often primary weapon	Accuracy and control emphasized
Ammunition	Finite; conservation required	Abundant but responsibility critical	Every round counts
Training	Stress inoculation, weapon transitions, CQB scenarios	Stress inoculation, scenario-based decision-making	Realistic, high-stress engagement training
Accountability	Mission success and operational risk	Legal and ethical responsibility	Both tactical and professional accountability

Conclusion

Across law enforcement and military domains, the guiding principle is clear: **every round counts**. Indiscriminate fire exposes personnel to operational failure, legal scrutiny, and increased risk to themselves and others. Training, doctrine, and operational planning must reinforce **precision, control, and accountability**—ensuring that every shot fired is both tactically effective and professionally defensible.

The Mind: Cultivating the Warrior's Edge

At the foundation of every elite performer — whether in combat, sport, or crisis lies a **sharpened mind**. The ability to remain calm under pressure, to act decisively in the face of chaos, and to maintain composure in life-threatening encounters is not an accident. It is the result of **intentional mental conditioning**. Skill with a firearm is important. But the ability to access and apply that skill when it counts — under stress, in low light, with lives on the line — is ultimately determined by **mental resilience, clarity, and control**.

Visualization and Mental Rehearsal

One of the most powerful and underutilized tools in the combative practitioner's arsenal is **positive mental imagery**, or **visualization**. This technique is widely employed by top-tier athletes, military professionals, and elite performers to **enhance proficiency**, especially when resources, time, or environmental constraints limit live training.

Even **fifteen minutes of focused dry practice per day**, performed in a safe and controlled environment, can drastically improve performance — particularly in weapon presentation, sight alignment, and trigger control. In fact, **fifteen minutes per week** of deliberate mental and dry-fire practice is often enough to maintain sharpness and build neural pathways that translate to increased real-world survivability.

The critical factor here is **self-motivation**. The responsible armed citizen must take ownership of their training. There is no external accountability in life-and-death moments — only the preparation you've done beforehand will matter.

Aggressive Mindset: From Reaction to Action

A **proactive mindset** — rooted in aggression and purpose — is essential to survival and success in armed conflict. An **aggressive mindset** is not about emotional aggression or recklessness. Rather, it is the mental readiness to seize initiative, dictate tempo, and **fight forward** when danger arises. This is the essence of the **Warrior Mindset**: being mentally, emotionally, and physically prepared to deal with any threat, at any time, even when it's forced upon you.

Once the need for force arises — once your life is on the line — **it is too late to begin learning**. If a citizen has never trained to respond with assertiveness, violence of action, and purpose, how will they suddenly summon those traits when crisis strikes? They won't. You **must train your mind** to respond the way your body will need to perform.

Ask yourself this:
Are you preparing to survive a gunfight, or to win one?

The difference between a slow, reactive mindset and a proactive, aggressive one is stark. The slow-reacting individual finds themselves **in a gunfight** — playing catch-up, under pressure, often behind the curve. The assertive, trained individual finds themselves **in a shooting** — dictating action, executing decisively, and ending the threat. The difference is mindset. And the time to develop it is **before the fight**.

Practical Mental Training Tools

Visualization:
Modern research confirms what warriors have known intuitively: **mental rehearsal improves real-world performance**. Fighters who visualize high-stress scenarios perform better under pressure. They show improved marksmanship, reduced anxiety, and

greater confidence when violence erupts. Why? Because the mind has already "seen" it before — the fight is not new.

- **Make it vivid.** Use all your senses — sight, sound, touch, even smell and emotion. Picture the environment, feel the weapon in your hand, hear the commands, and see yourself performing with precision.
- **Include adversity.** Visualize equipment malfunctions, multiple threats, environmental constraints — and most importantly, visualize yourself **successfully overcoming them**.
- **Never visualize failure.** Always conclude the mental scenario with a successful resolution.

Self-Talk and Instructional Cues:
In moments of stress, our inner dialogue shapes our actions. Use **task-relevant instructional self-talk** — short, positive, clear commands that reinforce action. Examples include:

- "Grip high. Front sight. Press."
- "Tap. Rack. Reassess."
- "Eyes up. Breathe. Move."

This kind of verbal reinforcement, especially when practiced consistently, can significantly improve both **cognitive focus** and **motor function** during high-stress engagements. Science backs this up: athletes and operators who engage in self-talk perform better across a wide range of cognitive and physical tasks.

Role Play and Dry Fire Integration:
Visualization and mental rehearsal must be **paired with physical practice**. Dry fire, scenario-based role playing, and force-on-force drills allow the mind and body to connect

— turning visualization into **habituated action**. These repetitions build a performance base that is not just conceptual but **neurologically imprinted**.

Closing Thoughts on the Mind

"I think anything is possible if you have the mindset and the will and desire to do it and put the time in."
— **Roger Clemens**

Mental preparation is **not optional**. It is a force multiplier that separates those who survive from those who dominate. As a practitioner of the combative arts — whether law enforcement, military, or responsibly armed citizen — your mind is the **first weapon** and the **last line of defense**.

Train it with the same discipline and seriousness you train your body.

The Human Response: Fight, Flight, Posture, or Capitulate

Understanding the spectrum of human responses to fear and violence—encompassing fight, flight, posture, and capitulate—stands as a cornerstone of effective self-defense training, particularly for those who choose to conceal carry a pistol. This knowledge empowers individuals by equipping them with the mental foresight to navigate high-stakes encounters, enabling quicker decision-making through tools like the OODA loop and fostering preparedness that can mean the difference between survival and victimization. For concealed carriers, it translates to enhanced situational awareness, strategic threat assessment, and the confidence to respond decisively rather than react impulsively, ultimately reducing the risks associated with armed self-defense. Instructors, meanwhile, must cultivate a profound grasp of these dynamics to impart not just technical skills but psychological resilience, ensuring their students internalize survival instincts and ethical considerations, thereby elevating the overall efficacy and responsibility of firearms education.

In the realm of self-defense and personal security, particularly for those who choose to conceal carry a firearm, understanding the spectrum of human responses to threats is paramount. Most practitioners of martial arts and self-defense disciplines are familiar with the classic dichotomy of "fight or flight" the instinctive reactions exhibited by individuals under duress. However, these represent only the most prevalent manifestations; human behavior in the face of danger encompasses a broader array, including posturing and capitulation. At its core, the response is governed by fear, one of humanity's most primal emotions, deeply rooted in our evolutionary survival instincts. These mechanisms, hardwired into our psyche, serve as the body's automatic defense against perceived threats, mobilizing resources to preserve life.

A fundamental principle in preparing for such encounters is the axiom that the body cannot venture where the mind has not first explored. This underscores the critical importance of mental rehearsal and visualization in self-defense training. Individuals must deliberately contemplate potential violent scenarios, immersing themselves in hypothetical situations of extreme vulnerability. For instance, in rape prevention seminars, instructors often guide participants to envision the most harrowing, isolated, and terrifying environments they might encounter—or be forcibly drawn into. By confronting these mental constructs in advance, the mind acclimates to the chaos, reducing the shock of real-world adversity.

This preparatory mindset directly enhances the OODA loop, a decision-making framework developed by military strategist John Boyd, comprising four stages: Observe (perceiving the threat), Orient (analyzing the situation within one's knowledge and experience), Decide (selecting a course of action), and Act (executing the response). When faced with violence, a pre-established plan, coupled with rigorous thought processes and practical training, becomes the linchpin of success. Procrastinating on such preparation until the moment of crisis is a grave error; by then, opportunities for effective intervention have often evaporated. For concealed carriers, this translates to not only physical proficiency with a firearm but also the psychological readiness to integrate these responses seamlessly, ensuring that fear does not paralyze but propels decisive action.

Fight

In this response, either the defender or the aggressor evaluates the confrontation and consciously elects to engage in physical combat. From a defensive standpoint, this might involve countering an attack with resolute force. Should the fight option be selected, commitment must be absolute: unleash violence with unyielding intensity. Empirical evidence from countless conflicts suggests that the individual who inflicts the most aggressive and sustained harm typically emerges victorious. As the Prussian military theorist Carl von Clausewitz aptly observed, "Courage, above all things, is the first quality of a warrior." For armed self-defenders, this means drawing and deploying a concealed pistol only when legally and ethically justified, but doing so with the ferocity required to neutralize the threat swiftly and decisively.

Flight

Here, the assessment leads to a deliberate choice to evade the danger through retreat or escape. This strategy often aligns with proactive situational awareness—such as altering one's path, crossing the street, or circumventing suspicious areas to preempt conflict. Wisdom dictates avoiding battles that cannot be won; discretion, in these cases, is the better part of valor. In the context of concealed carry, flight may involve creating distance to safely disengage, potentially allowing time to access a weapon if pursuit escalates the threat.

Posture

This involves adopting an aggressive stance or demeanor to dissuade the adversary from advancing or to prompt their withdrawal. The objective is akin to a peacock displaying its plumage: to project an aura of formidable readiness without necessarily escalating to violence. The intent is not combat itself but to convincingly signal preparedness, which may compel the opponent to flee—or, in rare instances, provoke an ill-advised attack. For those carrying concealed, posturing could manifest as a firm verbal command combined with a hand positioned near the holster, serving as a deterrent while adhering to de-escalation principles.

Capitulate

In capitulation, the individual succumbs to overwhelming fear, opting to submit, freeze, or plead for mercy in an attempt to mitigate harm. This passive yielding aims to appease the aggressor, hoping for minimal injury or reprieve. While it may occasionally preserve life in hopeless scenarios, it often stems from unchecked terror overtaking rational faculties. Concealed carriers must train to override this instinct when viable alternatives exist, as capitulation can forfeit the window for self-preservation through fight or flight.

Individuals instinctively respond to fear-driven threats through fight, flight, posture, or capitulation, survival mechanisms that martial artists recognize beyond the simplistic fight-or-flight dichotomy. Practitioners must mentally rehearse violent scenarios, visualizing the most harrowing vulnerabilities to prime their mindset and accelerate the OODA loop—observing, orienting, deciding, and acting decisively. In a confrontation, a preconceived plan and rigorous training propel victory; procrastination invites defeat. Fighters boldly engage adversaries with unrelenting ferocity, as the most aggressive contender often triumphs, embodying Carl von Clausewitz's axiom that courage defines a warrior. Fleers shrewdly evade unwinnable battles via heightened awareness, retreating to safety. Posturers aggressively bluff to deter foes, peacocking readiness to compel retreat without combat. Capitulators yield in terror, submitting to minimize harm. Mastering these responses remains paramount for concealed carriers, sharpening their defensive prowess, while instructors who deeply comprehend and articulate this wisdom forge resilient, proactive defenders capable of prevailing in chaos.

Understanding the Human Body and the Reaction to Stress

The Autonomic Nervous System (ANS) controls visceral organs such as heart, stomach, and intestines.

It is divided into two separate systems:

The Parasympathetic Nervous System (PNS) is in control in non-stress environments. While in this state our bodies are relaxed, deliberate, and precise. This is referred to as the "Rest and Digest" phase.

The Sympathetic Nervous System (SNS) activates when life is in jeopardy.

When activated we become quicker, stronger and, faster.

This is referred to as the "Fight or Flight or Freeze" phase. There are actually four possible responses.

Fight: You/Enemy assess the challenge and make the conscious decision to engage your adversary in physical combat or if challenged from a defensive posture, you decide to fight back.

Flight: You/Enemy assess the challenge and make the conscious decision to evade the threat by retreating or fleeing

Posture: You/Enemy assess the challenge and make the conscious decision to posture aggressively in an effort to influence your adversary to not fight or to flee.

Capitulate: You/Enemy assess the challenge and make the conscious decision to submit, freeze, lie down, and ask for mercy.

Instructors need to have a basic understanding of the Sympathetic Nervous System in order to comprehend what a shooter is most likely to do and what triggers to the sympathetic nervous system may cause.

The Sympathetic Nervous System may be caused by fear of death, fear of killing, fear of injury, fear of fear, physical exhaustion, lack of confidence in abilities, the perceived threat is a new experience, close proximity of threat.

Once the SNS is triggered, the student may experience negative effects in visual processing, motor skill performance, and cognitive processing.

Perceptual narrowing which consists of inability to focus with the dominant eye, night vision degradation and inability to distinguish colors, loss of depth perception, loss of peripheral vision, loss of near vision, involuntary tracking of the threat, increase of adrenalin, increased heart rate (>140), blood pressure, and respirations, deterioration of fine and complex motor skills, auditory exclusion, and lack of clarity of thought or irrational responses are primary results of SNS activation.

SNS can also cause the body to square off toward a threat (feet shoulder width apart rather than bladed or the traditional Weaver shooting stance).

This response is virtually automatic due to the startle effect, and the head squaring to receive all available visual input, and understanding this particular action has aided martial artists and those that participate in most combat sports, this will also allow the instructor to present a valid reason for a squared up shooting stance.

Motor Skills

The study of motor behavior classifies motor skills into three basic forms.

They are fine, complex, and gross motor skills.

The startle response is characterized by increased arterial pressure and blood flow to large muscle mass (enhancing gross motor skills and strength capabilities), and vasoconstriction of minor blood vessels at the end the appendages, this generally will lead to degrading fine and complex motor skills.

Fine motor skills are those that require hand/eye coordination and hand dexterity. These skills generally begin to deteriorate around 115 heartbeats per minute.

An example is precision shooting, firing a weapon for score in an effort to qualify requires a measure of concentration and can best be described as a fine motor skill.

Firing during lethal kinetic encounters is very different because of the many factors in play, with the skill component being better described as a complex motor skill.

Complex motor skills involve a series of muscle groups in a series of movements requiring hand/eye coordination, precision, tracking, and timing.

These skills generally begin to deteriorate around 145 heartbeats per minute. An example is Tap-Rack-Ready (cognitive due to proper sequencing and fine due to fine motor skills of weapons manipulation).

Gross motor skills involve the action of large or major muscle groups, essentially a pushing or pulling event.

Since gross motor skills utilize large muscle groups, they can also be referred to as strength events. As a strength event, a high level of arousal (motivation, excitement, or psyching-up) will increase the optimal performance level due to increased adrenal secretions.

Overcoming the effects of stress

The relationship between practice intensity, motivation, skill competency, and skill confidence are inseparable.

Well-rehearsed tasks are less prone to degradation under conditions of stress; well-rehearsed tasks become "automatic", thus requiring less of the individuals' attention; and well drilled tasks enhance a person's sense of predictability and control.

Instructors should understand that by teaching firearms tasks as almost religious rituals so that the tasks such as loading, unloading and malfunction clearing have predictability and the shooter is working in at a sub-conscious competency level so that they will better be able to solve tactical issues without distraction.

Performance is optimized (generally) when the heart rate is between 115 and 145 beats per minute. Complex motor skills, visual reaction time, and cognitive reaction time are all at their peak.

When learning skills in is important for the shooter to ingrain them into their neurological pathways creating effective neurological imprinting.

It becomes imperative that an instructor teaches the student one way to accomplish a task so that it can be mastered before a second way is taught.

W.E. Hicks 1952 study found that when the possible responses increased from one to two, reaction time increased by 58 percent.

Choosing between options takes time. The more options available, the greater the reaction time; thus, a simple set of skills, combined with actions requiring complex and gross motor skills, extensively rehearsed, allows for extraordinary performance levels under stress.

The loss of fine motor skills can be overcome with training. The ability of the US Military to train Fighter Pilots and Free Fall Parachutists proves this. It's possible to push the envelope of complex motor-skill performance under stress.

This generally occurs with specific, well-rehearsed skills.

For example, studies done on top Formula One and NASCAR drivers found that their heart rates averaged 175 bpm for hours on end. These drivers perform a limited set of finely tuned skills with extraordinary speed, under a good deal of stress.

As defined by Dave Grossman in another of his books, (Grossman & Christensen, 2004), stress inoculation is a process by which prior success under stressful conditions acclimatizes officers to similar situations and promotes future success.

Since patterns are ingrained with each repetition, it's crucial that any sort of technique be drilled flawlessly.

Even in a controlled environment, with a punching bag for an opponent, poor technique in training will be reproduced when it matters.

Training cannot be performed sloppy and then expect to perform well.

When the trained motor pattern is relegated to subconscious thought, there can be no question that it will be carried out correctly.

Complex motor control is going to diminish as heart rate increases; the exact heart rate at which this happens will depend on the level of fitness and the degree to which the shooter is inoculated against stress.

The best way to overcome the detrimental effects of stress on performance is inoculation through consistent, realistic training.

With proper, consistent, and realistic training, the shooter can hone their body to perform at optimal levels, even when the going gets the toughest.

Training under a steadily increasing level of stress and performance standards, the student's ability to control the adverse physical and mental reactions to stress is increased.

Using the concepts of: dominate the weapon, dominate the opponent, dominate the situation and dominate all visual areas, the student uses the specific techniques within the tactical shooting training to overcome and dominate all actual and potential threats generally within a close combat range.

I have learned that over the years of training that many instructors believe fine motor skills should not be used in training because these skills will be lost under stress. I disagree!

When teaching firearms it is important to have the shooter manipulate the trigger from front to rear without disturbing the sights. Trigger manipulation is a fine motor skill!

If you can manipulate the trigger under stress, then you can operate a slide catch with the proper training.

I will agree that fine and complex motor skills deteriorate under stress, but by training under stress the deterioration can be minimized. I am not telling you that you have to train in the use of fine and complex motor skills, just realize that their effective use requires more practice.

Mental Aspects

Positive mental imagery is a tool that those who are at the top of their game use to maintain and improve proficiency, even when they don't have the resources to actually practice the skills.

Fifteen minutes a day of dry practice will make an immense difference in the ability to deliver highly accurate fire during a life-threatening encounter.

Fifteen minutes a week would easily make the difference in terms of weapon presentation, sight alignment, and trigger control.

Aggressive mindset is an offensive mindset. This leads us to a warrior mindset.

As an instructor it is your responsibility to ensure that you are preparing the student not to just survive a lethal force encounter, but to actually win the encounter.

The student needs to be taught to have the mental preparation and mindset to be a winner.

The Warrior Mindset is being ready for every situation that may arise, wanted or unwanted.

The student should not be in a reactive mode, but if they find themselves in this situation, they should not react slowly.

The difference between slow reaction and an aggressive reaction is that slow reaction may result in a lethal force encounter, whereas an aggressive pro-active approach may result in the student dominating the encounter prior to any lethal force being applied.

Practice visualization shows that warriors who visualize hypothetical high-stress scenarios perform better in actual high-stress situations than those who don't.

For example, students who take part in visual exercises demonstrate better marksmanship than those who skip this technique.

Visualizing successful management of high-stress situations reduces a combatant's anxiety and stress response when the events actually occur, thus allowing the fighter to stay in an optimal response condition longer.

Convince your students to make the visualization as vivid as possible. Incorporate all the senses and emotions. Visualize problems and sticking points, but — and this is the critical part — always visualize the successful outcome of the problem or obstacle. Never visualize failure.
Never rely on visualization alone. It's important to combine it with tactical practice and role playing.
Use task-relevant instructional self-talk. To counter the detrimental performance effects of stress, talk through complex actions as if teaching these tasks to another.
Self-talk can increase performance on both cognitive and physical tasks. The key with this type of self-talk is to keep it brief and positive.

The Human response: Fight, Flight, Posture or Capitulate.

Most martial artists are aware of the fight or flight responses that most people display. These are the most common, but not the only responses. The human response will be determined by fear. This is one of the most basic of human responses. These are survival instincts.

Remember the body cannot go where the mind has not already been.

Take time to think about violent encounters. In my rape prevention classes I often tell my students to think about the darkest most vulnerable terrifying place they can go or be forcibly taken.

The mind has now been there, this will help with the **OODA loop. (Observe, Orient, Decide, and Act).** When you are confronted with a violent situation you should already have a plan, a though process and training to help you win. Do not wait until it happens to you to think about it, then it is too late!

Fight: You/Enemy assess the challenge and make the conscious decision to engage your adversary in physical combat or if challenged from a defensive posture, you decide to fight back. If this option is chosen, Be VIOLENT!!! Generally the person that is the most violent and doing the most violence prevails.

Flight: You/Enemy assess the challenge and make the conscious decision to evade the threat by retreating or fleeing. This may be part of situational awareness, go around, cross the street and avoid the potential conflict. Do not fight a fight that you cannot win.

Posture: You/Enemy assess the challenge and make the conscious decision to posture aggressively in an effort to influence your adversary to not fight or to flee. The ultimate goal is to "peacock" and to posture your way out of a fight. The goal is not to fight, but convince your adversary that you are prepared too. This may force your adversary to flee or possibly attack.

Capitulate: You/Enemy assess the challenge and make the conscious decision to submit, freeze, lie down, and ask for mercy. Capitulation is an effort to appease the adversary in hopes of little or no damage being done. Fear has taken over.

Remember and teach your students the old saying passed down amongst warriors: ***"We do not rise to the level of our expectations. We fall to the level of our training". Archilochus'***

Instructors must understand that in a lethal kinetic encounter that, you sink to the level of training and practice and reality the shooter will sink below their best level of training on the range!

Shooting is a very perishable skill.

The best way to overcome the detrimental effects of stress on performance is to inoculate yourself from it altogether through consistent, realistic training.

From a self-defense standpoint, this means you need to do more than just go to the gun range to practice your marksmanship or punch the heavy bag in your garage.

You'll actually need to train your techniques under the same sort of pressure you'd experience in a real-life situation.

Attack Indicators and Decision-Making in Firearms Training

As firearms instructors, we recognize that most range-based training does not require students to make a **use-of-force decision** in real time. Targets are presented, commands are given, and students execute. This controlled environment allows us to isolate skills, reinforce fundamentals, and build consistency. However, armed professionals must operate in environments where deadly force is not simply about pressing the trigger correctly—it is about recognizing **when and why to shoot.**

For that reason, instructors have a responsibility not only to teach technical execution, but also to **frame firearms use within human behavior, threat recognition, and proper articulation.**

Understanding Human Behavior

Armed professionals must learn to read and anticipate behavior. Before an armed encounter escalates, individuals often display **pre-assault cues** that fall within common behavioral patterns:

- **Fight:** Aggressive forward movement, clenched fists, tightening jaw, verbal escalation.
- **Flight:** Blading of the body, shifting feet, looking for exits.
- **Posturing:** Overconfidence displays, hands on waistband, hard stares, dominance gestures.
- **Capitulation:** Raised hands, backing away, verbal submission.

Within these categories lie **attack indicators**—behaviors that precede violence. A sudden glance to the hands, a bladed stance with the dominant side concealed, repeated touching of the waistband, or the lowering of the head with a forward lean can all signal imminent assault.

Hands Kill: The Core of Threat Recognition

Instructors must emphasize the reality that **hands are the delivery system for deadly force.** Whether it is a firearm, a knife, or an improvised weapon, the threat is revealed in the hands. Students must be conditioned to actively scan for, identify, and interpret hand movements in context:

- Hands disappearing into clothing or a waistband.
- Hands concealed behind the body or within an object.
- Rapid or furtive movements toward potential weapon-carry areas.

This scanning process becomes part of the **mental checklist** that determines when the transition from readiness to engagement is justified.

From Range to Reality: Incorporating Indicators into Training

While the range is primarily a technical environment, instructors can begin layering **decision-making and threat recognition** into drills as students progress:

- **Verbal Commands:** Integrating verbalization before shooting reinforces the mental process of commanding compliance and identifying non-compliance.
- **Target Discrimination:** Mixing threat and non-threat targets requires the shooter to observe, decide, and act rather than reflexively fire.
- **Behavioral Cues:** Using role-players or scenario targets with visual cues (e.g., hand on waistband, weapon partially concealed) conditions students to look for precursors of violence.

By gradually incorporating these elements, instructors help bridge the gap between **flat range repetition** and the **dynamic environments** where armed professionals must operate.

Articulation and Accountability

Firearms instruction is incomplete without preparing students to **articulate their decisions.** After a lethal encounter, the ability to clearly explain **what was observed, why it was perceived as a threat, and how the response was reasonable** is essential for both legal defense and professional accountability.

Instructors should deliberately weave articulation into after-action reviews. After drills that involve decision-making, students should be required to state:

1. **What indicators they observed.**
2. **Why those indicators suggested a lethal threat.**

3. **Why they acted (or withheld action) as they did.**

This habit of articulating reinforces awareness, strengthens judgment, and prepares professionals for the inevitable scrutiny that follows a use-of-force incident.

From Range To Reality

Instructor's Responsibility

As instructors, our duty goes beyond teaching grip, stance, or trigger control. We must ensure that every student understands the **intersection of behavior, indicators, and decision-making.** On the range, this means:

- Teaching mechanics first, but never separating them from the purpose they serve.
- Layering complexity—starting with fundamentals, then integrating cues, commands, and decision points.
- Holding students accountable not only for marksmanship, but for their **judgment and articulation.**

Ultimately, firearms training for armed professionals must produce shooters who are **technically proficient, tactically aware, and mentally prepared** to identify threats, respond appropriately, and defend their actions with confidence.

Instructor Module: Attack Indicators and Decision-Making for Armed Professionals

Module Purpose

This module equips firearms instructors with the tools to integrate **attack indicator recognition, decision-making, and articulation** into range training. It bridges the gap between technical marksmanship and real-world application, preparing armed professionals to recognize human behavior cues, act decisively, and justify their actions under scrutiny.

Learning Objectives

By the end of this module, students will:

1. **Identify** common behavioral precursors to assault (fight, flight, posturing, capitulation).
2. **Recognize** attack indicators, especially hand movements associated with weapon access.
3. **Integrate** decision-making into live-fire range drills through target discrimination and command drills.
4. **Demonstrate** appropriate shoot/no-shoot decisions under time pressure.
5. **Articulate** their observations and actions in clear, professional language.

Instructor Preparation

- **Safety First:** Decision-making drills introduce complexity—safety protocols must be uncompromising. Maintain strict muzzle discipline, range commands, and instructor oversight.
- **Targets:**
    - Standard silhouette targets.
    - Photo-realistic threat/non-threat targets.
    - Scenario targets depicting partial weapons, ambiguous hand placement, or innocent bystanders.
- **Props:** Replica firearms, cell phones, wallets, and other everyday objects for non-threat cues.
- **Range Setup:** Ensure clear lanes of fire and a safe backstop. Drills should progress from static firing lines to dynamic movement only when students demonstrate control.

Training Progression

Phase 1: Classroom/Briefing – Behavioral Foundations

Instructor Actions:

- Explain the four behavioral categories: fight, flight, posturing, capitulation.
- Show video clips of real encounters (LEO or CCTV footage) highlighting pre-assault cues.
- Discuss why **hands kill** and how to train students to constantly evaluate hand movement.

Student Takeaway:

- Build a mental library of observable cues.
- Understand that not all cues equal a shoot decision, but they guide readiness.

Phase 2: Dry-Fire Range Integration – Decision Before Trigger

Drill 1: Verbal Challenge

- Instructor calls out target numbers. Some are designated "compliant," some "non-compliant."
- Student must issue verbal commands before firing.
- If the target is compliant (hands raised or non-threat target), no shots are fired.

Purpose: Reinforces mental pause before shooting and conditions verbal articulation.

Drill 2: Indicator Recognition (Dry)

- Targets display different cues (waistband grab, hidden hand, raised hands).
- Student must call out their observation before engaging. Example: *"Target two—hand on waistband—engage."*

Purpose: Builds habit of linking observation to action.

Phase 3: Live-Fire Range Integration – Stress and Choice

Drill 3: Shoot/No-Shoot Discrimination

- Mixed target set (threat and non-threats).
- On instructor command, student must scan, identify, and engage only threats.

- Errors (engaging non-threats or failing to shoot threats) are corrected immediately.

Drill 4: Command and Fire Under Pressure

- Timer initiates the drill.
- Student issues a verbal challenge. Target exposure lasts 3–4 seconds.
- If target displays an attack indicator (e.g., gun, knife, or weapon draw), student fires. If not, student withholds fire.

Purpose: Introduces **time compression** and realistic engagement windows.

Drill 5: Scenario Stressor

- Multiple targets and role-play elements (moving non-threats, innocent cues like a phone or wallet).
- Student must move, issue commands, and decide.
- Instructor debriefs: Did the student shoot the right target, at the right time, for the right reason?

Phase 4: Articulation Training – After Action Reviews

Drill 6: Structured Articulation Exercise

- After each scenario, student must explain:
    1. **What they saw** (attack indicators, behavior cues).
    2. **What they decided** (shoot/no-shoot).
    3. **Why they acted** (reasonable fear, imminent threat).

Instructor Role: Guide the debrief. Reinforce professional articulation—"I saw the suspect's hand go to his waistband in a rapid movement; based on training and experience, I believed he was drawing a firearm; I fired to stop the threat."

Purpose: Conditions students to communicate clearly and defensibly in reports, court, or administrative review.

Evaluation Criteria

Students must demonstrate:

- **Technical:** Safe weapon handling and accuracy during all drills.
- **Cognitive:** Ability to correctly identify threat vs. non-threat under stress.
- **Verbal:** Clear, professional articulation of observations and decisions.

Key Instructor Points

- **Layer Complexity:** Start simple (commands and discrimination) before introducing stress and movement.
- **Correct Immediately:** Address judgment errors as firmly as marksmanship errors.
- **Link Everything:** Reinforce that technical skill is meaningless without proper decision-making and articulation.
- **End with Reflection:** After scenarios, students should leave the range thinking not only about *how they shot,* but *why they shot.*

Proprioception

Proprioception is one of those underlying, often overlooked, performance factors in shooting that separates "mechanical" shooters from highly skilled ones.

Definition

Proprioception is the body's sense of position, movement, and force without relying on vision. It's sometimes called the "sixth sense" of body awareness. In pistol shooting, it's what allows you to know where your hands, arms, and pistol are in space—even without consciously looking at them.

In Relation to Pistol Shooting

1. **Grip Consistency**
   - Proprioception helps you replicate the same grip pressure and hand alignment on the pistol every time.
   - Skilled shooters can "feel" if their grip is slightly off without needing to visually confirm.

2. **Presentation to Target**
   - When drawing from the holster, proprioception allows you to present the gun so the sights or red dot naturally align with your eyes.
   - With training, your body learns the exact angles and motions required so the gun "arrives" on target consistently.

3. **Trigger Control**
   - Proprioceptive awareness lets you sense the trigger press, reset, and weight without overthinking.
   - It helps you feel micro-errors in finger placement or excessive tension.

4. **Stability & Balance**
    - It controls stance, posture, and recoil management.
    - Your nervous system constantly makes micro-adjustments in balance and muscle tension to keep you stable under recoil or when moving between targets.

In Relation to Shooting Drills

Proprioception develops best under **repetition and feedback**, which is why certain drills are so valuable.

- **Dry Fire Reps**: Builds proprioceptive "maps" of the draw, trigger press, and reload.
- **Blind Draw Drill**: Present the pistol to eye level with eyes closed, then open eyes to check alignment—this sharpens proprioceptive alignment of sights to eyes.
- **Target Transitions**: Teach proprioceptive control of speed, stopping the gun precisely on new targets without overswing.
- **Strong-Hand/Support-Hand Only Shooting**: Forces your proprioception to adapt and refine motor control with reduced contact.

- **Low Light / No Light Drills**: Especially valuable because they force reliance on proprioceptive awareness instead of pure vision.

Bottom Line

Proprioception in pistol shooting is your **internal feedback system** that makes movements smooth, consistent, and repeatable. Visual confirmation (seeing the sights) tells you "when" you can shoot, but proprioception is what makes sure the gun, hands, and trigger are where they should be without conscious thought.

Instructors can think of it this way: *vision gives permission, proprioception builds precision.*

Proprioception is the body's sense of position, movement, and force without relying on vision. It's sometimes called the "sixth sense" of body awareness. In pistol shooting, it's what allows you to know where your hands, arms, and pistol are in space—even without consciously looking at them.

A **proprioception-focused drill progression** that you could use either as a personal training block or as an instructor module. The goal here is to develop body awareness, repeatability, and confidence in the gun's position without relying solely on vision.

Proprioception Drill Progression for Pistol Shooting

1. Foundation – Static Awareness

Purpose: Build proprioceptive maps for grip, trigger, and presentation.

- **Grip Reps (Eyes Closed):**
    - With eyes closed, build your grip on the pistol (dry).

- Open your eyes and check consistency (web of hand, support hand pressure, trigger finger placement).
- **Trigger Prep Drill (Dry Fire):**
  - With eyes closed, prep the trigger to the wall, press, and reset.
  - Open your eyes after 3–5 reps to confirm sight stability.

Vision gives you permission

Proprioception builds Precision

2. Alignment Awareness – Presentation

Purpose: Train proprioceptive alignment between pistol, eyes, and target.

- **Blind Presentation Drill:**
  - Stand in shooting stance, eyes closed.
  - Draw and present the pistol to where you believe sight alignment will be on target.
  - Open eyes and check sight picture/dot. Adjust as needed.
- **Wall Drill (Eyes Closed):**
  - From ready, close eyes, present pistol to a blank wall at one-inch distance.
  - Open eyes to confirm that sights are aligned.

3. Positional Awareness – Stability & Balance

Purpose: Develop proprioceptive control over body and recoil.

- **Balance & Recoil Drill:**
  - Fire slow pairs, focusing on stance and balance recovery.

- Between strings, close eyes, reset stance, and see if pistol naturally returns to point of aim.
- **One-Handed Drills (Dry + Live):**
  - Strong-hand only, then support-hand only.
  - Forces proprioceptive refinement since contact with pistol is reduced.

4. Movement Awareness – Transitions

Purpose: Build proprioceptive precision in moving the gun.

- **Target Transition Drill (Eyes Open → Closed):**
  - Present to first target with eyes open.
  - Close eyes, transition to second target by proprioceptive feel.
  - Open eyes and verify alignment.
- **Controlled Transitions:**
  - Shoot one shot per target across a line of 3–5 targets.
  - Focus on "stopping" the pistol exactly where it belongs—feel the stop, don't just see it.

5. Stress/Environmental Awareness

Purpose: Apply proprioceptive skills under stress or degraded conditions.

- **Low Light / No Light Drills:**
  - Dry fire draws and reloads in total darkness—then verify in light.
- **Timer-Induced Stress:**
  - Run blind draw drills or transitions on the timer to build proprioceptive trust under urgency.

Instructor Notes

- Start with **eyes open for reference**, then introduce **eyes closed** to force proprioceptive reliance.
- Always include a **visual check step** so students learn their proprioceptive "errors" and correct them.
- Emphasize *consistency before speed*. Proprioception builds in layers—the more consistent the motion, the more reliable it becomes under stress.

Here's a **ready-to-print instructor module** built around proprioception in pistol shooting. I've structured it in a professional lesson plan format with clear objectives, standards, drills, and coaching points.

Instructor Module: Proprioception in Pistol Shooting

Training Objective

Develop the shooter's proprioceptive ability to consistently control grip, presentation, trigger press, and target transitions without over-reliance on vision.

Performance Standards

- Shooter can achieve a consistent firing grip with eyes closed, verified visually after the fact.
- Shooter can present pistol from holster to eye line and achieve sight alignment within **3° of deviation** when checked.
- Shooter can execute controlled target transitions that stop cleanly on the intended aiming point.

- Shooter can perform reloads and manipulations by feel under low-light or no-light conditions.

Lesson Outline

1. **Introduction (5 min)**
    - Define proprioception: body's awareness of position and movement without sight.
    - Explain its role in pistol shooting: grip repeatability, sight alignment, balance, recoil control, transitions.
    - Stress vision confirms *when* to fire, proprioception ensures *how* movements are repeatable.
2. **Warm-Up (10 min)**
    - Dry fire grip reps (eyes closed → open and confirm).
    - Dry trigger press with eyes closed.

Drill Progression

1. Grip Awareness Drill

- **Setup:** Dry fire, no ammo.
- **Execution:**
    - With eyes closed, establish grip.
    - Open eyes to confirm placement and consistency.
- **Standard:** 10/10 reps should show consistent hand placement.
- **Coaching Point:** Feel backstrap pressure, support hand wedge, trigger finger isolation.

2. Blind Presentation Drill

- **Setup:** Holstered pistol, dry fire.
- **Execution:**
    - With eyes closed, draw and present to where sights should be.
    - Open eyes to confirm alignment.
- **Standard:** Sights aligned within 3° of correction on 8/10 reps.
- **Coaching Point:** Focus on indexing off body mechanics, not chasing sights.

3. Wall Drill (Proprioceptive Alignment)

- **Setup:** 1 inch from a blank wall.
- **Execution:**
    - With eyes closed, present pistol.
    - Open eyes to verify alignment on wall.
- **Standard:** 9/10 reps aligned.
- **Coaching Point:** Helps eliminate reliance on external targets.

4. One-Handed Awareness Drills

- **Setup:** Dry and live fire.
- **Execution:**
    - Draw and fire strong-hand only, then support-hand only.
- **Standard:** 5-shot groups remain inside 8" circle at 7 yards.
- **Coaching Point:** Refines proprioceptive control under reduced contact.

5. Transition Awareness Drill

- **Setup:** 3–5 targets spaced 2–3 feet apart.

- **Execution:**
    - With eyes open, shoot first target.
    - Close eyes, transition to next target by proprioceptive feel, then open and confirm.
- **Standard:** Alignment on target within 5° of correction.
- **Coaching Point:** Feel the *stop* of the gun, don't overswing.

6. Environmental Stressors (Low-Light / Timer)

- **Setup:** Range lights dimmed or turned off.
- **Execution:**
    - Reloads, draws, and manipulations in low or no light.
    - Add timer for speed stress.
- **Standard:** Perform all manipulations safely and correctly without light, consistent hits inside 8" circle at 7 yards.
- **Coaching Point:** Builds trust in proprioception when vision is degraded.

Debrief / Wrap-Up (10 min)

- Discuss observations: where shooters relied on vision, where proprioception took over.
- Reinforce that proprioception creates **repeatability and consistency**, while vision confirms the result.
- Assign dry practice homework: 25 blind presentations nightly.

Through Repetitions: A Firearms Instructor's Proven Path to Mastery

In the high-stakes world of firearms training, inductive learning stands as the cornerstone of building unshakeable proficiency. This approach, where trainees derive general principles from repeated, specific experiences, transforms novices into experts by forging neural pathways through relentless practice. As a seasoned professional firearms instructor with roots in Special Forces, I assert without reservation that repetitions form the bedrock of effective training. They do not merely build skills—they etch them into muscle memory, ensuring split-second decisions under pressure become instinctive. Repetitions drive results, as evidenced by the rigorous protocols of elite units, and they remain the method I champion in my instruction today.

Inductive learning thrives on experiential immersion rather than abstract theory. Trainees encounter real-world scenarios repeatedly, allowing them to observe patterns, adjust techniques, and internalize lessons organically. In firearms training, this manifests through high-volume repetitions that simulate combat's chaos. Consider the pistol, often relegated to a secondary weapon system in Special Forces operations. Yet, programs like the Special Operations Target Interdiction Course (SOT) and the Special Forces Advanced Reconnaissance, Target Analysis, and Exploitation Techniques Course (SFARTEAC) prioritize it with an initial 80 hour -point-of-instruction curriculum. Instructors demand 1,000 live rounds per day, supplemented by two hours of nightly dry-fire practice. This regimen compels shooters to confront variables—recoil, sight alignment, solid grip, trigger control—time and again, inductively refining their approach until precision emerges as second nature.

The training day commences with a deliberate challenge: a B8 bullseye target at 25 yards, completed within a 10-minute limit. The standard? A minimum of 70/100 for ten days in a row with a culmination of 700 out of 1,000 points. This serves as the critical first gate, barring progression to rifle work or close-quarters battle (CQB) until mastered. Instructors enforce this threshold actively, knowing it separates competent operators from the elite. Even-numbered shooters position themselves in front of their targets while odd-numbered ones fire, then switch roles. With targets spaced just one yard apart center-to-center, this setup builds unyielding confidence. It prepares trainees for the intensity of live-fire CQB, where proximity to teammates and adversaries demands flawless execution amid distraction.

Vision reigns supreme in this process, as instructors emphasize acquiring and maintaining a crisp sight picture. However, the grip receives relentless focus from cadre members. They drill it into trainees through verbal cues, physical corrections, and endless repetitions, recognizing that a firm, consistent grip stabilizes the weapon and mitigates errors under stress. This emphasis aligns with inductive principles: repeatedly establishing the grip under varying conditions teaching the body to adapt, revealing that subtle wrist angles or finger placements yield monumental differences in accuracy.

Why do repetitions yield such transformative results? Neuroscience provides the answer. Each repetition strengthens synaptic connections in the brain's motor cortex and cerebellum, accelerating the transition from conscious effort to automated response. In Special Forces, this methodology produces operators for one of the planet's most lethal organizations, where hesitation equals failure. Repetitions simulate the unpredictability of real engagements, allowing trainees to inductively learn from misses, near-misses, and hits. Dry-fire sessions amplify this, enabling cost-effective refinement without ammunition expenditure, while live-fire cements the lessons in high-fidelity scenarios.

Critics may argue that modern simulations or virtual reality could supplant traditional repetitions, but I counter that nothing replicates the tactile feedback of actual rounds downrange. Inductive learning via repetitions builds not just technical skill but mental resilience. Trainees confront fatigue, frustration, and failure head-on, emerging with the authoritative confidence that defines professionals. In my practice, I replicate these elements, starting sessions with bullseye drills and progressing only when standards are met. This mirrors the Special Forces model, ensuring my students—law enforcement, military personnel, and civilians alike—achieve mastery.

Inductive learning through repetitions propels firearms training beyond rote memorization into true expertise. Special Forces protocols demonstrate this unequivocally: they forge warriors who perform under duress because they have lived the repetitions. As an instructor, I teach this way because it works—it saves lives, enhances lethality, and instills discipline. Embrace repetitions, and watch proficiency soar.

Repetitions drive transformative results in skill acquisition through neuroplasticity, the brain's capacity to reorganize and adapt by forming and strengthening neural connections. Hebb's rule—"neurons that fire together wire together"—captures this essence: repeated actions activate neural pathways, triggering biochemical changes that enhance synaptic efficiency and forge robust, enduring connections. Mechanisms such as long-term potentiation (LTP) amplify this process, as recurrent stimulation boosts neurotransmitter release and receptor sensitivity, facilitating quicker future activations. In motor learning, these changes prominently occur in the motor cortex, which orchestrates movement planning and execution, and the cerebellum, which fine-tunes coordination, timing, and error correction for seamless performance. Over iterations, skills shift from deliberate, conscious control—often engaging the prefrontal cortex for decision-making—to automated, subconscious responses managed by subcortical structures, liberating cognitive resources for higher-order tasks.

This neurological framework underpins the efficacy of repetitions in elite training regimens, such as those employed by Special Forces units, which rank among the world's most formidable military organizations. These programs forge operators who excel under extreme duress, where hesitation invites catastrophe. Repetitive drills cultivate "muscle memory," enabling instinctive responses to volatile scenarios like close-quarters combat or split-second decisions amid chaos. Trainees inductively refine their techniques by dissecting misses, near-misses, and hits across countless iterations, systematically minimizing errors and variability. Dry-fire sessions—practicing without ammunition—provide a cost-effective means to master fundamentals such as trigger control and sight alignment, accelerating synaptic reinforcement without depleting resources. Live-fire exercises then consolidate these gains in realistic, high-stakes environments, embedding the neural adaptations under pressure.

The intensity of such training reveals stark disparities in repetition volume. Special Forces soldiers often fire up to 10,000 live rounds over a 10-day period, immersing them in high-repetition drills that build unyielding proficiency. In contrast, federal law enforcement trainees typically expend fewer than 3,000 live rounds across 10 weeks, reflecting a more measured pace that prioritizes foundational skills but yields slower mastery. This gap underscores why I mandate that my students commit to at least 10 minutes of dry-fire practice each night: it bridges the divide, propelling them toward journeyman-level shooting competence—where reliability meets efficiency—through consistent, deliberate repetitions. Ultimately, repetitions do not merely hone skills; they rewire the brain, transforming novices into adept performers equipped for real-world demands.

Doctrinal

Live-Fire Demonstrations

I firmly believe that Instructors must conduct live-fire demonstrations for any technique, drill, or concept that is new to the student. Demonstrations establish the standard, display proper execution, and confirm the instructor's own level of skill and proficiency. This practice not only provides a clear model for students to emulate but also reinforces the instructor's credibility. Without demonstration, there is no proof of competence; and without competence, credibility is lost.

Motivational

Why Live-Fire Demonstrations Matter

If a student has never seen a skill performed, the instructor must show it—live, on the range. A live-fire demonstration does more than display technique; it proves ability, sets expectations, and shows the student that the instructor has walked the path they are teaching. When students see their instructor execute with precision and confidence, they trust the lesson and push themselves to meet that standard. No demonstration means no example, no proof, and ultimately, no credibility.

The Professional Standard of Live-Fire Demonstrations

Live-fire demonstrations are not optional—they are essential. As a student in high-level courses, I have always expected the instructor to conduct them, and I hold myself to that same standard. A professional instructor does not simply explain a drill; he proves it, breaking it down in real time so students can see, hear, and understand the process.

The most effective demonstrations follow a structured approach. The first run is conducted at approximately 25% speed while the instructor narrates, allowing students to observe the fine details and nuances of technique. The second run is delivered at 85–90% speed, showing students what competent execution looks like under realistic conditions. The third demonstration slows back down to roughly 50%, reinforcing key points while still showcasing elements of speed. This progression allows students to both see the subtleties and grasp the standard of performance they should strive toward.

As a Special Forces instructor, live-fire demonstrations were not optional—they were expected. At that level, both instructor and student were professionals, and credibility was inseparable from performance. The same held true at SIG Academy, where Adam demanded that instructors demonstrate any drill the students had not previously seen. That expectation of professionalism shaped the way I run all courses under Modern American Combative Arts LLC: I demonstrate everything, because that is what a professional instructor does.

Unfortunately, at the Federal Law Enforcement Training Center, live-fire demonstrations are often discouraged, usually under the justification of time constraints or concerns that a mistake will undermine instructor credibility. The reality is that only about a third of the staff demonstrate live fire, and we are the minority. I reject the notion that a mistake erodes credibility. On the contrary, if a draw stroke is sloppy or a shot is missed, it

becomes a valuable teaching moment. Stop, ask the students what went wrong, discuss it openly, and then perform the demonstration again—this time correctly. That transparency builds trust, reinforces learning, and models professionalism in a way that simple lecture never could.

Live-fire demonstrations are not about ego or performance; they are about setting the standard, teaching through action, and proving to the student that what is being taught works. Anything less falls short of professional instruction.

Live-Fire Demonstration Standard

1. **Requirement**

   Live-fire demonstrations are mandatory. Professional firearms instruction requires the instructor to demonstrate every drill or skill the student has not seen before.

2. **Demonstration Method**

   - **First Demonstration (25% speed):** Instructor narrates while performing the drill slowly to highlight details and technical points.

- **Second Demonstration (85–90% speed):** Instructor performs at near-real speed to show proper execution under realistic conditions.
- **Third Demonstration (50% speed):** Instructor slows back down to reinforce nuances while maintaining elements of speed.

3. **Professional Expectation**
   - Special Operations, SIG Academy, and Modern American Combative Arts LLC standard: live-fire demonstrations are a professional requirement.
   - Federal Law Enforcement Training Center: practice is inconsistent, with many instructors citing time constraints or credibility concerns.

4. **Credibility and Teaching Moments**

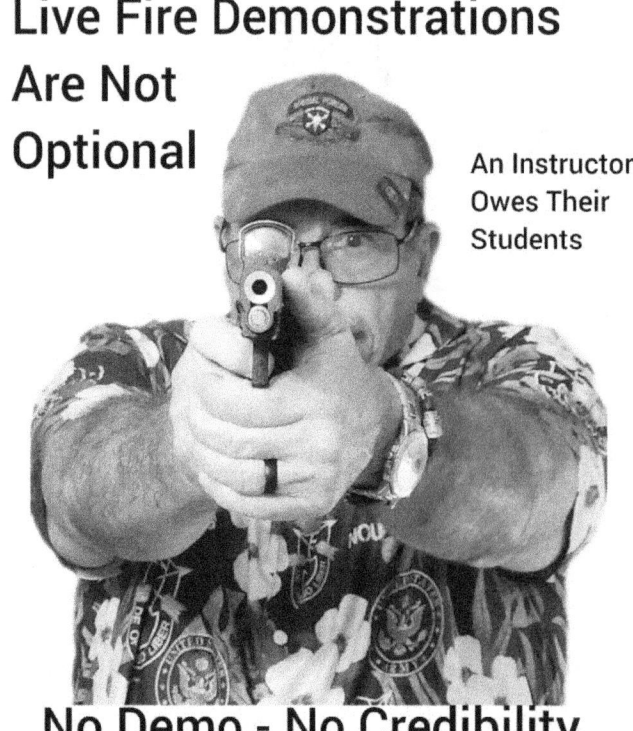

- A mistake during a demonstration is not a failure—it is a teaching opportunity.
- Instructors will pause, ask students to identify the error, explain the cause, and then repeat the drill correctly.
- This transparency reinforces learning, builds trust, and demonstrates professional integrity.

5. **Instructor Standard**

Live-fire demonstrations are not optional. They set the performance benchmark, establish credibility.

Instructor Live-Fire Demonstrations

Beginner Level (Student Perspective)

- When learning something new, students need to see the correct way to do it.
- A live-fire demonstration shows exactly what "right" looks like, giving the student a clear visual reference.
- Watching an instructor shoot builds confidence that the technique works and is achievable.
- *Key Point:* If you haven't seen it done, it's harder to believe you can do it.

Intermediate / Advanced Level (Developing Shooter Perspective)

- Demonstrations provide more than a basic example—they show consistency, efficiency, and attention to detail under real conditions.
- Advanced shooters benefit from observing the finer points: grip pressure, sight tracking, cadence, movement efficiency, and recovery.
- By seeing skills executed under live-fire conditions, the shooter can model proper standards for speed and accuracy.
- *Key Point:* A live-fire demonstration does not just show "what to do," but "how it should look" when performed correctly.

Instructor Level (Professional Application)

- Demonstrations are a professional obligation. Instructors must validate their credibility through performance, not just explanation.
- Every new concept should be introduced with a live-fire demonstration. This shows mastery, sets the standard, and proves the instructor's ability to perform under the same conditions expected of students.

- A demonstration should highlight fundamentals executed at speed and under control, reinforcing the training objective.
- Failure to demonstrate erodes credibility; students will doubt both the skill and the instructor.
- *Instructor's Creed: No demonstration, no standard. No standard, no credibility.*

Instructor Live-Fire Demonstration Checklist

1. Preparation

- Ensure the drill/skill has been fully explained before live-fire.
- Confirm the objective (what students should focus on observing).
- Conduct a personal gear check (holster, mags, weapon condition, PPE).
- Verify range is safe, clear, and ready for demonstration.

2. Positioning & Presence

- Stand where all students have clear visibility.
- Use body orientation and voice projection to maintain command of the group.
- Brief students on what to *watch for* (grip, sight alignment, cadence, movement, etc.).

3. Execution

- Demonstrate at a deliberate pace first, with exaggerated fundamentals.
- Perform again at full speed to show the expected standard.
- Maintain accuracy, efficiency, and composure — the goal is consistency, not "flash."

- Reinforce safety throughout (finger off trigger, muzzle awareness, follow-through).

4. Post-Demonstration

- Re-holster or clear the weapon in a safe, visible manner.
- Reiterate the key training objective: *"This is the standard I expect you to achieve."*
- Allow students to ask questions and clarify before their repetitions.
- Transition smoothly into student execution.

5. Instructor Reminders

- You are always teaching — even when shooting.
- Demonstration is not about showing off; it's about showing *standards.*
- Consistency earns trust; trust builds credibility.
- ***No demonstration, no credibility.***

In the first book I authored, *Responsible Citizens Seeking Responsible Training: A Guide for Self-Defense with a Pistol* (ISBN 978-0692114452), I introduced a survival formula drawn from my martial arts teaching experience. This formula was originally shared with me by Brian Mayfield, a skilled Hop Gar practitioner and accomplished martial artist.

Following the publication of my second book, *A Green Beret's Guide to Enhanced Pistol Shooting Skills* (ISBN 979-8218640354), I was approached by my friend and fellow firearms instructor, Kevin Austin, a self-described mathematics enthusiast who spent much of his career as a federal officer with the United States Immigration and Naturalization Service (INS) and later U.S. Customs and Border Protection. Kevin's office is adjacent to mine, and over the years, we have engaged in numerous insightful discussions.

Kevin felt compelled to apply his mathematical expertise to refine and enhance the original formula. I am grateful for his contributions and wish to extend him the recognition he deserves.

It is often said that all phenomena can be expressed mathematically in some form. As an instructor in martial arts and indeed, firearms training qualifies as a martial art, with roots traceable to the Japanese discipline of Hojutsu in the 1500s it is essential to comprehend not only the history of the art but also the rationale behind its techniques and teaching methods. I will incorporate such historical insights throughout this presentation

Barrington Survival Formula

$$\left(\frac{IQ_D}{IQ_A} + \frac{Aw_D}{Aw_1}\right)\left(\frac{F_D}{F_A} + \frac{H_D}{H_A}\right)\left(\frac{L_D}{L_A} + \frac{S_D}{S_A}\right) = \text{Chances of Victory/Survival}$$

Mental factors / Personal Physical factors / Location and overall environment factors

IQ_D Intelligence of defender

IQ_A Intelligence of attacker

Aw_D Situational Awareness of defender

Aw_A Situational Awareness of attacker

F_D Fitness level of defender

F_A Fitness level of attacker

H_D Health level of defender

H_A Health level of defender

L_D Location factors that favor defender

L_A Location factors that favor attacker

s_D Scenario factors that favor defender

s_A Scenario factors that favor attacker.

Defender/Attacker: Understand who you are, who your enemy is. What is your level of training? What is the training level of your adversary?

Intelligence + Awareness: What is your awareness level? What fighting systems have you learned? What targets are accessible to you? What targets are accessible to your adversary? Did you make the conscious decision to enter this area or where you surprised?

Athletic Ability + Health: What shape are you in? What shape is your adversary in? What is your current health status? What is your cardio shape? What is your mat shape? Are medications or alcohol affecting your health?

Arena + Scenario: Are you in a Do Jo? Is this a street fight? Are you in a sporting event? Is it day or night? Is there one opponent or multiple opponents? Are there by standers? Are you armed? Is your adversary armed?

The principles of combat that I have learned consist of various concepts: Know the Mission, Decisiveness, Surprise, Speed and Violence of Action and keep it simple. . This is true in martial sports, arts that are truly martial, fighting and combat in general.

The Principles of Combat: Surprise, Speed, and Violence of Action (Appropriate Use of Force)

Being a retired "Green Beret" Assualter, I developed a very good grasp of the fundamental principles of combat and the need to apply them correctly. As a firearms instructor for those that wish to protect themselves and those that they hold dear, I have found that they need to understand the overriding principles that will allow them success. If your goal as an instructor is to teach pistol skills to those individuals you need to have a firm grasp of the principles that are the foundation of your martial art.

The foundational principles of effective combat—**Surprise**, **Speed**, and **Violence of Actionta**—are not merely tactical preferences; they are decisive elements that, when applied with precision and intent, overwhelm adversaries, disrupt their decision-making cycles, and achieve dominance in dynamic engagements. Each principle has unique applications based on the adversary's awareness, posture, and reaction time, and their interplay forms the basis of many successful offensive and defensive actions.

1. Surprise

Definition:
Surprise is the deliberate imposition of the unexpected. It is the creation of tactical, psychological, or positional advantage by catching the adversary unprepared, unready, or unaware.

Applications:

- **Tactical Surprise**: Striking from an angle, location, or timing that the enemy does not anticipate. This could be through deception, concealment, or distraction.

- **Temporal Surprise**: Acting at a time when the adversary is least prepared—during rest, transition, or movement phases.
- **Psychological Surprise**: Employing tactics, weapons, or levels of aggression that exceed the enemy's expectations or disrupt their mental readiness.

Impact on the Adversary:

Surprise shatters the adversary's plan and forces a reactive posture. When caught off guard, most opponents default to delay, confusion, or a freeze response, providing a critical window of dominance for the aggressor.

2. Speed

Definition:

Speed is the rapid execution of movement or decision-making that compresses the enemy's ability to perceive, orient, decide, and act. It is not recklessness; rather, it is controlled urgency and efficient aggression.

Applications:

- **Physical Speed**: Moving swiftly through spaces, around obstacles, and into dominant firing positions.
- **Cognitive Speed**: Making faster, more accurate decisions under pressure—often enhanced by training to a level of unconscious competence.
- **Tactical Speed**: Rapid tempo of engagements that outpaces the adversary's ability to adapt or communicate.

Impact on the Adversary:

Speed denies the enemy time to organize an effective response. It overwhelms their processing cycle and forces them into disorganized reaction. When speed is properly employed, it leaves the adversary struggling to keep up and often leads to panic, hesitation, or surrender.

3. Violence of Action

Definition:
Violence of Action is the unapologetic, immediate, and overwhelming use of force to seize control of a situation. It reflects a commitment to total dominance during the engagement window.

Applications:

- **Explosive Entry or Contact**: Breaching, clearing, or engaging with maximum intensity and volume of fire.
- **Overwhelming Force Projection**: Rapid, aggressive movement combined with deliberate, accurate application of force.
- **Commitment to Action**: No hesitation; a full, all-in mentality that dominates both the physical and psychological battlespace.

Impact on the Adversary:
Violence of Action breaks the will of most adversaries. It can trigger a freeze or capitulation response by presenting a threat level that surpasses their threshold for resistance. Even a prepared opponent can be stunned or overwhelmed by the sheer ferocity and dominance of aggressive force.

Integration and Layered Response

While each principle is powerful in isolation, their integration is what creates true combat superiority. When Surprise initiates the action, Speed capitalizes on the disruption, and Violence of Action seals the advantage with overwhelming force. The combined effect collapses the adversary's decision cycle and often concludes the engagement before a response can be mounted.

Adversary Reactions and Adjustments:

- If the adversary **freezes**, apply decisive Violence of Action to end the engagement.
- If the adversary **flees**, Speed allows pursuit or control of the battlespace.
- If the adversary **fights back**, cycle back to Surprise through unorthodox positioning or tactics, then re-engage with Speed and Violence.

Compare & contrast — *Violence of Action* (military) vs *Appropriate Use of Force* (law enforcement) — and how to implement each

Violence of Action is a military principle that emphasizes rapid, decisive, and overwhelming application of force to seize the initiative and accomplish an objective. **Appropriate Use of Force** (law enforcement) is an operational and legal framework that requires force to be necessary, proportionate, and minimized consistent with public safety, officers' safety, and legal/ethical norms. They share tactical thinking and the need for training and control — but their goals, legal limits, audiences, and measures of success are fundamentally different.

Below I lay out the differences, the similarities, and practical steps for implementing each in an organization (doctrine, training, leadership, oversight, measurements).

1) Core definitions & intent

Violence of Action (VOA) — military

- Goal: achieve a decisive advantage quickly; destroy or rout the enemy; seize/hold ground or an objective.
- Character: aggressive, overwhelming, offensive, tempo-driven.
- Legal/ethical frame: governed by the law of armed conflict (LOAC) and rules of engagement (ROE) — but those permit lethal force against valid military targets.
- Measure of success: mission accomplishment, force preservation, enemy incapacitation, initiative maintained.

Appropriate Use of Force (AUOF) — law enforcement

- Goal: protect life and enforce the law while respecting constitutional and statutory constraints; restore or preserve public order and safety.
- Character: graduated, necessary, proportionate, with emphasis on minimizing harm and preserving rights.
- Legal/ethical frame: civil law, constitutional protections, departmental policy, criminal law, and community expectations.
- Measure of success: lawful resolution, minimized injury, legal defensibility, public trust.

2) Key differences (side-by-side)

- **Primary end-state**

- o VOA: mission success; suppress or eliminate opposition.
- o AUOF: lawful resolution and public safety; compliance or safe arrest.

- **Legal constraints**
    - o VOA: LOAC + ROE allow lethal force against enemy combatants; broader latitude in wartime.
    - o AUOF: criminal law, constitutional limits (e.g., proportionality, necessity), civil liability risk, internal discipline.
- **Use-of-force philosophy**
    - o VOA: overwhelming and rapid to exploit momentum.
    - o AUOF: escalation / de-escalation continuum; force only as necessary.
- **Public & political context**
    - o VOA: primarily a military-civilian relationship in the operational theater; political oversight but less immediate civilian scrutiny at the point of action.
    - o AUOF: direct community scrutiny, media, legal processes, and immediate civil accountability.
- **Tactics & equipment**
    - o VOA: heavy weapons, sustained engagement, area effects permitted within LOAC.
    - o AUOF: non-lethal tools prioritized (tasers, OC, baton), negotiation, containment, minimization of bystander harm.
- **Training focus**
    - o VOA: combined arms, tempo, rapid decision loops, lethal marksmanship, and suppressive fires.
    - o AUOF: threat assessment, tactics to minimize force, communication, legal training, medical response, de-escalation, evidence preservation.

3) Key similarities

- Both require clear doctrine and command intent.
- Both depend on disciplined decision making under stress.
- Both require rehearsals, after-action review (AAR), and accountability.
- Both rely on well-maintained equipment, effective leadership, and timely medical care/casualty management.
- Both benefit from scenario-based training and cross-discipline coordination (e.g., military with civil affairs; police with EMS and community partners).

4) Implementation — practical steps for each

Implementing Violence of Action (military context)

1. **Doctrine & ROE**
   - Codify VOA in operations doctrine with clear ROE that define when and how overwhelming force is to be used.
   - Define intent, objectives, target types, authorized weapon systems, and limits.
2. **Command intent & mission command**
   - Clear commander's intent that emphasizes tempo, initiative, and permissible bounds.
   - Decentralized execution with centralized intent (empower subordinate leaders).
3. **Training & rehearsals**
   - Combined-arms live/virtual force-on-force training emphasizing tempo and decisive maneuver.
   - Train decision loops under degraded comms, time pressure, casualty events.

4. **Force posture & logistics**
   - Ensure the ability to mass fires, mobility, ammunition resupply, casualty evacuation, and sustainment to maintain momentum.

5. **Targeting & legal support**
   - Quick-access legal advice (judge advocate) integrated into planning to ensure LOAC compliance.
   - Robust intelligence and positive target identification to limit collateral damage.

6. **Medical & humanitarian considerations**
   - MEDEVAC and field medical capability scaled to tempo.
   - Civil-military coordination for civilian protection and post-engagement stabilization.

7. **After action & measurement**
   - Fast AARs focused on tempo, attrition rates, collateral damage, and whether initiative was maintained.
   - Metrics: mission accomplishment timeline, casualty ratios, sustainment tempo.

Implementing Appropriate Use of Force (law enforcement context)

1. **Clear policy & legal framework**
   - Write policies that define necessity, proportionality, de-escalation obligations, and use-of-force continuum.
   - Include definitions of survival-based threats, imminent danger, and acceptable tactics.

2. **Training: decision-making + skills**
   - Scenario-based, high-fidelity training that combines verbal tactics, containment, non-lethal tools, duty handgun skills, and medical response.

- Train for perception, time-pressure, and dynamic threat assessment; emphasize "if/then" decision rules.

3. **Emphasize de-escalation**
    - Tactics and language that reduce need for force: time, distance, containment, negotiation, tactical repositioning.
    - Reward de-escalation in evaluations.

4. **Equipment & non-lethal options**
    - Maintain and train with less-lethal options.
    - Ensure body-worn cameras, communication tools, and medical kits are standard and reliable.

5. **Supervisory oversight & backup**
    - Rapid supervisory review for critical incidents; clear escalation and support rules.
    - Teams trained in coordinated containment and tactical entry with medical support present when possible.

6. **Reporting, review & accountability**
    - Immediate reporting of force incidents, with independent review units and transparent AAR processes.
    - Data collection for trends: use-of-force rates, complaints, injuries.

7. **Community engagement & transparency**
    - Publish policies, provide community training sessions, and use civilian oversight where appropriate to build trust.

8. **Post-incident care & legal process**
    - Ensure immediate medical aid for injured persons.
    - Preserve evidence and coordinate with prosecutors to ensure legal defensibility.

5) Examples of doctrinal language

VOA (military) — commander's line

"When enemy contact threatens our objective and the commander's intent requires seizure of terrain or decisive defeat of hostile forces, units will apply Violence of Action: coordinated, overwhelming fires and maneuver to seize and exploit the initiative in accordance with ROE and LOAC."

AUOF (law enforcement) — policy excerpt

"Officers shall use only the force necessary and proportionate to effect lawful objectives. Every reasonable effort to de-escalate shall be made when safe to do so. Excessive or unnecessary force is prohibited. All use-of-force incidents will be documented and subject to supervisory and independent review."

Leadership & culture differences

- **Military leaders**: reward initiative and tempo; tolerate higher risk of casualty in exchange for strategic effects. Training should reinforce disciplined aggression within legal bounds.
- **Police leaders**: reward restraint where possible, emphasize community trust, legal defensibility, and minimizing harm. Promotions should reflect sound judgment and legal/ethical awareness as much as tactical skill.

Metrics & evaluation

VOA metrics

- Time to objective.

- Enemy's ability to resist post-engagement.
- Friendly casualty rate vs enemy attrition.
- Sustainment tempo (ammo, fuel, medevac).

AUOF metrics

- Number of force incidents per 1,000 contacts.
- Rate of complaints, civil lawsuits, and their outcomes.
- Percentage of incidents with body-cam/video corroboration.
- Rate of de-escalation (contacts resolved without force).
- Training completion and scenario proficiency scores.

Common pitfalls to avoid

- Treating VOA doctrine as "anything goes" — must be bounded by ROE and LOAC.
- Treating AUOF as only legal text — it must be operationalized through realistic training and leadership.
- Failing to integrate medical and legal advice into planning for both.
- Poor data collection — makes it impossible to correct bad practices.

Quick actionable checklist (for a commander or police chief)

1. Publish clear, concise intent/policy (VOA or AUOF), unambiguous language.
2. Integrate legal advisors into planning and training.
3. Build and fund a recurring, scenario-based training program tied to evaluations.
4. Ensure equipment & medical capabilities are aligned with doctrine (non-lethal for police; sustainment for military).

5. Create a rapid reporting and independent review mechanism for all significant force events.
6. Use transparent metrics and publish periodic summaries to stakeholders.
7. Conduct honest AARs and adapt doctrine/training based on findings.

Instructor Handout: Military — Violence of Action (VOA)

Definition

Violence of Action (VOA) is the rapid, decisive, and overwhelming application of combat power to seize the initiative, destroy the enemy, and accomplish the mission.

Core Principles

- **Decisiveness**: Act before the enemy can react; seize momentum.
- **Overwhelm**: Apply force in mass to shock, disrupt, and break enemy cohesion.
- **Tempo**: Maintain pressure; do not allow the enemy recovery time.
- **Discipline**: Aggression must remain within ROE and Law of Armed Conflict (LOAC).

Implementation

1. **Doctrine & ROE**: Ensure soldiers know the commander's intent and the limits of authorized force.
2. **Training & Rehearsals**: Conduct force-on-force, live fire, and degraded comms drills to prepare for decisive execution.
3. **Combined Arms Integration**: Coordinate maneuver, fires, sustainment, and medical support to maintain tempo.
4. **Positive Identification (PID)**: Ensure lawful targeting — balance speed with accuracy of identification.

5. **After-Action Review (AAR)**: Assess tempo, initiative, mission accomplishment, and collateral damage control.

Measures of Success

- Objective seized or enemy neutralized rapidly.
- Friendly forces preserved relative to mission accomplishment.
- Momentum maintained — enemy cannot regroup.
- LOAC and ROE compliance.

Instructor Note

Violence of Action is not "reckless aggression." It is disciplined, coordinated, and mission-driven application of overwhelming force within lawful limits.

Instructor Handout: Law Enforcement — Appropriate Use of Force (AUOF)

Definition
Appropriate Use of Force (AUOF) is the application of force that is **necessary, proportionate, and lawful** to achieve a legitimate law enforcement objective while protecting life, upholding rights, and maintaining public trust.

Core Principles

- **Necessity**: Force only when no reasonable alternatives exist.
- **Proportionality**: Match the level of force to the threat.
- **De-Escalation**: Whenever safe, reduce confrontation through time, distance, and communication.

- **Accountability**: Every use of force must be documented, reviewed, and legally defensible.

Implementation

1. **Policy & Training**: Officers must know departmental standards, constitutional limits, and the force continuum.
2. **Scenario-Based Practice**: Role-play high-stress encounters integrating verbal skills, non-lethal tools, and firearms.
3. **Non-Lethal Options**: Ensure availability and proficiency with tasers, OC spray, batons, and control tactics.
4. **Supervision & Oversight**: Rapid supervisor involvement and mandatory reporting for every force incident.
5. **Community Transparency**: Publish policies, provide public briefings, and maintain video accountability.

Measures of Success

- Incidents resolved with minimal injury to officers and civilians.
- Use of force is rare relative to total contacts.
- Body-worn camera footage supports decisions.
- Public trust maintained through transparency and accountability.

Instructor Note

Appropriate Use of Force is not about hesitation or indecision. It is about **measured, legally sound, and ethically defensible action** that protects life and maintains public confidence.

Conclusion

The principles of Surprise, Speed, and Violence of Action, (Appropriate Use of Force) are time-tested and real world-proven. Their value lies not only in their power but in their adaptability to varied threats and environments. When executed with training, discipline, and decisiveness, these principles become more than tactics—they become a combat philosophy capable of overwhelming even the most determined adversary.

Teaching the principles of **Surprise, Speed, and Violence of Action (Appropriate Use of Force)** to everyday Armed Professionals may require **translating military doctrine into practical, legally sound, and morally responsible concepts** applicable in Law Enforcement defensive scenarios. The key is to **adapt the spirit of the principles**—not the battlefield aggressiveness—into a framework that enhances survivability, decision-making, and lawful force application in the context of armed self-defense.

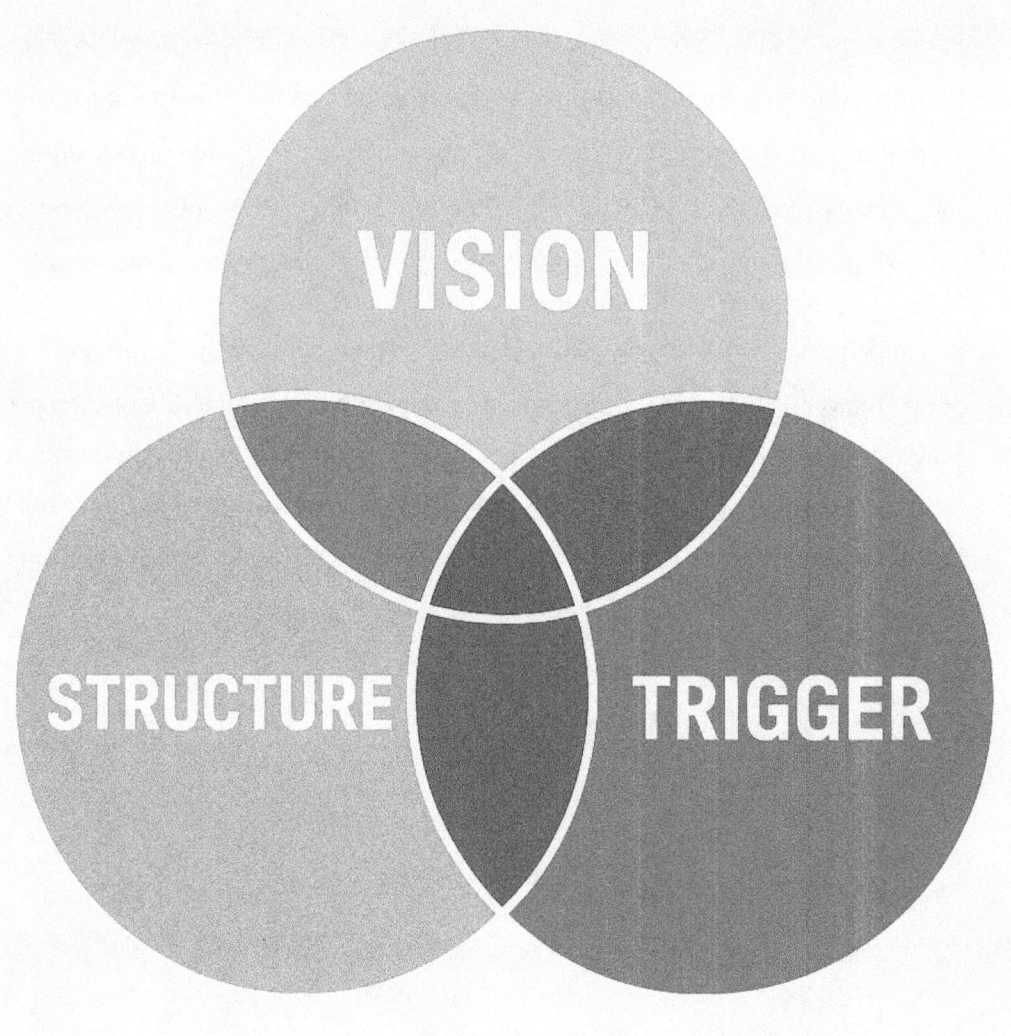

Vision as the Deciding Factor in Shooting and Combat

Vision is not just the mechanical act of seeing—it is the conscious processing of information in real time that dictates a shooter's actions. In the Trinity Triangle of marksmanship—**vision, mechanics, and mindset**—vision stands at the apex because it governs decision-making.

1. **Vision Determines Timing**

    Every shot should be visually confirmed. Whether at a subconscious level in close, high-speed shooting, or through deliberate sight refinement at distance, vision dictates when the shot breaks. The trigger press is not an independent action—it is *triggered by the eyes*. If the shooter cannot clearly see the sight package aligned on target, or cannot visually verify a threat, the shot is not yet ready to be fired.

2. **Vision Directs Mechanics**

    The body follows the eyes. Target acquisition, transitions, recoil management, and recovery all begin with vision. Mechanics without vision are blind motions. Vision provides the feedback loop—calling shots, diagnosing errors, and confirming hits—that allows mechanics to refine and adapt.

3. **Vision Drives Decision-Making in Combat**

    In a lethal encounter, vision is more than aiming—it is survival. Peripheral awareness, recognition of movement, and rapid threat identification all stem from vision. The shooter's ability to shift from target to sight focus and back to environmental awareness is what allows them to shoot what matters, when it matters, and not be deceived by distractions.

4. **Vision as the Governor of Speed**

    Many shooters believe they are limited by their hands or their trigger finger. In truth, speed is always governed by vision. The faster the eyes can acquire, process, and confirm sight alignment, the faster accurate shots can be delivered. When vision lags behind mechanics, rounds are wasted. When mechanics are tuned to vision, accuracy and speed merge.

5. **Vision Decides Life or Death**

    Ultimately, in a kinetic encounter, vision is the deciding factor. It tells the shooter not only when to shoot, but when *not* to shoot. Vision confirms the threat, evaluates the backdrop, and ensures that lethal force is applied with precision and restraint. Mechanics and mindset prepare the shooter, but vision makes the call.

This concept is crucial to emphasize in your framework: **Vision is both the steering wheel and the brake pedal of lethal force application.**

Vision — Layered Teaching Progression (Beginner → Intermediate → Advanced → Instructor)

Overview (common to all levels)

Core idea: Vision is the primary decision-maker — it tells the shooter *when* and *what* to shoot. Training objective is to develop reliable, repeatable visual processes: target acquisition, sight focus, threat discrimination, and visual timing under increasing speed, complexity, and stress.

Key training vocabulary: focal vision (central), peripheral vision, target-sight-target cycle, visual confirmation, visual latency, visual anticipatory timing.

Beginner (Foundations — conscious, slow, deliberate)

Goal: Teach the student to *use* vision deliberately: acquire a target, achieve proper sight picture, and press the trigger only when the visual confirmation is present.

Learning outcomes

- Slow, correct target-sight-target cycle.
- Consistent sight alignment verified visually before trigger break.
- Awareness of background and muzzle direction.

Drills

1. **Sight-Pick Drill (25 reps, static target, 3–5 yards)**
   - Start from low-ready. Present, pick the front sight, confirm alignment, break the shot.
   - Emphasize: eyes FIRST, hands follow; verbalize "sight" before shot.
2. **Dot-to-Target Focus (10 reps)**
   - Use a large target with a small center dot. The shooter calls "dot" when the sight sits on the dot, then fires.
3. **Slow Transitional Awareness (5 × 2-target transitions at 7 yards)**
   - Move between targets slowly, fix vision on each target before firing.

Instructor cues

- "Eyes first, then hands."
- "Find the dot — don't guess."
- Give immediate visual feedback: "You pulled early; your eyes were still moving."

Assessment

- 80% of shots within acceptable group while following sight-confirmation protocol.
- Verbal confirmation from shooter that they saw the sight on target before each shot.

Intermediate (Speed and decision integration)

Goal: Reduce visual latency and incorporate visual threat discrimination while increasing speed.

Learning outcomes

- Faster target-sight-target cycles with maintained visual confirmation.
- Effective use of peripheral vision for threat detection while sighting.
- Smooth transitions with visual lead-in.

Drills

1. **Speed Bullseye Progression (10 rounds / 10s at 10–15 yards; scale speed down as needed)**
   - Emphasize that speed must still be governed by sight confirmation. Pause drills if shooter sacrifices visual confirmation.
2. **Index & Snap (multiple small targets at 7–10 yards)**
   - Shooter uses peripheral to capture target, then brings focal vision to the sight quickly to confirm.
3. **Background Check Drill**
   - Shots only allowed when shooter visually confirms safe backdrop; instructor occasionally adds non-threat objects to reinforce discrimination.

Instructor cues

- "Let the eyes lead the hands — don't outrun your sight."
- "Use your peripheral to find; bring central vision to finish."

Assessment

- Time-to-first-shot metric (e.g., average) while maintaining acceptable accuracy; >90% of shots made after visual confirmation.

Advanced (Complexity, stress inoculation, tactical application)

Goal: Make vision reliable under dynamic movement, threat ambiguity, and physiological stress.

Learning outcomes

- Rapid visual acquisition at varying distances and angles.
- Maintain environmental awareness (multiple threats, bystanders, cover) while engaging.
- Visual decision discipline under stress inoculation.

Drills

1. **Dynamic Transition with Threat Discrimination**
    - Multiple targets with "no-shoot" and "shoot" identifiers. Add movement and cover. Shooter must visually confirm correct target.
2. **Moving Target / Tracking + Sight Reset**
    - Engage a moving target; emphasize quick re-acquisition of the front sight and visual confirmation between shots.
3. **Stress-Load Visual Confirmation**
    - Combine physical exertion (sprints) with immediate target engagement to force the visual system to perform while heart rate is elevated.
4. **25-Yard Diagnostic Speed Bullseye (10 rounds in time limit — diagnostic)**
    - Use this as a periodic evaluator for visual and mechanical deficiencies.

Instructor cues

- "Find the threat, verify, then apply lethal."
- "Don't trade accuracy for speed — sight will tell you when."

Assessment

- Accuracy under stress: acceptable hit percentage on threat targets and zero hits on no-shoots.
- Ability to articulate visual decision process post-run (after-action debrief).

Instructor (Teaching, diagnosing, and remediating visual failures)

Goal: Train instructors to evaluate visual processes, identify visual-cued errors, and prescribe corrective progressions.

Make your eyes the Governor.

Instructor competencies

- Diagnose visual timing problems (anticipation, lag, and fixation) and correlate to mechanical errors.
- Teach focal/peripheral drills and prescribe corrective sensory cues.
- Design progressive lesson plans and measure visual improvement quantitatively.

Common visual failure modes & corrections

1. **Anticipation (shooting before sight confirmation)**
   - Correction: mirror drill — shooter must call "sight" aloud before each shot; add stricter penalties for anticipations.
2. **Tunnel Vision / Over-Fixation (loss of peripheral awareness)**
   - Correction: peripheral drills — hold a target in central vision while instructor moves objects in periphery; train to notice movement without leaving sight.
3. **Visual Latency (eyes too slow to get on target)**
   - Correction: sprint-to-acquire drills; incremental distance challenge; visual pre-indexing.
4. **Sight Blur under Stress**
   - Correction: focus drills under elevated heart rates and breath control integration.

Instructor drills & tools

- **Slow-Motion Video Review**: record and show eye-sight-hand sequencing to the shooter.
- **Eye-Tracking Cues**: use verbal and tactile prompts to re-establish proper visual sequence.

- **Checklist for Visual Diagnosis**: (1) where were the eyes at trigger pull, (2) was there a verbal confirmation, (3) was peripheral awareness present, (4) did the sight return quickly after recoil.

Lesson plan template (30, 60, 90 min)

- 0–10 min: Visual warm-up & dry-fire focal drills.
- 10–30 min: Skill block (progression of drills from current student level).
- 30–50 min: Stress/complexity block (transitions, no-shoots).
- 50–60 min: Diagnostics & homework prescription.
- 60–90 min (advanced/instructor): Video review and remediation drills.

Measurement & Progress Tracking

- **Metrics to record:** time-to-first-shot, time-between-shots, hit percentage (threat/no-shoot), visual-confirmation compliance (% of shots accompanied by verbal/visual cue), and error taxonomy (anticipation, target discrimination failure, poor re-acquisition).
- **Benchmarking:** set level-appropriate benchmarks and require consistent performance across multiple runs before advancing.

Short, Instructor-Ready Teaching Points (soundbites)

- "Vision tells you when to shoot; your hands only obey."
- "Make your eyes the governor — speed without sight is wasted."
- "Train peripheral awareness as aggressively as you train sight alignment."
- "If the shot feels right but your eyes disagree — stop."

Vision Checklist

Purpose: Quick-reference checklist for teaching, coaching, and diagnosing the shooter's visual process (target acquisition → sight confirmation → trigger decision).

Pre-Range / Dry-Fire Warmup
- ☐ 1. Dry-fire: 10 slow sight-pick repetitions (eyes lead, hands follow).
- ☐ 2. Dot focus: 5 reps on a small dot target — call "dot" aloud before each press.
- ☐ 3. Peripheral scan: 1-minute drill — notice movement in periphery without leaving sight.

During Live Fire (Single-Session Protocol)

Before each drill: state objective and visual cue (e.g., "Find the front sight — call 'sight'").

- ☐ 4. Visual Intent: Shooter verbalizes visual cue before first shot.
- ☐ 5. Sight Confirmation: Every shot accompanied by visual confirmation (verbal or nod).
- ☐ 6. Background Check: Shooter visually confirms safe backdrop before shooting each target.
- ☐ 7. Speed Governor: If accuracy drops, pause and reset visual focus before continuing.

Common Failure Modes — Quick Remedies
- ☐ Anticipation (shoots before sight): reintroduce mirror drill & require verbal "sight" before shot.
- ☐ Tunnel Vision (lost peripheral): insert quick peripheral awareness games; limit focus time.
- ☐ Visual Latency (slow acquisition): sprint-to-acquire progressions and pre-indexing.
- ☐ Sight Blur under Stress: add elevated HR reps with breath control & immediate sight re-acquisition.

Drills to Reinforce Vision (pick 2 per session)
- ☐ Sight-Pick (25 reps, 3–5 yds)
- ☐ Dot-to-Target (10 reps)

- ☐ Speed Bullseye Progression (10 rounds/time-set)
- ☐ Dynamic Transition with No-Shoots (accuracy + discrimination)
- ☐ Stress-Load Visuals (sprint + engage)

Metrics to Record (for progression)
- ☐ Time-to-first-shot _____ s
- ☐ Time-between-shots _____ s
- ☐ Threat hit % _____
- ☐ No-shoot hit % _____
- ☐ Visual-confirmation compliance % _____

Instructor Remediation Checklist (if shooter fails)
- ☐ Video review of eye-sight-hand sequence
- ☐ Re-introduce slow deliberate sight-pick
- ☐ Add verbal call-outs for every shot
- ☐ Prescribe 5 dry-fire sessions + 1 live-fire progression

Soundbites for Coaching: - "Eyes first — hands obey." - "If your eyes say stop, stop." - "Speed is governed by sight."

End of checklist — keep on your range clipboard.

Instructor Knowledge: Current Methodologies and Terminologies in Pistol Shooting

As a shooting instructor, maintaining proficiency in contemporary methodologies and terminologies is essential. In the realm of competitive and tactical pistol shooting, certain concepts and naming conventions are attributed to influential figures such as JJ Racaza and Ben Stoeger. While the origins of these ideas may spark debate—much like the attribution of various shooting drills—their precise provenance is secondary to their practical utility. What matters most is a thorough understanding of the terms, conventions, and underlying principles, enabling instructors to effectively convey them to students.

I have tried to provide a structured breakdown and comparison of key visual processing and decision-making models: JJ Racaza's "Attack vs. Control," Ben Stoeger's "Predictive vs. Reactive" shooting, his Visual Confirmation Levels (1–3), and the generalized 5 Levels of Focus. These frameworks are particularly relevant to transitions, visual processing, and performance under speed and pressure in pistol shooting.

1. JJ Racaza's Attack vs. Control

JJ Racaza's model articulates the dynamic balance between velocity and precision in high-stakes shooting scenarios.

- **Attack Mode**
    - Characterized by aggressive, rapid movements.
    - Employed for low-difficulty targets, such as those at close range or with open presentations.
    - Requires minimal visual confirmation.

- o Emphasizes speed at the expense of meticulous precision.
- **Control Mode**
    - o Focuses on deliberate, precision-driven actions.
    - o Applied to challenging shots, including distant targets, partials, or those adjacent to no-shoots.
    - o Demands heightened visual confirmation before and during the shot.
    - o Prioritizes accuracy over rapidity.

Purpose: This dichotomy equips shooters to discern when to accelerate aggressively ("attack") and when to moderate pace ("control"), thereby minimizing avoidable errors or excessive verification.

2. Ben Stoeger's Predictive vs. Reactive Shooting

Ben Stoeger's approach delineates visual and temporal strategies contingent on target characteristics and shooter assurance.

- **Predictive Shooting**
    - o Involves discharging the firearm in anticipation of an adequate sight picture.
    - o Suitable for straightforward targets or scenarios where confidence in sight alignment is high.
    - o Commonly utilized during transitions or while in motion.
- **Reactive Shooting**
    - o Entails withholding the shot until the sight picture is visually verified.
    - o More methodical and slower; reserved for demanding shots.
    - o Relies on explicit visual cues to affirm alignment prior to firing.

Purpose: The framework differentiates shots amenable to intuitive rhythm and proprioception (predictive) from those necessitating explicit validation (reactive).

3. Ben Stoeger's Visual Confirmation Levels (1–3)

This tiered system quantifies the extent of visual input required prior to trigger break, calibrating effort to target demands.

- **VC 1 (Minimal Confirmation)**
    - Involves scant or absent clear sight picture.
    - Aligns with predictive shooting.
    - Ideal for expansive targets at proximity.
    - Sufficient peripheral awareness permits confident firing without intensive aiming.
- **VC 2 (Moderate Confirmation)**
    - Features distinct visibility and alignment of the front sight or dot, though briefly.
    - Appropriate for intermediate distances, partials, or moderate-risk engagements.
    - Alignment is verified, but the shot is executed promptly thereafter.
- **VC 3 (Extensive Confirmation)**
    - Demands a sustained, deliberate sight picture.
    - Essential for extended ranges, hard cover, or stringent no-shoots.
    - Necessitates reactive shooting protocols.

Purpose: It enables shooters to modulate visual rigor according to target complexity, avoiding both under- and over-verification.

4. The 5 Levels of Focus (Attributed to Steve Anderson; Generalized Framework)

This progressive model elucidates stages of visual engagement and cognitive integration in shooting.

- **Level 1: No Focus**
    - Absence of directed attention; minimal awareness.
    - Results in frequent misses without comprehension of causation.
- **Level 2: Target Focus**
    - Attention confined to the target, yielding broad but superficial detail.
    - Prevalent among novices or under duress.
- **Level 3: Sight Awareness**
    - Sights enter the field of view but lack fixation.
    - Common in developing shooters.
- **Level 4: Front Sight Focus**
    - Precise alignment is observed, fostering reliable accuracy.
    - Enables consistent shot calling; correlates with VC 2 and VC 3.
- **Level 5: Visual Patience/Mastery**
    - Comprehensive perception encompasses target, sights, motion, and transitions.
    - Facilitates real-time adaptations.
    - Exemplifies elite proficiency, blending reactive and predictive elements as warranted.

Purpose: The levels cultivate heightened awareness and command over visual focus, progressing from rudimentary to sophisticated application.

Comparison Matrix

The following table synthesizes these concepts, highlighting emphases on speed, accuracy, target dependency, visual processing, and typical applications.

Concept	Speed-First	Accuracy-First	Based on Target Difficulty	Visual Processing Emphasis	When Used
JJ Attack	Yes	No	Yes	Moderate	Close/fast targets
JJ Control	No	Yes	Yes	High	Hard/technical shots
Predictive	Yes	No	Yes	Moderate	Close/familiar targets
Reactive	No	Yes	Yes	High	Long/tight targets
VC 1	Yes	No	Yes	Low	Hoser stages
VC 2	Balanced	Balanced	Yes	Moderate	Most targets
VC 3	No	Yes	Yes	High	Far/partial targets
Focus Levels 1–2	No	No	No	Poor	Novice/poor performance
Focus Level 3	Balanced	Balanced	Inconsistent	Moderate	Mid-level
Focus Levels 4–5	No	Yes	Yes	Excellent	Expert shooters

Nuanced Breakdown for Instructors and Advanced Shooters

Beyond foundational comprehension, instructors must delve into the subtleties of these methodologies. This deeper analysis illuminates the rationale, timing, and integration of each, fostering adaptive instruction for advanced practitioners.

JJ Racaza's Attack vs. Control

- **Attack Mode**
    - **Mindset**: Emphasize aggressive pacing, propelling the firearm through sequences with elevated confidence and low error tolerance.
    - **Applications**: Proximity engagements (<7 yards), rapid steel arrays (3–5 yards), or ambulatory shooting where exactitude is subordinate.
    - **Visual Behavior**: Prioritize target fixation over sight-centric detail; rely on kinesthetic indexing from extensive repetition.
    - **Risks**: Outpacing visual acuity or premature trigger breaks sans stabilization.
    - **Prerequisites**: Robust indexing and autonomic firearm handling; hallmark of elite performers.
- **Control Mode**
    - **Mindset**: Adopt a respectful, measured approach to ensure sight dominance.
    - **Applications**: Constricted partials, extended distances (15–25+ yards), or unstable postures (e.g., barricades or kneeling).
    - **Visual Behavior**: Constrict focus to the dot or front sight, incorporating intentional pauses for validation.
    - **Risks**: Excessive scrutiny leading to hesitation or anxiety-induced disruption.

Integration: Proficiency emerges from fluid alternation, even mid-array—escalating to attack when viable, reverting to control as exigencies demand.

Ben Stoeger's Predictive vs. Reactive Shooting

- **Predictive Shooting**
    - **Definition**: Trigger activation synchronized with anticipated alignment, bypassing exhaustive confirmation.
    - **Traits**: Optimal for oscillating targets, close doubles, or sequential arrays; involves preemptive grip and trigger preparation.
    - **Visual Element**: Awareness of projected sight trajectory via biomechanics.
    - **Success Indicators**: Tight groupings and efficient splits absent pursuit.
    - **Pitfalls**: Erroneous assumptions yielding misses or recoil-induced flinching if fundamentals falter.
- **Reactive Shooting**
    - **Definition**: Deferral of the shot pending visual affirmation of alignment.
    - **Necessity**: Precision demands like distant headshots, obscured dots, or single-shot evaluations.
    - **Timing**: Perceived as slower yet efficient by averting corrections.
    - **Risks**: Prolonged fixation or immobilization under competitive strain.

Pro Tip: Hybridize by prepping predictively during transitions while reserving reactive confirmation for the shot itself.

Ben Stoeger's Visual Confirmation Levels (1–3)

The table below details visual cues, contexts, and exemplary drills for each level.

VC Level	What You See	Used When	Example Drill
VC 1	Fleeting glimpse of dot/sight in vicinity	Expansive targets at close range	3-yard Bill Drill
VC 2	Distinct entry of front sight/dot into target center	10–15 yards with adjacent no-shoots	15-yard Accelerator Drill
VC 3	Sustained, intentional sight picture	20–30 yards on diminutive steel or tight partials	25-yard Head Box (Static)

The 5 Levels of Focus: Detailed Framework

This model transcends mere observation, probing the depth of visual assimilation and its influence on decision-making. It empowers instructors to pinpoint deficiencies, customize interventions, and guide evolution from deliberate to instinctive execution.

Overview Table:

Level	Focus Description	Shooter Behavior
Level 1	No visual focus	Looking without perceiving
Level 2	Target-focused only	Disregarding sights
Level 3	Sights enter awareness	Inconsistent sight utilization
Level 4	Conscious sight alignment	Initiation of accurate shot calling
Level 5	Visual control mastery	Intuitive, responsive management

- **Level 1: No Visual Focus**
  - **Description**: Indiscriminate gaze or erratic scanning; prevalent in novices or amid overload.
  - **Mental State**: Overwhelmed reactivity sans planning or anchors.
  - **Visual Behavior**: Open eyes yield no actionable data; possible recoil-induced blinking.
  - **Instructor Notes**: Incapacity for shot calling; tied to inexperience, poor preparation, or exhaustion.
  - **Remediation**: Employ dry-fire with focal points; query post-shot observations to instill engagement.
- **Level 2: Target Focus Only**
  - **Description**: Exclusive target fixation, evoking instinctive point shooting.
  - **Mental State**: Prioritizing haste over precision, often stress-induced.
  - **Visual Behavior**: Alignment overlooked; reliance on indexing or urgency.
  - **Instructor Notes**: Viable at ultra-close ranges (3–5 yards) but deficient beyond.
  - **Remediation**: Introduce dot drills or graduated-distance controlled pairs with mandatory calling.
- **Level 3: Sights Enter Awareness**
  - **Description**: Emerging sight recognition without full exploitation; a pivotal intermediate stage.
  - **Mental State**: Dividing attention, with resultant indecision on shot timing.
  - **Visual Behavior**: Transient sight appearances, susceptible to overrides or blinks.
  - **Instructor Notes**: Prone to excessive validation; hesitation risks.
  - **Remediation**: Incorporate VC 2 exercises (7–15 yards on partials); advocate firing upon acceptable sights.
-

- **Level 4: Conscious Sight Alignment and Shot Calling**
    - **Description**: Intentional sight prioritization, leveraging visuals for informed actions.
    - **Mental State**: Directed focus yields a feedback cycle.
    - **Visual Behavior**: Tracks dot elevation and recovery; sustains on complexities.
    - **Instructor Notes**: Enables modality blending (predictive/reactive); handles diverse arrays.
    - **Remediation**: Accelerate under duress via Accelerator Drills, Dot Torture, or El Presidente variants.
- **Level 5: Visual Mastery (Focus on Demand)**
    - **Description**: Adaptive focus allocation across multiple elements in real time.
    - **Mental State**: Subconscious mechanics liberate consciousness for strategy.
    - **Visual Behavior**: Multifaceted perception (e.g., dot path, recoil, target contours).
    - **Instructor Notes**: Attained by few; vital for pinnacle performance and adaptability.
    - **Remediation**: Reinforce with advanced regimens like 3-2-1 Drills, partial transitions, or reactive scenarios.

Definition: Visual Confirmation Levels 1, 2, and 3

Visual Confirmation Levels are a framework for categorizing the amount of visual input and sight refinement a shooter uses before and during the firing of a shot. These levels guide shot accountability, speed of engagement, and decision-making in various threat or training scenarios. The levels correspond with the degree of visual detail and focus a shooter applies to the sights or optic before breaking the shot.

Visual Confirmation Level 1 (Confirmation One)

Definition:

Minimal or flash sight picture—rapid visual alignment sufficient to confirm the presence of the front sight (iron sights) or dot (optic) on target without pausing to refine alignment or clarity.

Use:

- **Predictive shooting**
- **Close-range threats**
- **High-speed engagements**
- **Hammer pairs / rapid strings**

Characteristics:

- Extremely fast.
- Front sight or dot may be slightly blurry or misaligned.
- Accepts minimal deviation as acceptable for center-mass hits.
- Often subconscious after strong reps.

Example:

Shooting a target at 3-5 yards with rapid follow-up shots while relying on acceptable deviation and recoil control.

Visual Confirmation Level 2 (Confirmation Two)

Definition:

Deliberate sight picture—front sight or dot is visibly on target with moderate alignment and clarity, though not perfectly refined.

Use:

- **Transitional distances (7–15 yards)**
- **Controlled pairs or follow-up shots**
- **Moderate-threat environments requiring increased accountability**

Characteristics:

- Visual check on alignment, but not full precision.
- Brief pause to ensure shot will land within the desired target zone.
- Balances speed and control.
- Common in competitive shooting and real-world CCW/LE engagements at moderate range.

Example:

Engaging a target at 10 yards with two controlled shots, ensuring acceptable sight alignment before breaking each shot.

Visual Confirmation Level 3 (Confirmation Three)

Definition:

Highly refined, deliberate sight picture—perfect front sight (iron) or dot alignment with clarity, usually with an intentional pause for maximum precision.

Use:

- **Reactive shooting**
- **High accountability situations (e.g., headshots, partial targets, hostage rescue scenarios)**
- **Longer distances (15+ yards)**
- **Low probability hits / tight accuracy requirements**

Characteristics:

- Slowest of the three.
- Prioritizes accuracy over speed.
- Visual confirmation includes clear sight alignment and specific point of aim.
- Often accompanied by breath control and greater trigger discipline.

Example:

Taking a precision shot on a 25-yard head plate or a hostage-taker silhouette with minimal target exposure.

Comparison and Contrast

Feature	Confirmation 1	Confirmation 2	Confirmation 3
Speed	Fastest	Moderate	Slowest
Accuracy requirement	Low to moderate	Moderate to high	High to surgical
Use case	Close-range, multiple shots	Medium-range, controlled engagements	Long-range or high-risk shots
Visual clarity of sight/dot	Minimal or flash confirmation	Reasonable alignment and clarity	Clear, refined, deliberate alignment
Shooting style	Predictive	Blended (Predictive/Reactive)	Reactive
Threat distance	<7 yards	7–15 yards	15+ yards or tight shots
Accountability	Acceptable deviation	Moderate accountability	Maximum accountability
Examples	Hammer pairs, speed drills	Controlled pairs, qualification shots	Hostage shots, tight zones, head shots

Instructional Notes

- **Instructor Tip:** Introduce these levels using real targets with scaled scoring zones to show students how much deviation is acceptable per level.
- **Layered Teaching:**
    - *Beginner:* Focus on Level 2 to build fundamentals.
    - *Intermediate:* Learn to switch between Level 1 and 2 based on distance.
    - *Advanced:* Master Level 3 under stress and on demand, while fluidly shifting levels as needed.
- **Practical Application:** On the range, instructors should link each level to a type of drill or threat scenario, helping students build visual processing speed, shot timing, and discrimination.

Standard Comparable Systems for Iron Sights

What is old is new again! When I attended the US Army Special Forces Special Operations Techniques Course (SOT), I was first exposed to fast distance shooting (Speed Bulls) and to the various sighting packages required to achieve the course goals. These sighting packages almost fell to the wayside because of Pistol Mounted Optics with Visual Confirmations 1,2 and 3.

This is nothing new! Like all martial arts, there are not many new things, just things we as instructors seem to forget. I will be the first to admit I am an optics guy! As my eyes aged, the incorporation of pistol optics rejuvenated my pistol shooting. But as a Senior Firearms Instructor at the Federal Law Enforcement Training Center I still have to teach agencies that use various pistol setups. I coordinated a class from the Department of State (DSS) and then followed that class up with Capital Police agents. The DSS used Glock 19s with iron sights, so one on the cart for my demos! The Capital Police were using Glock 22 which in the long run also are and excellent way to work grip issues!

My current class is DSS and I am back to Glock 47s. All iron sights, all the time! I will say that because of my age and eyes that I most do all my live fire demos using target focused shooting techniques. Target focused out to the 25 yard line on a DHS Tran Star Target is a relatively easy task.

I often work with the US Marshal Service who transitioned from Glock 17 to Glock 47, but are still using iron sights. It is always gratifying to borrow and student gun and put on a live fire demo using the "old school" methods to demonstrate abilities!

In a review, Ben Stoeger's **Visual Confirmation 1–3** system for red-dot sights is essentially a tiered sight-processing model, how much visual information the shooter takes in before breaking the shot, based on distance, difficulty, and acceptable accuracy standards. While that terminology is fairly specific to Stoeger and the red-dot community, the **concept itself is not new** and there *are* comparable models historically used for **iron-sighted pistol shooting** across competitive and defensive shooting communities.

Industry-Standard Comparable Systems for Iron Sights

There isn't a universally agreed-upon, trademarked term like "Visual Confirmation 1–3" for irons, but the same principles have long been taught using different language. The closest and most widely accepted frameworks include:

1) Acceptable Sight Picture / Sight Confirmation Levels

- **Jeff Cooper and Modern Technique lineage** often used the concept of *acceptable sight picture*.
    - At close range on a large target: *coarse alignment* (flash sight picture or even target-focused shooting).
    - At longer range or on a small target: *refined front-sight focus* and more precise alignment.
- Some instructors break this into **three levels of sight focus**:
    - **Level 1:** Target-focused, coarse alignment (for very close, high-speed engagements).
    - **Level 2:** Front sight focus, hard edge visible but less refined (for moderate difficulty).
    - **Level 3:** Crisp front sight, perfect alignment (for long-range or precision shots).

This is nearly identical to Stoeger's dot levels but adapted for irons.

2) Flash Sight Picture (FSP) Concept

- Taught widely in defensive handgun training since the 1980s (Cooper, Ayoob, etc.).
- FSP describes the shooter firing as soon as the sights *flash into acceptable alignment* in their peripheral vision—this is essentially **Visual Confirmation 1** with irons.
- More precise, deliberate alignment at increased difficulty mirrors Stoeger's **VC 2 and VC 3**.

3) Brian Enos' Sight Focus Continuum

- Competitive shooters using irons (USPSA/IPSC) often reference Brian Enos' model:
    - Sight focus is a **continuum, not a switch**, where visual processing varies based on required precision.
    - Enos discussed "awareness of the front sight" vs "hard focus on the front sight," which maps almost perfectly to Stoeger's VC 1–3.

4) Dot vs. Iron Translation Used by Many Instructors

When adapting Stoeger's system to irons, instructors typically describe it as:

- **VC1 (Dot):** "Target focus + superimposed dot" → **Iron equivalent:** Target focus with coarse sight alignment (or even point shooting at bad-breath distance).
- **VC2 (Dot):** "Acceptable dot in the window, not perfectly centered" → **Iron equivalent:** Front sight sharp, rear sight slightly fuzzy; not perfect equal height/light.
- **VC3 (Dot):** "Perfect dot alignment" → **Iron equivalent:** Crisp front sight, precise equal height/light, perfect focus.

Key Takeaway:

While Stoeger gave formal names (VC1–3) for red-dot users, **iron-sight shooters have long used the same concepts under terms like**:

- *Acceptable sight picture*
- *Flash sight picture*
- *Coarse vs. refined sight alignment*
- *Sight focus continuum*

These frameworks are the de facto industry standard and are functionally equivalent. The difference is that red dots separate target vs. dot focus differently due to the parallax-free nature of the optic, while irons require more eye accommodation for hard front-sight focus.

I have mapped out a **direct instructor-level mapping** of Ben Stoeger's Visual Confirmation 1–3 (for red dots) to the **industry-standard iron-sight equivalent system**, along with examples of when and how to train each level. This can be used in your curriculum or professional publication.

Stoeger (Dot) Level	Iron Sight Equivalent	Visual Focus & Alignment	Typical Use
VC1 – Dot visible anywhere on target, coarse confirmation	**Flash Sight Picture / Coarse Alignment**	Target focus or soft front-sight awareness; minimal alignment check. The sights flash into your vision and are "good enough."	Extreme close range (3–7 yds), large target areas (A-zone or larger), speed priority over precision.
VC2 – Dot roughly centered, acceptable wobble	**Moderate Sight Picture / Acceptable Alignment**	Front sight more defined; equal height/light is close but not perfect. Rear sight blur acceptable; focus between front and target.	7–15 yds on A/C zone, or partial targets closer; balance of speed and accuracy.
VC3 – Dot perfectly centered, crisp hold	**Refined Sight Picture / Hard Front-Sight Focus**	Crisp front sight focus; perfect equal height/light and clear edges. Rear sight and target intentionally blurry.	15–25+ yds, B8 bull or small plates; accuracy prioritized over speed.

2) Instructor Teaching Points

- **Key Principle: The amount of visual confirmation must match the shot difficulty.**

  Over-confirmation slows you unnecessarily; under-confirmation causes misses.
- **Iron Sight Nuance vs Dots:**
  - Dots let you stay **target-focused** across all levels.
  - Irons require shifting eye focus **onto the front sight** for refined shots, which adds an accommodation step.
- **Industry Terminology to Use:**
  - Flash Sight Picture (VC1)
  - Acceptable Sight Picture (VC2)
  - Refined/Precision Sight Picture (VC3)

3) Training Drills & Progressions
VC1 / Flash Sight Picture (Close & Fast)

- **Drills:**
  - Bill Drill at 7 yards (6 shots from draw; focus on speed)
  - 1-reload-1 at 5 yards
- **Target:** IPSC/USPSA A-zone, 8" circle
- **Coaching:** Emphasize reacting as soon as the sights enter the target area; no over-confirmation.

VC2 / Acceptable Alignment (Balanced Speed & Accuracy)

- **Drills:**
  - El Prez (10 yds, 6 shots/two targets/reload)
  - Doubles at 10–15 yds (pairs, calling shots)
- **Target:** A-zone or 6" circle

- **Coaching:** Work on front-sight awareness and smooth trigger; acceptable wobble zone.

VC3 / Precision Sight Picture (Accuracy Priority)

- **Drills:**
    - 25-yard B8 bull: 10 shots in 10–15 sec.
    - The Test (10 rounds, 10 yds, 10 sec, B8; scale for 25 yds for advanced shooters)
- **Target:** B8 bullseye or 4" plate
- **Coaching:** Crisp front-sight focus; emphasize equal height/light; perfect press.

4) Integration & Instructor Notes

- **Progression:** Train shooters to start with VC3 (hard focus, slow fire) to build fundamentals, then expand to VC2 and VC1 for speed and dynamic shooting.
- **Adaptive Loop:** Encourage calling shots (knowing where they hit based on sight picture) to develop automatic selection of the right confirmation level.
- **Mixed Drills:** Use variable-distance targets (3–25 yds) in the same string to force adaptation of confirmation levels.

Summary for Curriculum

- Stoeger's VC1–3 is simply the *dot-optics expression* of a long-standing **acceptable sight picture continuum**.
- For irons, use **Flash Sight Picture → Acceptable → Precision Sight Picture** with clear definitions and drill progressions.
- The principle is universal: *"Match the visual confirmation to the shot difficulty."*

Color Confirmation in Predictive Shooting (Confirmation Two)

Definition, Application, and Role in Performance-Based Engagements

Definition:

Color Confirmation is the process by which a shooter recognizes, interprets, and responds to the **visual presence and position of color-based sighting cues** (typically the front sight post or red dot) to **validate alignment and orientation** during high-speed engagements.

In a **Confirmation Two or Predictive shooting context**, Color Confirmation acts as a **non-focal visual verification**—a rapid, subconscious assurance that the pistol is aligned *enough* to deliver effective hits on target without requiring full sight refinement

What is Confirmation Two / Predictive Shooting?

In shooting taxonomy, **Confirmation Two** refers to:

- **Two shots fired** with **one quick sight reference** before or during the first shot.
- Sights or dot are **verified only once** before the engagement.
- Used in **close to moderate distances** or **high-confidence scenarios** where speed takes priority over precision.
- Examples include **hammer pairs**, **rapid transitions**, or **engaging large high-center-mass targets** at close range

Color Confirmation with Iron Sights in Predictive Shooting

With **iron sights**, the shooter typically confirms:

- The **colored front sight** (often orange, red, or green) appears **within the rear sight notch**.
- This appearance is processed not with **precise focal alignment**, but with **visual confirmation of the color** in the expected place.

Application:

- Shooter drives the gun out and **detects the flash of the front sight color** in the sight window.
- This color presence signals that the gun is generally aligned and shots can be broken.
- The second shot in the pair is delivered based on **visual memory and recoil pattern**, not re-acquisition of sights.

Key Observation:

Color Confirmation becomes a **"go signal"**—not perfect, but **good enough** for acceptable hits under speed.

Color Confirmation with Red Dot Optics in Predictive Shooting

With **RDS**, color confirmation is even more streamlined:

- The shooter confirms the **red or green dot appears on or near the intended target zone**.
- Precision is replaced by the **recognition of the dot's color presence** in a general location.

Application:

- Dot appears in the window during presentation and is **superimposed over the target**.
- Shooter may **never fully stabilize the dot** before or during the first shot.
- The second shot is fired as the dot **recoils and returns**, relying on muscle memory and natural point-of-aim.

Key Observation:

Color equals confirmation. If the red/green dot is on target—even fleetingly—it's green-light time in predictive mode.

Iron Sights vs. Optic Color Confirmation in Predictive Shooting

Attribute	Iron Sights	Red Dot Optic
Confirmation Type	Flash of color front sight within notch	Appearance of colored dot over target
Focus Type	Primarily front sight (brief focal contact)	Target focus with dot as overlay
Sight Stability Needed	Minimal (just enough to flash center)	Minimal (dot can be moving slightly)
Visual Signature	Flash of orange/green front sight	Flash or smear of red/green dot

Attribute	Iron Sights	Red Dot Optic
Application Range	3–10 yards (combat speed)	3–15 yards depending on shooter skill

Instructor Insights: Teaching Color Confirmation in Predictive Shooting

1. **Clarify Purpose:**

   Emphasize to students that in predictive shooting, **we're not waiting for perfect**. We're training our eyes and brain to say *"Yes, that's good enough—shoot."*

2. **Drills That Reinforce Color Confirmation:**
   - **Flash Sight Picture Drill (Iron Sights):**

     Present and fire two shots the moment the **front sight color is visible**—do not delay for perfect alignment.
   - **Dot-on-Target Drill (RDS):**

     Engage as soon as **colored dot touches high center mass**, no further refinement allowed.
   - **Target-Focus Transitions:**

     Keep eyes on the target, and engage as soon as the **color appears** (sight or dot).

3. **Feedback Tools:**
   - Use video playback to show shooters how often they "pause" or over-confirm.
   - Encourage dry fire presentations where the **front sight color or dot** appears **consistently in the same place**.

4. **Progression:**
   - Start slow and allow shooters to "see it happen."

- o Progress to timed or stress-based drills to train subconscious response to color cues.

Advanced Interpretation: Color as a Predictive Index

- In speed shooting, **color becomes a prediction engine**—if it's where you expect it to be, the rest of the system (grip, stance, recoil control) is likely aligned.
- **The absence of color**, or a color in the wrong place (off-center, tilted, flaring), tells the shooter **not to shoot** or to recalibrate.

Summary

Color Confirmation in predictive shooting is not about precision—it's about confidence.

It's the brain's shortcut to say, *"I recognize this flash of red/orange/green in the right space. I've seen this before. The shot will land."*

It enables shooters to apply speed, maintain flow, and execute rapid engagements **without compromising the fundamentals of control**.

Clean Sight Package in Reactive (Confirmation Three) Pistol Shooting

Definition, Application, and Critical Role in Precision-Based Engagements

Definition:

A **Clean Sight Package** is a visually stable, properly aligned, and clearly resolved sight picture that meets the required standard for **high accountability or precision shots**. It indicates the pistol is in a firing condition where the **sights (iron or optic)** are not only present but also **aligned, stable, and visually confirmed** in relation to the target.

In the context of **Confirmation Three or Reactive Shooting**, a clean sight package is **the shooter's final visual checkpoint** before pressing the trigger. It ensures the decision to shoot is based on **maximum visual accountability**, especially under high-consequence or low-margin conditions.

What is Confirmation Three / Reactive Shooting?

Confirmation Three refers to:

- **One shot** fired.
- **Two or more visual confirmations**—once during the presentation, and again before the shot breaks.
- Used in **precision or high-consequence engagements**: headshots, partial exposures, hostage rescue scenarios, long-distance pistol shooting.
- Prioritizes **accountability over speed**.

This style is **reactive**—the shooter **waits until** the clean sight picture presents itself. There is **no guessing, no predictive action**. The shooter reacts to precise visual input.

Iron Sights: Clean Sight Package Characteristics

A **clean iron sight package** in reactive shooting includes:

- **Front sight** clearly in focus.
- **Rear notch alignment** is correct—equal height and equal light.
- **Front sight post** centered horizontally and vertically.
- Sights are **motionless or minimally moving** in the sight plane.
- **Sight picture is stable**, and shooter is visually locked in on front sight clarity.

Example Use Cases:

- Hostage headshot at 10+ yards.
- Shooting between no-shoots or barricade slots.
- Tight scoring zone or steel at distance.

Shooter Behavior:

The shooter recognizes the alignment, pauses to confirm it, then reacts by breaking the shot.
No visual slop is tolerated. No rushing.

Red Dot Optics: Clean Sight Package Characteristics

A **clean red dot sight package** includes:

- The **dot is clearly visible**, crisp, and not flaring or ghosting.

- The dot is **motionless or tracking cleanly** in the intended point of impact.
- The shooter's **focus remains on the target**, but the dot is superimposed with precise placement.
- There is **no hunting or fishing**—the dot appears where the shooter expects and remains stable before the shot breaks.

Example Use Cases:

- High-center mass shot on a partially obscured threat at 20 yards.
- Precision dot placement on an active shooter threat behind cover.
- Long-range steel or anatomical targets at 25+ yards.

Shooter Behavior:

The dot is not just seen—it is stabilized.
The shooter waits until it confirms *perfect placement*, then reacts with controlled trigger execution.

Comparison: Clean Sight Package by System

Feature	Iron Sights	Red Dot Optic
Focal Plane	Front sight focused, rear sight aligned	Target focused, dot resolved on focal plane
Sight Picture	Equal height/light, front sight sharp	Crisp dot, stable, no parallax drift
Shooter Focus	Front sight clarity	Dot on target clarity
Stability Expectation	Minimal movement or oscillation	Dot motion stops or tracks predictably

Feature	Iron Sights	Red Dot Optic
Engagement Priority	Precision, accountability, surgical shots	Same—especially under pressure or distance

Instructor Notes: Teaching the Clean Sight Package in Reactive Shooting

1. **Explain the Trigger Discipline Connection:**
   - A clean sight package **demands a clean trigger press**.
   - Teach students that sight clarity and trigger control are **co-dependent** in this style of shooting.
2. **Reinforce Visual Patience:**
   - Shooters must be taught to wait—not out of hesitation, but from discipline.
   - Reactive shooting rewards shooters who react only to **confirmed information**.
3. **Key Drills for Development:**
   - **One-Shot Accuracy Drill (Iron or RDS):**
   Shooter may fire *only* when the sight picture is clean and stabilized—add time pressure slowly.
   - **Hold and Break Drill:**
   Present to the target, hold for 3–5 seconds while maintaining sight picture, then break the shot clean.
   - **No-Shoot Overlay Training:**
   Use targets with hard consequences for bad sight pictures—force sight picture discipline.

4. **Common Student Errors:**
    - **Rushing the trigger** before the sight picture is complete.
    - **Failing to focus on front sight** (irons) or shooting with an unstable dot (RDS).
    - **Trigger flinch** during the visual hold phase.

Advanced Interpretation: Sight Package = Decision Matrix

For advanced shooters, the clean sight package is more than alignment—it's a **decision threshold**.

- **Is the gun in the right place?**
- **Are the sights telling me the truth?**
- **Do I trust this moment to deliver the shot I need?**

If any of those answers are **no**, the shot is not taken.

Summary

A **Clean Sight Package** is the shooter's highest standard of visual confirmation.
It is slow only by comparison—it is deliberate, controlled, and exact.

It belongs in the most **consequential moments** of pistol shooting, where the **cost of a miss is high** and **confidence must be absolute**.

In Confirmation Three or Reactive engagements, a clean sight package is not just desired—it is required.

Grip -Instructor Viewpoint

I've been teaching firearms for over 30 years, and after watching tens of thousands of students, I can tell you this: in the trinity of shooting—vision, grip, and trigger—your vision will always tell you *when* you can shoot. But the moment speed or urgency comes into play, grip outweighs the trigger every single time.

A strong, consistent grip gives you predictability. When your grip is durable—meaning it doesn't break down under stress, speed, or volume of fire—it will take care of most of your trigger problems before they even start.

Think of it this way: your grip lays the foundation for everything that follows. With a solid grip, you can reset the trigger faster, get deeper into the wall, and complete the press with confidence. Without it, accuracy falters, speed breaks down, and the trigger becomes inconsistent.

So remember: the grip is not just how you hold the gun—it's the anchor that allows you to apply vision and trigger control under stress. Build it strong, make it consistent, and you'll have the durability to perform when it matters most.

Grip: At the Instructor Level

For over three decades of professional instruction, one truth has never changed—**grip is king.** Everything else builds from it. Without a proper grip, nothing else matters.

A good grip must meet three standards: it must be **consistent, predictable, and durable.** Consistent—applied the same way every time. Predictable—because it delivers the same results under stress or fatigue. Durable—capable of withstanding hundreds of rounds in a single session or a lethal-force encounter without breaking down.

Grip is about friction, pressure, and control. The debate has raged for years: 50/50 push-pull, 60/40 support-to-strong hand, even 90/10 ratios. In reality, we've always been talking about the same principle. **The strong hand holds the pistol tightly enough to never lose it. The support hand manages recoil.** Nothing more, nothing less.

Here's what matters: the tendons that connect the forearm to the back of the hand must be locked in. The wrist must be rigid, forming a stable platform so the pistol's recoil spring can cycle properly. Without this locked platform, you invite malfunctions. The grip begins in the forearms, drives tension through the wrist, and clamps the pistol in a 360-degree vise—**all without choking off the independence of the trigger finger.**

A proper grip not only mitigates recoil, it also masks flaws in trigger press and prevents many mechanical malfunctions outright. Done correctly, it frees the shooter to see faster, press smoother, and deliver accurate rounds at speed.

Understand this: **the grip is not new, not revolutionary, and not negotiable.** Look at the martial arts. Study how the Japanese sword masters taught the decapitation cut thousands of years ago—locked wrists, full tension, vise-like control, with the weapon acting as an extension of the body. The mechanics are the same today. The principles are eternal.

In the hierarchy of pistol performance—vision, structure, and trigger—grip is the cornerstone of structure. And in real-world lethal encounters where speed and survival are non-negotiable, grip becomes the fulcrum. Without it, you lose the fight before it starts.

The Non-Negotiable Standard

Your grip is not optional—it is the foundation of pistol shooting. A proper, vise-like hold gives you control of the weapon, manages recoil, and speeds recovery between shots. The stronger and more stable the grip, the more aggressively you can run the trigger without losing accuracy. It also keeps the pistol oriented on the threat, reducing the need for fine, time-consuming sight alignment when fighting for your life.

A correct grip must meet three standards: **consistency, predictability, and durability.**

- **Consistency** means you grip the pistol the same way every single time. No exceptions. Every draw, every presentation, every shot. Consistency builds reliability.
- **Predictability** follows. When the grip is consistent, the pistol recoils the same way every time and the sights return to the same spot. That predictable behavior allows you to track the sights through recoil and fire as fast as you can process the sight picture.
- **Durability** seals the deal. Your grip must withstand pressure, stress, and fatigue for as many shots as the fight demands. A grip that loosens, slips, or collapses destroys predictability, and without predictability there is no consistency.

The key factors are **pressure and friction.** Apply enough pressure to lock the gun in, and maximize friction between your hands and the pistol. That is what creates the 360-degree vise that controls recoil and keeps the weapon running.

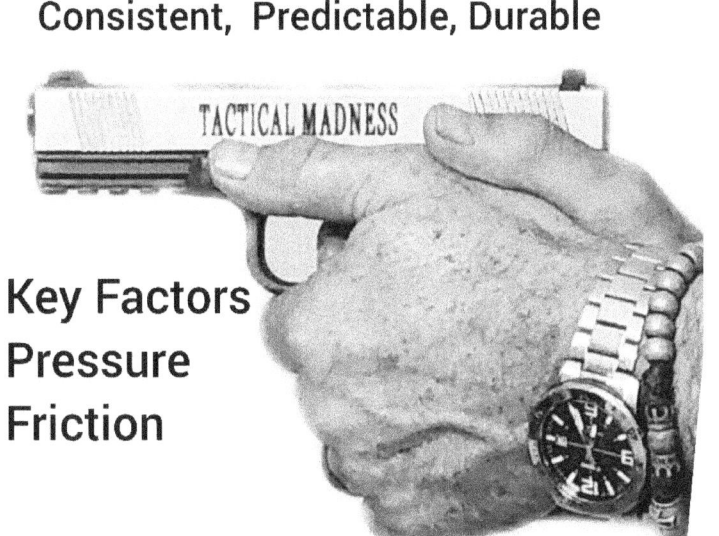

Instructor's Command: *Lock the gun in, lock the wrists, and do not let it change from the first round to the last. A weak grip is unacceptable. A durable, consistent grip wins fights.*

Anatomical and Biomechanical Foundations of the Grip

This exposition delves into the grip's role in fostering consistency, predictability, and durability, illuminated through anatomical and biomechanical lenses. Such insights equip instructors to convey these principles with precision, enhancing shooter performance.

1. Grip Consistency and Predictability

- **Biomechanical Rationale**: Consistency arises from the body's capacity to replicate the grip configuration reliably. Proprioceptors—sensory receptors in the hands and forearms that detect positional cues—require a stable, repeatable hold to minimize recoil variability and bolster shooting reliability.
- This uniformity yields a foreseeable recoil pattern, facilitating swift follow-up shots and sustained accuracy.
- **Anatomical Insights**: Synchronized engagement of forearm and hand musculature is essential, with balanced tension across flexors and extensors. This orchestration stabilizes the grip under duress, preventing deviations.

2. Head and Eye Positioning

- **Head Up, Eyes Up**: The eyes serve as the primary conduit for aiming; thus, maintaining an upright head aligned with the target is vital for precision.
- Anatomically, this posture relaxes the sternocleidomastoid and associated neck muscles, averting tension in the shoulders and upper back that could compromise stability.
- **Aim Small, Miss Small**: Concentrating on a diminutive focal point leverages the fovea's acute central vision. Proper head alignment permits independent eye and neck mobility, mitigating extraneous strain.

3. Shoulder Relaxation and Elbow Positioning

- **No Shoulder Tension**: Shoulder rigidity impairs grip integrity. Elevating the head alleviates this, preserving fluidity in the arms.
- **Muscles Involved**: The deltoids and trapezius govern shoulder posture; their tension induces arm rigidity, hindering recoil absorption and realignment.

4. Forearm Tension from Elbows to Wrists

- **Biomechanics**: Engaging musculature from elbows to wrists—via flexors and extensors—fortifies recoil control. This tension locks the wrists forward, channeling energy efficiently.
- **Anatomical Details**:
    - Brachioradialis: Stabilizes wrist and elbow.
    - Flexor Carpi Radialis and Ulnaris: Facilitate forward wrist flexion.
    - Extensor Carpi Radialis: Counterbalances flexors for a rigid lock.

5. Wrist Tendons and Locking Forward

- **Wrist Locking Mechanism**: Active tendon engagement prevents backward collapse under recoil. Balanced flexor activation (e.g., Flexor Carpi Radialis and Ulnaris) sustains forward stability.

6. Thumb and Palm Positioning

- **Thumbs High**: Position thumbs maximally elevated without impeding slide function, curbing muzzle rise and averting limp-wristing. The thenar eminence presses firmly against the backstrap.
- **Pressure Distribution**: Support-hand dominance in pressure application optimizes recoil mitigation, with strong-hand alignment ensuring aim integrity.

7. The Role of the Fingers

- **Strong Hand**: Middle, ring, and pinky exert rearward force, securing the grip via flexor tendons. Anatomically, palmar interossei aid in finger compression.
- **Support Hand**: Index and middle fingers nest in strong-hand knuckle grooves for uniform pressure.
- **Trigger Finger**: Operates autonomously to preclude sympathetic disruptions, isolating flexor tendon action.

8. 360-Degree Grip Pressure

- **Vise-Like Grip**: Omnidirectional pressure engages flexors (e.g., Flexor Digitorum Superficialis) and extensors (e.g., Extensor Digitorum Longus), governing recoil holistically.
- **Durability**: Unyielding pressure sustains focus on trigger work, obviating mid-sequence adjustments.

9. Misconceptions about Grip Pressure

- **Dispelling Myths**: Antiquated notions (e.g., "hold until it shakes, then ease") have evolved; contemporary emphasis favors support-hand predominance for recoil mastery.
- **Special Forces Legacy**: Wrist-rolling and thumb-pointing techniques lock tendons, enhancing control—a precursor to modern methods.

A meticulously formed grip, when consistent and predictable, applies optimal tension and friction, neutralizing trigger anomalies at engagement ranges.

Grip: Built From the Draw

The grip begins the instant you touch the pistol. It is built during the draw stroke, and it starts with the **strong hand leveraging the holster's stability.** If the grip is wrong here, you will never recover it later.

Strong Hand Responsibilities

The strong hand establishes dominance from the start. It must:

- **Seat the web of the thumb and forefinger high into the tang/beavertail.** High purchase reduces muzzle flip and maximizes leverage.
- **Assert control from the top and rear.** The strong hand locks the pistol down so it cannot shift.
- **Disengage holster retention with the thumb.** This must be automatic—no wasted movement.
- **Apply firm front-to-rear pressure** so that when the support hand joins, the pistol is already locked in.

The fingers matter. The middle, ring, and pinky fingers wrap forward with even pressure, pulling the pistol straight back into the hand. The trigger guard should index against the middle finger as a tactile anchor. The thumb and palm provide rearward friction, while the trigger finger rides rigidly along the frame until it's time to fire.

Support Hand Responsibilities

The support hand must not float—it stages across the body during the draw for immediate, efficient union. As the pistol clears the holster and levels to the threat, the support hand drives into position. It overlays the exposed grip, palm sealing into the open panel left by the strong hand. Fingers wrap forward and interlock at the knuckles, with the index finger high under the trigger guard to maximize upward leverage and recoil control.

Final Grip Formation

Once both hands are joined:

- **Strong hand pressure never changes.** Any adjustment introduces instability.
- **Support hand clamps down.** It provides the majority of recoil management, ensuring the pistol cycles smoothly and returns to target fast.
- **Both hands form a 360-degree vise.** This is not gentle contact—it is a locked enclosure that eliminates pistol movement not initiated by the trigger press.

Why This Matters

This configuration produces three non-negotiable results:

1. **Trigger stability:** A locked grip mitigates the natural disturbances of pressing the trigger.
2. **Recoil control:** The pistol cycles predictably, sights track straight, and recovery is immediate.
3. **Speed under stress:** With the grip built correctly in the draw, there is no hesitation, no correction, no wasted motion. The gun is ready to fight the moment it is presented.

Instructor's Command: *Build the grip correctly from the draw—high, tight, locked, and vise-like. Strong hand controls, support hand clamps, wrists rigid. If you miss this step, you will chase the pistol and lose the fight. Do it right, or don't draw at all.*

Quick Review: 13 Points of Proper Pistol Grip Structure

1. **Head & Eyes Up**: Upright posture; eyes fixed on a precise target point. "Aim small, miss small."
2. **Relaxed Shoulders**: Tension-free; head elevation dissipates strain.
3. **Forearm Tension**: Uniform from elbows to wrists for foundational control.
4. **Wrist Tendons Engaged**: Locked forward with isometric balance.
5. **Thumbs High**: Maximized elevation sans mechanical interference.
6. **Palm Pressure In**: Inward drive; support hand predominates.

7. **Frozen Finger Pressure**: Immutable once set.
8. **Support Index Finger Placement**: Firmly under trigger guard for lateral stability.
9. **Support Finger Integration**: Even pressure into strong-hand knuckles.
10. **Strong Hand Fingers (Rearward Pressure)**: Middle, ring, pinky secure durability.
11. **Strong Thumb Forward Pressure**: Counters rearward forces.
12. **Trigger Finger Isolation**: Independent motion.
13. **360° Vise-like Tension**: Multi-directional for comprehensive recoil mastery.

Inductive Learning

Employ inquiry-based methods, wherein shooters discern optimal support pressure, friction, and thumb placement through iterative observation and experience, rather than didactic instruction. Repetitions reveal personalized efficiencies.

Grip efficacy manifests in rapid engagements: Minimal sight lift, with symmetric rise and return velocities, signaling structural and grip synergy.

A steadfast, predictable grip, imbued with apt tension and friction, obviates trigger concerns at fighting ranges.

Beginner Level – Establishing the Foundation

- **Non-Negotiable Rule:** Grip the pistol the same way every single time. Consistency is survival.
- **Strong Hand:** Wrap the dominant hand high on the backstrap. Hold tight enough that you will not drop the pistol, but not so tight that you shake.

- **Support Hand:** Lock into the open space left on the grip, fingers wrapped, thumbs forward. The support hand adds pressure from the side, controlling recoil.
- **Wrist Position:** Straight, locked, rigid. No bending or breaking.
- **What to Expect:** A proper grip reduces muzzle rise, helps you see your sights faster, and keeps the gun running without malfunctions.

Instructor's Command: *If your grip changes from shot to shot, your hits will too. Lock it in, every time, the same way.*

Intermediate Level – Building Pressure and Control

- **Hand Pressure Ratio:** Think **60% support hand / 40% strong hand.** The strong hand holds firmly; the support hand crushes in to stabilize and fight recoil.
- **Tendon Lock:** Drive tension through the forearm into the back of the hand. Feel the tendons tighten. That tension locks the wrist and stabilizes the platform.
- **Trigger Finger Isolation:** The grip clamps with 360-degree pressure, but the trigger finger stays free—straight, smooth, and independent.
- **Predictability:** The goal is a **predictable gun cycle.** Every shot should feel the same in your hands—recoil straight back, slide cycles clean, sights return to target.

Instructor's Command: *You do not adjust your grip after the shot. You grip correctly before the shot and never let it degrade.*

Advanced Level – Performance Under Stress

- **Durability of Grip:** Your grip must hold through long strings of fire, high round counts, sweat, stress, and fatigue. Weak grips collapse; strong grips endure.

- **Recoil Management:** Aggressive thumbs-forward, elbows slightly locked out, full 360-degree vise. The pistol recoils, but your locked structure drives the gun back on target.
- **Error Mitigation:** A proper grip masks minor trigger errors. A poor grip magnifies them.
- **Combat Application:** In real-world violence, there is no time to "fix" your grip. It must be there from the draw—immediately correct, immediately aggressive.

Instructor's Command: *If your grip is not perfect on the first shot, the fight is already moving faster than you are. Train until perfection is automatic.*

Instructor Level – Teaching the King

- **Principle:** Grip is not negotiable. It is the primary mechanical control of the pistol. Everything else—sight picture, trigger press—fails without it.
- **Error Diagnosis:**
    - Shots left/right? Trigger finger or weak wrist.
    - Muzzle flip too high? Weak support hand or unlocked wrist.
    - Malfunctions? Inconsistent grip, limp-wristing, poor platform.
- **Historical Context:** The mechanics of grip are not new. From ancient swordsmanship to modern combatives, the body mechanics are universal: locked wrists, full-arm tension, weapon as extension of the body.
- **Standard:** Every student must meet the same baseline—**a durable, repeatable, 360-degree vise grip that manages recoil and preserves trigger function.** No excuses, no exceptions.

Instructor's Command: *Do not pass a student who cannot grip properly. The grip is the foundation of shooting and fighting with a pistol. If you allow weakness here, you set them up for failure in the fight.*

Grip: The Non-Negotiable Standard

Your grip is king. It is not optional. Without it, everything else fails—sight picture, trigger press, and ultimately, survival. A proper, vise-like hold gives you absolute control of the weapon, manages recoil, speeds recovery, and keeps the pistol oriented on the threat. It must be **consistent, predictable, and durable.** Nothing less is acceptable.

Grip -Instructor Viewpoint

I've been teaching firearms for over 30 years, and after watching tens of thousands of students, I can tell you this: in the trinity of shooting—vision, grip, and trigger—your vision will always tell you *when* you can shoot. But the moment speed or urgency comes into play, grip outweighs the trigger every single time.

A strong, consistent grip gives you predictability. When your grip is durable—meaning it doesn't break down under stress, speed, or volume of fire—it will take care of most of your trigger problems before they even start.

Think of it this way: your grip lays the foundation for everything that follows. With a solid grip, you can reset the trigger faster, get deeper into the wall, and complete the press with confidence. Without it, accuracy falters, speed breaks down, and the trigger becomes inconsistent.

So remember: the grip is not just how you hold the gun—it's the anchor that allows you to apply vision and trigger control under stress. Build it strong, make it consistent, and you'll have the durability to perform when it matters most.

Instructor Checklist: Pistol Grip Structure

☐ 1. Head upright, eyes on small point
☐ 2. Shoulders relaxed, not rolled
☐ 3. Forearm tension from elbow to wrist
☐ 4. Wrist tendons locked forward, equally engaged
☐ 5. Thumbs high on frame, non-interfering
☐ 6. Palms pressing inward; support dominant
☐ 7. Finger tension unchanged
☐ 8. Support index under trigger guard

☐ 9. Support fingers in strong-hand knuckles

☐ 10. Strong fingers rearward

☐ 11. Strong thumb/palm forward

☐ 12. Trigger finger independent

☐ 13. Full 360° vise-like tension

A robust, uniform grip neutralizes trigger flaws at operational distances.

The essence: A high two-handed grip maximizing surface contact, gripped firmly and consistently for predictable recoil and enduring performance.

Dispelling Grip Myths of Old

Evolutions in pedagogy mirror those in martial arts, refinements in articulation. Early queries on grip intensity elicited responses like Fairbairn and Sykes' "hold till it shakes, then back off a wee bit" for the Colt 1911. Subsequent ratios (90/10 to 70/30) underscored support-hand emphasis for recoil, though unquantifiable.

Special Forces' wrist-rolling and thumb-pointing locked tendons, amplifying efficacy. "Aim small, miss small" and augmented support pressure endure as validated tenets.

A solid well-formed grip will mitigate most trigger manipulation issues. A solid well-formed grip that is consistent and predicable will apply the proper tension and friction will mitigate trigger issues at pistol fighting distances!

The bottom line is that a two-handed grip must be as high up on the pistol as possible and still allow the slide to function, the two hands should utilize as much of the gripping surface as possible, grip the pistol as hard as possible.

Be **consistent**. Grab the pistol the same way every time. This will allow the pistol to perform and recoil in a **predictable** manner. The grip should remain **durable** for the number of rounds being fired.

I firmly assert that a solid, well-formed grip stands as the unbreakable foundation for resolving most trigger manipulation issues in pistol shooting, leaving no room for debate on its primacy. Vision always dictates the precise moment to shoot, yet shooters who master a consistent, predictable hold—applying unyielding tension and friction—directly mitigate the majority of trigger problems, especially at pistol fighting distances where hesitation proves fatal. In lethal kinetic encounters under extreme stress, this grip elevates survivability by transforming the pistol into a seamless extension of the body: grip it two-handed as high as possible while allowing flawless slide function, cover every inch of the gripping surface for maximum contact, and squeeze with unrelenting force short of tremor to deliver instinctive, life-saving accuracy.

Trigger Control

The Importance of a Well-Formed Grip in Trigger Control

A well-formed**, consistent, predictable, and durable** grip serves as the bedrock of effective trigger control, profoundly impacting the performance of individuals who conceal carry a pistol. This foundational element ensures that the firearm remains stable and aligned during the recoil cycle, mitigating common trigger manipulation errors that can compromise accuracy and speed in high-pressure defensive scenarios. For concealed carriers, mastering a reliable grip translates to enhanced confidence, precision, and control, enabling rapid and accurate shot delivery when seconds matter most. Instructors must possess a comprehensive understanding of grip dynamics and their interplay with trigger control, as this knowledge allows them to teach students how to establish and maintain a robust grip that minimizes disruptions to sight alignment. By emphasizing this critical skill, instructors empower shooters to execute responsible and effective self-defense, fostering both technical proficiency and psychological resilience in life-threatening encounters.

Trigger control as a foundational skill

In the discipline of marksmanship, particularly within the context of concealed carry and defensive pistol use, trigger control emerges as a foundational skill that bridges the gap between intention and impact. It encompasses the deliberate and precise manipulation of the trigger to discharge the firearm with minimal disruption to sight alignment, ensuring shots are both rapid and accurate. This control is not merely a mechanical action but a synthesis of mental discipline and physical execution, influenced by factors such as target distance, size, and the inherent characteristics of the pistol. Mastering trigger control demands consistent practice, as it must remain reliable under the duress of high-stress encounters, where rhythm and predictability become vital allies in maintaining composure.

Regardless of a shooter's proficiency, the ability to press and release the trigger at a uniform speed fosters rhythm, which serves as a stabilizing force during adrenaline-fueled situations. Trigger control integrates seamlessly with other shooting fundamentals—grip, stance, sight alignment, and breath control—forming a cohesive system that optimizes performance. The physical application of pressure on the trigger varies by individual physiology and firearm design, yet through disciplined training, it converges toward a standardized technique that prioritizes stability and precision.

At its essence, trigger control involves manipulating the trigger to facilitate swift, accurate shooting while preserving sight alignment on the target. The speed and method of manipulation are dictated by the target's distance, dimensions, associated risks, and the shooter's skill level. A key rule of thumb governs this process: vision dictates trigger speed. As the shooter refines the sight picture, they should progressively engage the trigger's "wall" or resistance point. Once the sights achieve the necessary alignment for the given target, the press completes without hesitation. Efficiency demands that trigger manipulation not impede visual processing; rather, the aligned sights signal the culmination of the press.

Trigger control comprises two interdependent components: mental control and physical manipulation. Mentally, it requires managing emotions and arousal levels to sustain focus—cultivating a state of "calm aggression" where determination and confidence prevail without escalating into panic. This arousal threshold for precise shooting is notably lower than that required for physical altercations, emphasizing the need for emotional regulation. Physically, proficient trigger handling ensures control even at elevated firing rates, preventing deviations that could compromise accuracy.

Types of Triggers

Firearms triggers vary in design, each demanding tailored manipulation techniques.

Double Action: When initiating double-action trigger control, the shooter should momentarily pause upon settling into the aiming area, minimizing the arc of movement. In double-action mode, trigger pull weights typically range from 9.5 to 16.5 pounds. The shooter acquires a sight picture and applies smooth, consistent rearward pressure until the shot breaks, avoiding abrupt jerks that could disturb alignment.

Single Action: For single-action triggers, slack removal begins as the weapon rises toward the target, with initial pressure applied early. Pull weights generally fall between 4.0 and 6.5 pounds. Upon entering the aiming area, the shooter secures the sight picture and executes a steady, uninterrupted increase in pressure to the rear. Post-shot, the trigger is released without disengaging the finger, slack is taken up anew, and focus remains fixed on the front sight throughout the sequence.

Trigger Finger Placement and Isolation

Effective trigger manipulation hinges on a stable grip and balanced stance, which unify the hands and pistol into a single recoiling unit. Proper balance positions the center of gravity slightly forward, allowing the body to absorb recoil naturally without unnecessary tension.

Trigger finger placement is paramount for isolating its movement and preventing sight disturbance. The finger must press the trigger straight rearward, maintaining constant grip tension once established—only the trigger finger articulates. Under stress, trigger control often deteriorates first, underscoring the challenge of mastering it during timed drills or real-world scenarios.

No universal finger placement exists; it must feel natural and enable a fluid pull, accommodating variations in hand size and pistol ergonomics. Typically, the pad centers between the fingertip and first knuckle. Excessive finger insertion pulls impacts toward the strong hand, while insufficient contact pushes them away. The goal: a straight-back press at consistent speed, undisturbed sights.

Trigger Manipulation Concepts

Isolation of the trigger finger remains the cornerstone of manipulation, blending mental fortitude with physical precision. Challenges arise from anticipating recoil and noise, which provoke flinching, and from sympathetic finger movements at higher speeds. Dry fire practice—conducting drills with an unloaded firearm, airsoft replica, or training tool—proves invaluable for honing these skills without ammunition expenditure. It reveals subtleties obscured during live fire, particularly in aligning sights with trigger presses.

Two primary dry fire variants exist, with "dead trigger press" offering superior feedback by simulating post-discharge conditions (detailed further in discussions linking grip to trigger). This method exposes hand inputs affecting the pistol, enabling inductive learning: slap the trigger aggressively in dry fire, observe sight deviations, and apply corrections.

Follow-Through and Recovery

Follow-through entails sustaining focus on sight alignment beyond the shot's discharge, encompassing the ignition, bullet launch, recoil cycle, and slide return. This surprise break mitigates anticipatory reflexes, allowing the shooter to "call" their shot pre-impact. Instructors emphasize follow-through's role in enabling rapid, multiple accurate shots.

Recovery swiftly restores the pistol to its original aiming position and natural point of aim, absorbing recoil directly rearward. Fundamentals resume immediately for subsequent shots, prioritizing speed without sacrificing precision.

Achieving Accurate Hits at Speed

Training begins with perfecting sight pictures in basic presentations, evolving to rapid alignments during speed drills. With practice, shooters discern essential visual cues for fight-stopping hits, accountable for every round. The objective: deliver multiple rounds into vital zones swiftly to neutralize threats.

Instructor Note: A consistent, solid grip mitigates most trigger issues at close-range engagements, providing tension and friction to counteract deviations.

Types of Trigger Manipulation

Prep and Press: Remove pre-travel (slack) initially, then complete the press upon sight confirmation. Ideal for reactive shooting at moderate distances or obscured targets, it aligns with "Confirmation Three" (clear sight/dot return post-recoil). Prep occurs during sight refinement, culminating in a press on alignment.

Rolling Trigger Press: Execute a continuous, smooth rearward motion, akin to revolver firing, resetting promptly for repetition. Suited for mid-to-close ranges and some obscured targets with "Confirmation Two" (color/shape verification). A firm grip minimizes pistol movement.

Slapping: Despite controversy, this technique accelerates firing on close, low-risk targets by pulling through the entire trigger without staging. Proper grip eliminates recoil anticipation inputs, achieving speed and acceptable accuracy in fast, violent encounters. Low impacts often stem from pre-ignition pushes, not slapping itself. Employed in "Confirmation One" scenarios (spatial orientation recognition), it supports predictive shooting sans per-shot sight confirmation.

For all methods, monitor pistol feel, isolate the trigger finger, and avoid firing-hand curling from excess tension. Observe sight lift and return in recoil for grip and press adjustments.

Trigger Control at Speed

Ensure straight-rearward presses, with hand tension influencing finger efficiency. Heightened tension risks sympathetic movements, often causing low-opposite impacts. Anticipation—pushing downward against expected recoil—exacerbates errors. Isolate the finger to counteract.

Concepts reiterate: manage recoil/noise anticipation and multi-finger sympathy via "dead trigger" dry fire, simulating live inputs for corrective feedback.

Trigger Freeze

This phenomenon halts trigger reset for follow-ups, typically from excessive firing-hand tension. Training emphasizes relaxation and isolation to prevent it.

A robust, unwavering grip empowers concealed carriers to execute precise, rapid shots, anchoring their defense against threats with steadfast control. Shooters actively refine a consistent, predictable grip to stabilize the firearm, neutralizing trigger manipulation errors and preserving sight alignment under duress. This disciplined foundation, paired with rhythmic trigger presses, drives effective responses across diverse target scenarios. Instructors, armed with deep expertise, instill this critical skill, guiding students to master grip mechanics and mental fortitude. Such mastery proves vital, enabling shooters to neutralize dangers decisively while underscoring the instructor's role in forging resilient, proficient defenders.

Symbiotic Relationship between Grip and Trigger Control

One cannot function optimally without the other

In pistol shooting, **grip and trigger control** are two of the most critical fundamentals. When executed properly and consistently, they **support and reinforce each other**, leading to faster, more accurate, and repeatable shooting — even under stress, fatigue, or speed.

GRIP – The Structural Foundation of Pistol Shooting

A **consistent, predictable, and durable grip** provides the physical *anchor* for the gun's movement and your visual reference (the sight or dot). It controls recoil, keeps the gun indexed to the eye line, and enables **repetition under pressure**.

Key Grip Elements:

- **Consistent Placement**: Both hands must meet the pistol in exactly the same location and orientation every time.
- **Predictable Pressure**: 360° pressure applied by the support hand and firing hand must be balanced and repeatable.
- **Durable Under Recoil**: The structure must not collapse, shift, or fatigue under recoil, multiple shots, or time.

An effective grip **minimizes muzzle movement** during trigger manipulation — meaning the sights stay aligned with the shooter's intended point of impact *while the trigger is being moved.*

TRIGGER CONTROL – The Precision Input

Trigger control is **the only input that causes the gun to fire**. Even with perfect alignment and stance, if the trigger is pressed incorrectly, the shot will miss.

Essential Aspects of Trigger Control:

- **Isolated Finger Movement**: The trigger finger must move independently of the rest of the firing hand.
- **Straight Rearward Path**: The press must not cause lateral displacement of the gun.
- **Timing with Visual Input**: Trigger press must coincide with the required level of sight confirmation.

The trigger press **has a direct effect on the orientation of the muzzle** at the moment the shot breaks. If done improperly, it undermines even the most solid grip.

How Grip and Trigger Control Reinforce Each Other

Grip Supports Trigger Control	Trigger Control Protects the Grip
A stable grip **anchors the gun**, reducing motion and allowing the trigger finger to **move independently**.	Smooth, straight trigger presses prevent **torque or lateral pressure**, which could **disrupt the grip** or sight alignment.
Proper grip tension allows the shooter to **press the trigger without inducing movement** in the frame.	Clean trigger control minimizes over-travel and sympathetic tension, which **preserves grip structure** and recoil integrity.

Grip Supports Trigger Control	**Trigger Control Protects the Grip**
A predictable grip **manages recoil**, helping the shooter reset the trigger during recoil and maintain cadence.	Controlled, rhythmic trigger manipulation **avoids grip breakdown**, especially during fast strings.
A durable grip withstands **trigger slapping or aggressive presses** during high-speed engagements.	Trigger control ensures that **rapid shots do not introduce chaos** into the gun-hand interface.

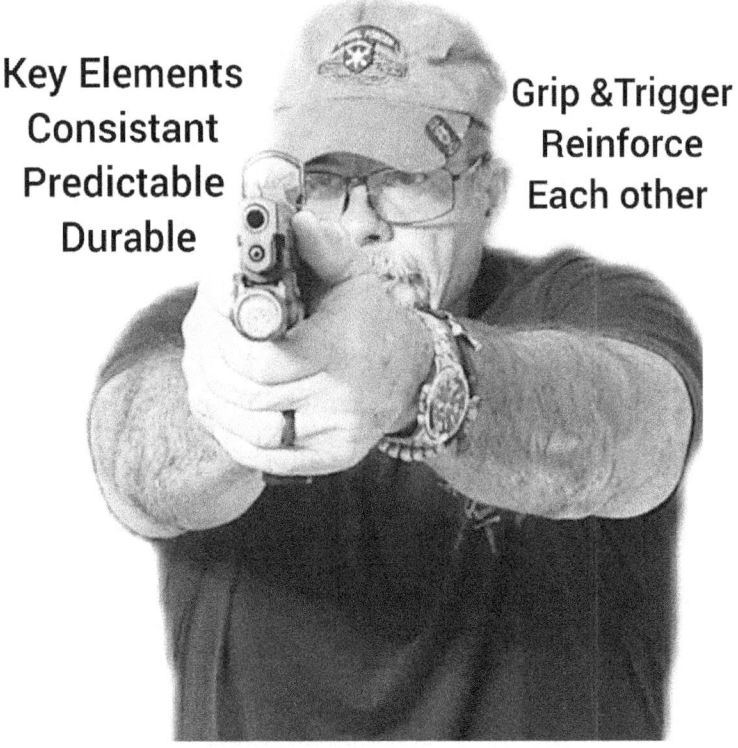

GRIP
The Structural Foundation
Of Pistol Shooting

Key Elements
Consistant
Predictable
Durable

Grip &Trigger
Reinforce
Each other

Effective Grip Minimizes Muzzel Movement

Performance Outcome: When Both Are Working Together

When grip and trigger control are **properly synchronized**:

- The dot or front sight **tracks predictably in recoil**.
- The shooter maintains **sight integrity during the trigger press**.
- The gun **returns to the same place** shot after shot.
- The shooter can transition between **reactive and predictive shooting** without changing grip or technique.
- **Trigger freeze, anticipation, and low-left hits** are dramatically reduced.

When the Relationship Fails

Bad Grip → Poor Trigger Control	Bad Trigger Control → Poor Grip
Inconsistent grip tension causes **gun movement during trigger press**.	Jerking or slapping the trigger distorts the firing hand, which **breaks grip stability**.
Lack of grip structure forces the shooter to **over-control with the trigger finger**, introducing sympathetic movement.	Poor control causes recoil to impact **unevenly**, wearing out grip endurance.
Grip failure forces compensations (e.g., more finger on trigger), leading to **non-isolated movement**.	Abrupt trigger press causes grip to **slip, shift, or open**, especially during rapid fire.

Instructor Tip – Diagnostic Cue:

"If the dot moves **before** the shot, it's your trigger.

If it moves **after** the shot and doesn't return, it's your grip.

If it moves **before, during, and after**, it's both."

REAL-WORLD DIAGNOSTICS & TEACHING CUES

Dot or Front Sight Movement before the Shot:

- Problem: **Trigger control error**
- Cue: "You moved it before it went bang — slow down the press."

Dot Does Not Return to the Same Spot After Recoil:

- Problem: **Grip collapse or asymmetrical tension**
- Cue: "You're losing your grip in recoil — fix your support hand."

Gun Jumps Sideways on Shot Break:

- Problem: **Combined grip and trigger failure**
- Cue: "Relax your firing hand — the finger is fighting the frame."

ANATOMICAL & NEUROMUSCULAR COMPONENTS

Grip:

- Muscular tension comes from **flexors and extensors** in the forearm.
- A strong grip with the **support hand** allows the **firing hand** to relax, preserving finger isolation.

Trigger Finger Isolation:

- The **flexor digitorum profundus** and **superficialis** control the fingers.
- Tension in the palm or pinky/ring fingers of the firing hand creates **sympathetic movement**, causing the **trigger finger to arc or pull sideways**, disrupting alignment.
- Over-gripping or squeezing the entire firing hand during the press causes **"milking"**, collapsing the structure and disrupting the sights.

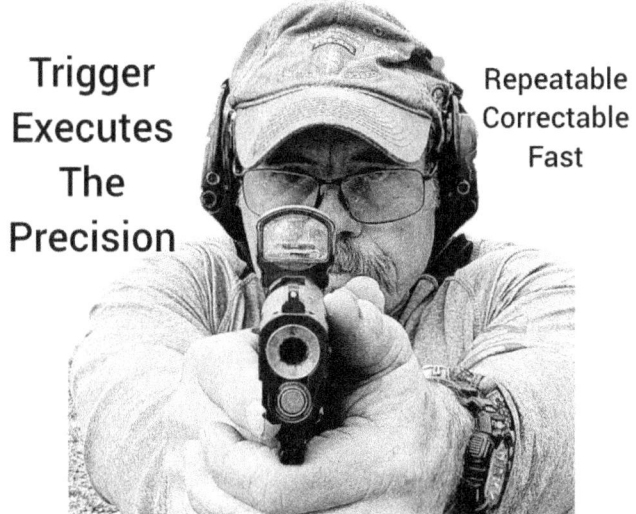

THE FEEDBACK LOOP IN SHOOTING

- A good grip **reduces the visual and mechanical penalty** of minor trigger errors.
- Good trigger control **maximizes the benefit** of a stable grip.
- The shooter can then **learn from the visual feedback of the sight package** — seeing exactly what their mechanics produced.
- Over time, this allows for **inductive learning** and **intuitive correction**.

"You won't see what matters in recoil unless your trigger press and grip let you."

How to Train the Symbiosis

- **Dry Fire with Live Trigger Press**

    – Watch for dot or sight movement during the press.

    - Watch the dot or front sight for *pre-ignition movement*.
    - Focus on maintaining grip pressure while pressing cleanly.

- **"Dot Bounce" Recoil Observation Drill**

    – Watch how the dot lifts and returns under recoil to analyze grip recovery.

    - Fire multiple shots and **observe dot lift and return**.
    - If it doesn't return to the same point, it's a grip failure.
    - If it jitters before the shot, it's a trigger failure.

- **Trigger Isolation + Grip Endurance**

    – Conduct cadence drills at different paces (Bill Drill, 1-2-3-4 Drill).

- **Ball and Dummy Live Fire**

    – Isolate unexpected shot breaks and grip collapse moments.

    - Mix dummy rounds into mags.
    - When the dummy round is encountered, *observe sight movement on trigger press*.
    - Was it the grip or the finger?

- **"Dead Trigger" Follow-Through Drill**

    – Press the trigger on an empty chamber and **observe what moved** when recoil doesn't distract.

- After a dry fire press, the trigger goes dead.
- Attempt a second press to observe *what the hand does* without the "click" or distraction.
- This reveals true grip vs. trigger separation.

The **grip stabilizes the platform**; the **trigger executes the precision**.

A durable grip allows you to press the trigger **without disturbing** the gun.

Good trigger control allows the gun to **behave predictably** under recoil — protecting your grip.

Together, they produce a shooting experience that is **repeatable, correctable, and fast**.

Pistol Presentation – Index Point Breakdown

Position 1 – Grip and Retention Defeat

The presentation begins before the gun leaves the holster. Establish a full, master grip with the strong hand, high on the tang, with web of the hand fully seated. Defeat any and all retention devices in a deliberate and efficient motion. A compromised grip here cannot be corrected later—this is non-negotiable.

Position 2 – Initial Rotation and Support Hand Index

As the pistol clears the holster, it begins to rotate toward the target, but it is not yet leveled. At this point, the support hand moves to its first index. The support-hand index finger should slide directly under the trigger guard as the gun rotates, guiding the establishment of a proper two-handed firing grip. This indexing ensures consistency and eliminates guesswork in grip formation.

Position 3 – Grip Integration and Forward Drive

With the gun rotated toward the target and both hands meeting, the two-handed grip is locked. From here, the pistol begins its drive toward full extension. This forward motion is purposeful and efficient—no wasted movement.

Position 4 – Spatial Orientation and Visual Index

As the pistol continues to extend, spatial orientation takes over. The slide, or the optic housing if equipped, enters the lower portion of the shooter's visual plane. At this precise moment, the pistol is guided into alignment with the line of sight. From here, it is permissible to place the strong-hand trigger finger on the trigger and begin prepping—removing mechanical slack and pressing to the wall in anticipation of the shot.

Position 5 – Full Presentation and Break

At full extension, the pistol settles naturally into the sight picture. The sights or dot confirm alignment. The trigger press continues seamlessly from the wall, breaking the shot without hesitation. At this point, all earlier work in indexing, grip, and orientation manifests in a controlled, accurate first round on target.

This indexed method ensures that every movement has purpose. Each position builds upon the previous, eliminating inefficiency and reinforcing consistency. A student who masters these positions will be fast, accurate, and repeatable under pressure.

Pistol Presentation from the Holster – Layered Instruction

Beginner Level – The Basics

At this stage, simplicity and consistency matter most.

1. **Grip the Gun (Position 1):** Strong hand high on the tang, full firing grip established. Defeat any holster retention.
2. **Bring the Gun Up (Position 2):** As the gun clears, it starts to turn toward the target.
3. **Meet the Hands (Position 3):** Support hand meets the gun and locks into grip.
4. **Push Toward the Target (Position 4):** Gun moves forward and into your line of sight.
5. **Shoot (Position 5):** At full extension, sights settle, press the trigger smoothly.

Instructor Note: Keep it simple—focus on repeatable mechanics, not speed.

Intermediate Level – Building Efficiency

Here we introduce indexing and prepping the trigger.

1. **Position 1:** Master grip must be established in the holster. No exceptions.
2. **Position 2:** Gun rotates toward the target. Support-hand index finger slides under the trigger guard to guide hand placement.
3. **Position 3:** Two-handed grip fully established. Gun drives forward with no wasted motion.
4. **Position 4:** As the slide/optic enters line of sight, begin prepping the trigger—finger to the wall, mechanical slack removed.
5. **Position 5:** At full extension, sights or dot settle naturally, shot breaks cleanly.

Instructor Note: Emphasize consistency, efficiency, and introducing the concept of visual and trigger prep timing.

Advanced Level – Performance Under Pressure

Now we connect mechanics with speed, accountability, and real-world conditions.

1. **Position 1:** Immediate, master grip—done aggressively, but without compromise.
2. **Position 2:** Early rotation, support-hand index guarantees repeatable grip under stress.
3. **Position 3:** Grip pressure set—crush with strong hand, lock with support hand. Gun drives forward explosively, economy of motion only.
4. **Position 4:** Visual orientation is aggressive. As soon as optic housing or front sight enters vision, trigger prep begins. This buys time and ensures first-round accountability.

5. **Position 5:** Full extension is not always necessary. Gun stops where sights confirm. Press breaks as sights stabilize—speed with accountability.

Instructor Note: Train advanced shooters to process visually faster and break the shot sooner without sacrificing accuracy.

Instructor Level – Teaching and Diagnosing

Here the focus is not just on execution, but on teaching others and correcting errors.

- **Key Principles to Teach:**
    - *Master Grip in the Holster:* Cannot be fixed later. Diagnose students who grab low or adjust after draw.
    - *Support-Hand Indexing:* Correct sloppy or delayed support-hand contact. Emphasize sliding under the trigger guard as a tactile reference.
    - *Spatial Orientation:* Teach shooters to recognize optic/sight housing entering vision. Many fail here by over-driving or hunting for the dot.
    - *Trigger Prep Timing:* Stress that trigger finger should move with the gun, not after it. This is where speed meets accountability.
    - *Shot Break:* Coach follow-through—watch for students "stabbing" at the trigger instead of pressing through.
- **Corrections to Watch For:**
    - Scooping the draw (lifting and then leveling late).
    - Weak or inconsistent support-hand placement.
    - Over-extending before sights are confirmed.
    - Finger to trigger too early (before spatial orientation).

Instructor Note: Teach positions as a framework, not rigid steps. The positions are learning points that blend together fluidly under pressure.

In my view as a long time instructor it is pretty simple in totality. Grab the gun, aim the gun, and shoot the gun with proper timing, that is the draw-stroke in one sentence and the standard you will demand until it is instinct. Grab the gun: index the strong hand to the same contact point every rep, seat the grip slightly toward the rear so your thumb defeats retention without searching, and pull straight up to clear the holster — vertical extraction first, no premature rotation. Aim the gun: once clear, rotate the muzzle to level and drive the pistol on the shortest, most efficient line (roughly a 45° path) into your line of sight while the support hand moves across to meet and lock; build the two-handed grip as the sight package enters your spatial orientation, use the trigger finger to remove mechanical pre-travel and "find the wall," and keep the presentation deliberate and repeatable so the sight picture is consistent with the target difficulty. Shoot the gun with proper timing: press the trigger to the rear at a steady, practiced cadence so the round breaks at or immediately near full presentation, control recoil, reset the trigger, and recover the sights to the original line for follow-on shots. Teach this sequence in reverse when instructing — put students at full presentation, drill the end state, then chain backward into the holster — and always enforce muzzle discipline, trigger finger discipline, and immediate correction of faults. Repeat the mantra: grab the gun, aim the gun, shoot the gun with proper timing — say it, demonstrate it, demand it, and measure it until the draw-stroke is automatic and uncompromising under stress. As instructors we must remember the goal of the pistol draw-stroke is to present the pistol from the holster to the target with **maximum efficiency, consistency, and alignment**, ensuring the shooter is able to fire accurately and rapidly under stress.

The Draw-stroke — Core Concepts

This is the tactical draw-stroke: reliable, repeatable, and fast. Your job as the instructor is to remove doubt, enforce fundamentals, and demand consistent execution. Teach it in layers, drill it to habit, and correct failures immediately.

Ensure the shooter finds their economy of motion, properly indexing and effectively using body contact points with proper symmetry and natural biomechanics

One-line definition

Grip the pistol, clear the holster, join the support hand, present to the target, index the trigger, and break the shot at presentation; every repetition, the same sequence.

Step-by-step method

1. **Index and secure the weapon in the holster.**
    - Place the strong-hand in the same pocket on the frame every time.
    - Grip slightly to the rear so your thumb can instantly defeat any retention device. No searching. No hesitation.
2. **Drive the gun straight up to clear the holster.**
    - Vertical extraction first. Clear the mouth completely before any rotation.
    - If the gun is not clear, stop and reset — do not rotate against the holster.
3. **Rotate the muzzle to level.**
    - Rotate the pistol so the barrel (and sight assembly) becomes parallel with the ground.
    - The rotation is controlled and intentional — not a snap or a lazy flop.
4. **Stage the support hand to meet.**
    - As the strong hand begins extraction and rotation, the support hand moves across the body into the "meet-and-greet" position.
    - The support hand must already be committing to consistent placement — not searching.
5. **Drive the pistol on a straight, efficient path to presentation.**
    - The trajectory is roughly a 45° line upward into the firing line.

- Move the gun in the shortest, most efficient line from holster to cheek/eyes — eliminate wasted arcs.

6. **Establish two-handed grip as the pistol approaches presentation.**
   - Support hand provides consistent friction and pressure, not a limp touch.
   - Strong hand secures the grip: high, tight, and repeatable.

7. **Index the trigger and find the wall.**
   - As slide or red-dot housing meets the shooter's spatial orientation, run the trigger finger along the trigger, remove any mechanical pre-travel, and find the wall.
   - This is a tactile confirmation — do it every time.

8. **Apply rearward pressure at a controlled speed.**
   - As the pistol completes its final pathway to full presentation, press the trigger to the rear at a consistent, practiced cadence.
   - The round should break at, or immediately near, full presentation consistent with the target difficulty.

9. **Control recoil and reset for follow-ups.**
   - Allow the gun to lift on recoil and then allow the sight package to settle back to the same line.
   - Reset the trigger and prepare for the next shot — timing and rhythm are taught and enforced.

Drive the Pistol

Trigger Prep Begins When the Optic Housing Or Slide Enter into The visual Pathway

Use Spatial Orientation

Fine Tune Adjustments for Individual Biomedicanics

Teaching progression (inductive method — instructor-led)

- **Reverse presentation drill:** Start students at full presentation and work backward into the holster. This builds the correct endpoint first, then connects the pathway.
- **Segmented practice:** Break the draw-stroke into micro-segments (grip → clear → rotate → meet → present → trigger) and chain them together. No skipping.
- **Live integration:** Once mechanical proficiency is consistent, fuse the sequence under stress (time, movement, retention drills, or malfunction clears).

Instructor cues — short, hard, repeatable

Use these as one-sentence commands on the line:

- "High, tight, thumb—clear."
- "Vertical extract—rotate level."
- "Meet hands—drive straight."
- "Find the wall—press to the rear."
- "Reset—follow up."

Say one cue per rep. Demand immediate correction on any deviation.

Common errors and corrections

- **Searching for the grip:** Cue: "Index—high and tight." Drill: dry draws with eyes closed until placement is consistent.
- **Rotating before clearing:** Cue: "Clear first." Drill: slow repetition emphasizing vertical pull.
- **Support hand late or sloppy:** Cue: "Meet and lock." Drill: dry meet-and-greet — no release until grip locked.

- **Trigger slap or surprise break:** Cue: "Find the wall." Drill: trigger index and wall-finding with the pistol staged at eye level.
- **Throwing the gun to the target (wide arcs):** Cue: "Straight line." Drill: draw to a low target at varying distances — reward shortest path.

Press and Break

- Trigger Prep Completed
- Arms extended Naturally
- Sight Picture Stabilizes
- Target Focused Presentation

Visual Verification

Instructor Emphasis:

- Emphasize **straight-line extension**—no scoop or arc.
- Use of **target-focused presentation drills** to teach press-and-break cadence.
- Integrate **visual verification drills** (Confirmations 1, 2, 3) into this position.

Safety enforcement (non-negotiable)

- Muzzle discipline and finger off trigger until ready to fire — absolute.
- If the student breaks a rule, stop the drill. Correct immediately. Safety comes before speed.

Measurement and standards

- **Benchmark dry:** 90% of repetitions produce correct grip, clear, and presentation sequence without coach intervention.
- **Benchmark live:** Under timed conditions appropriate to skill level, student must present, acquire sights, and break the first shot within instructor-set time windows. Adjust window by experience level.

Train the draw-stroke like a skill you will depend on under duress. Teach forward: demand the endpoint, work backward, and chain the movements until the sequence is an unthinking reflex. Correct deviations instantly, keep safety absolute, and measure progress with repeatable standards. The draw-stroke is simple in concept — rigorous in execution. Insist on perfection in practice so performance becomes unavoidable in the fight.

Draw-stroke Drill Sequence — Instructor-Led, Step-by-Step

Purpose: turn the draw-stroke into a repeatable, safe, and fight-ready reflex. This sequence is modular — run the whole block or pick segments to fix specific faults. Use firm, one-line commands. Stop and correct immediately on safety or gross technique failure.

Quick setup (range / gear / safety)

- Equipment: duty holster **(same retention as students use),** duty belt, service pistol (cleared for dry drills), snap-caps, live ammo, eye/ear protection, timer, target (A-zone silhouette or 6–8" dot), stopwatch or shot timer.
- Range layout: 3–7 yards for most live reps; 1–3 yards for close-up retention/fast presentation.
- Safety brief (non-negotiable): muzzles up/downrange, finger off trigger until on target and ready, holster manipulations only when pointed downrange in instructor control, stop command enforced.
- Instructor placement: behind or to side where you can observe muzzle, grip indexing, and support-hand meet.

Block A — Foundation (Dry, no live ammo) — 15–20 minutes

Goal: grip consistency, vertical clear, muzzle leveling, meet & greet, straight-line path.

1. **Grip indexing (5 min)**
    - Drill: From low-ready, strong-hand only draw to waist level, index grip high & tight, return. 20 reps.
    - Coaching cue: "Index — high, thumb ready."
    - Correction trigger: stop after 3 faulty reps; re-demonstrate.
2. **Vertical extract only (5 min)**
    - Drill: With holster, strong-hand draw straight up, stop at holster mouth height — no rotation. 15 reps.
    - Cue: "Vertical—clear."
    - Objective: clear first, then rotate.
3. **Rotation + level (5 min)**
    - Drill: Draw, clear, rotate muzzle parallel to ground, re-holster. 15 reps.

- Cue: "Clear—rotate level—re-holster."
- Fault correction: if rotating early, make student slow to emphasize clear-first.

4. **Meet-and-greet (5 min)**
   - Drill: Add support hand meet at mid-chest—no squeeze yet. 15 reps.
   - Cue: "Meet hands—lock."
   - Focus: consistent placement and timing.

Block B — Integration (Dry to Snap-Caps) — 15–20 minutes

Goal: two-handed grip timing, trigger index, find the wall, press cadence.

1. **Drive-to-presentation (dry, eyes open) — 10 reps**
   - Start holstered. Draw to full presentation (aim point), index trigger and hold at wall, then re-holster.
   - Cue: "Drive straight—find the wall."
   - Instructor: observe straight-line path and grip improvement.

2. **Trigger wall and press on snap-caps — 2 sets x 10 reps**
   - Use snap-caps. Student draws, finds the wall, presses at a slow controlled cadence so "click" corresponds to presentation.
   - Tempo: 1.5s presentation → 0.8s press.
   - Scoring: coach notes any surprise breaks or trigger slap.

3. **Reverse chain drill — 8–10 reps**
   - Student starts at presentation, moves back to holster in the exact reverse sequence.
   - Purpose: reinforce endpoint and pathway.

Block C — Live Fire (Progressive, safety-first) — 20–30 minutes

Goal: break the shot at or near full presentation; build follow-up rhythm.

1. **Baseline single (3–5 yards) — 5 rounds**
   - On signal, draw and deliver 1 round to the A-zone. Return to holster. Time cap per rep by skill level (see Standards).
   - Cue: "Draw—present—press—reset."
   - Scoring: Hit/Miss; time.
2. **Controlled pairs — 3–5 yards — 5 reps**
   - Draw, fire two shots at a steady cadence, managing recoil and reset.
   - Coaching points: sight recovery and trigger reset.
3. **Timed draw (par time) — 5 reps**
   - Set a time standard (e.g., 1.2–1.6s for advanced, 1.6–2.2s for intermediate, adjust per student). Student must present and break within time while maintaining hits. 5 reps.
4. **Close-quarters fast presentation — 1–3 yards — 5 reps**
   - Focus: muzzle control, aggressive presentation, immediate hits. Use shorter magazine counts as needed.

Block D — Fault-Conditioning & Retention (Optional, high-fidelity) — 10–15 minutes

Goal: handle retention, unexpected contact, and imperfect draws.

1. **Retention interference (dry, instructor-applied)**
   - Instructor applies light contact to arm/shoulder during draw. Student must complete draw without losing grip. 6–8 reps.
   - Safety: no live ammo for these drills.

2. **Malfunction transition (dry or snap-cap)**
   - Simulate failure to fire: student performs immediate tap-rack or transition drill per system taught, then re-engages. 6–8 reps.

Block E — Stress & Scenario (Optional advanced) — 10–15 minutes

Goal: apply under stress: movement, time pressure, decision-making.

1. **Move-and-draw**
   - Student moves laterally 3–5 yards then draws and fires. 6 reps.
2. **Dual-task (verbal challenge)**
   - Instructor issues a quick verbal math problem during presentation; student must answer after firing to simulate cognitive load. 6 reps.

Cool-down / Debrief — 5–10 minutes

- Instructor-led review: 1–2 observed strengths, 1–2 corrections.
- Assign homework dry reps (e.g., 100 quality dry draws this week), and specific remediation (e.g., trigger index drills).

Standards & Scoring (simple instructor rubric)

- **Green**: Grip correct, vertical clear, muzzle level, meet hand consistent, first-shot hit, presentation within time window (as set).
- **Amber**: Needs coaching — minor issues (late support hand, slow trigger), hits inconsistent.
- **Red**: Safety fault, holster contact on rotation, surprise break, muzzle discipline error — stop; remediate.

Record times and hits for each student; require improvement or repeat until green for 90% of reps in two consecutive sessions.

Common teacher interventions (one-line cues)

- Searching grip → "Index, high, thumb."
- Early rotation → "Clear first."
- Support hand late → "Meet and lock."
- Surprise break → "Find the wall."
- Wide arc → "Straight line, shortest path."

Progressions & Variations

- Progress distance: 3 → 5 → 7 yards.
- Decrease allowed time window as skill improves.
- Add movement, retention, malfunction, or low-light presentations for advanced students.
- For new shooters, extend dry-phase and reduce live reps until competency reached.

Sample 45-minute drill block (single class plan)

1. Setup & safety brief — 3 min
2. Block A foundation — 15 min
3. Block B integration — 12 min
4. Block C live fire — 10 min
5. Debrief & homework — 5 min

The Pistol Draw-stroke — A Layered Instructor-Level Breakdown (4-Position Model)

Objective:

The pistol draw-stroke is a motor sequence: a repeatable, gross-motor program that reliably brings the pistol from holster to effective alignment with the target under stress. The instructor's responsibility is to convert the draw-stroke from a fragile, individually variable action into a dependable, biomechanically sensible skillset that students can execute consistently, safely, and with appropriate decision-making. The four positions below are a pedagogical scaffold — a teaching map that separates cognitive decision points from motor execution so instructors can diagnose, correct, and layer complexity without sacrificing safety.

Core Instructional Concepts

- **Economy of motion.** Minimize unnecessary micro-adjustments and lateral motion that create variability under stress. Teach a limited set of gross movement patterns that scale to stressors.
- **Indexing & body contact points.** Use consistent body contacts (ribcage, sternum, pectoral area) as proprioceptive references so the draw-stroke survives time pressure and startle responses.
- **Symmetry & natural biomechanics.** Align movement patterns with natural shoulder, scapular and hip mechanics so students use larger muscle groups and preserve fine motor function for trigger control.
- **Decision readiness.** Integrate clear decision cues at each position so presenting the pistol is always coupled with conscious threat assessment and legal/ethical checks.

- **Stress-hardened consistency.** Build the sequence through progressive overload: mental rehearsal → dry practice with inert trainers → scenario decision drills → graded stress; only progress when measurable consistency is demonstrated.

Position-by-Position Instructor Narrative

Position 1 — Grip Establishment & Access

Cue: "Grip and clear."
Purpose: Establish a repeatable, high-quality interface with the pistol and a reliable proprioceptive reference for the entire sequence.

Begin by teaching the body as the first reference system. The shooter's dominant hand should locate the holster via a consistent pathway that creates the same torso contact points every repetition. Instructors should insist on an immediate and secure grip in the holster — not tentative "fishing" or repeated thumb adjustments — because a correct grip formed at the holster reduces remedial adjustments later in the stroke. The support hand must move to the sternum or midline with open fingers and a ready palm so it can meet the pistol predictably in the subsequent phase. Train students to treat these contact points as mechanical bookmarks; under stress, proprioception will out-perform visual memory.

Instructor emphasis / coaching notes:
• Cue the torso contacts (ribcage, pectoral stretch) as a repeatable starting geometry.
• Insist that grip formation be a single deliberate action at the holster — graders should mark attempts where the grip was not complete prior to extraction.
• Reinforce a non-clamping thumb posture on the dominant hand to preserve the later support-hand interface.

Position 2 — Draw & Orientation

Cue: "Lift and rotate."

Purpose: Transfer the pistol from holster retention into a retention-ready orientation that allows early sighting, immediate defensive response, and consistent presentation alignment.

Instructor narrative

The weapon must be cleared from the holster in a manner that keeps it tight to the body and introduces the muzzle into the sight plane as early as practical. Teach students to lift with intent and then orient the pistol into line of engagement. Emphasize that premature rotation or wide arcing movements compromise both speed and alignment; the vertical component of extraction creates the space for a controlled rotation into the firing plane. Where the system uses manual retention devices, the instructor should incorporate retention defeat into this phase as a deliberate, trained subtask — demonstrated and rehearsed only with inert trainers and in an appropriately controlled environment.

Instructor emphasis / coaching notes:

• Avoid teaching an immediate outward arc; teach the separation of vertical clearance then orientation.

• Reinforce muzzle awareness and index the trainee's perception of when the pistol is in a retention-ready posture.

• Stress that disengagement of external retention mechanisms is a trained movement to be practiced only with training gear.

Position 3 — Close-Quarters / Grip Completion

Cue: "Meet and drive."

Purpose: Finalize the two-handed grip, establish control for recoil management, and prepare for either retention firing or transition to full presentation.

Instructor narrative (publication text):

Position 3 is the convergence point. The support hand must meet the pistol predictably at the midline or slightly to the strong side so a stable two-handed platform can be formed without costly late-stage grip adjustments. The instructor should coach the support hand to wrap under the dominant thumb in a manner that creates web tension for recoil control while avoiding downward pressure that would compromise the grip's elastic integrity. At this point the student also begins the cognitive transition to trigger readiness — removing slack in the finger pathway and refining sight alignment — but must not execute trigger manipulation absent a clear, trained decision to fire. Scenario work at this stage trains the student to choose between retention-based responses and full presentation.

Instructor emphasis / coaching notes:

• Early grip completion reduces the number of corrective motions during presentation.
• Tailor support-hand placement to individual anthropometrics (eye dominance, shoulder width).
• Use dry drills to practice close-quarters firing concepts without live fire.

Position 4 — Presentation to Target

Cue: "Press and break."

Purpose: Drive the weapon into the firing line with minimal deviation, stabilize the sight picture, and execute controlled trigger press if justified.

The final presentation is the outward manifestation of the previous three positions' work. The pistol is driven into the target line with efficient extension and body weight transfer, allowing the dominant eye to acquire the sight plane and the trigger hand to complete depressor preps in a controlled manner. Emphasize that follow-through — immediate trigger reset, sight re-acquisition, and reassessment — is as critical as the initial press. Under instructor supervision, students should practice follow-up engagement sequencing and transitions between aggression and de-escalation. Re-holstering or securing the pistol remains a deliberate decision that is part of the presentation cycle.

Instructor emphasis / coaching notes:

- Teach linear drive into the target line rather than exaggerated arcs.
- Reinforce body weight transfer and follow-through discipline for follow-ups.
- Re-holstering is a distinct safety decision and must only happen after the scene is controlled.

Teaching Progression

1. **Concept & language:** Introduce the four positions and their decision points in lecture form.
2. **Proprioceptive rehearsal:** Mental visualization and tabletop walk-throughs with inert trainers.
3. **Dry rehearsal with trainers:** Repeated, slow, and assessed dry sequences under instructor observation; no live ammo in the area.
4. **Scenario decisions:** Low-complexity role-play focusing on threat identification, presentation withholding, and abort cues.
5. **Incremental stressors:** Add time pressure, physical exertion, and auditory distractions— only after consistent dry performance.
6. **Supervised live work:** Only when formal criteria (safety, consistency, coaching sign-off) are met.

Instructor Assessment Rubric

Use a simple pass/fail + scaled metrics approach in performance checks.

- **Safety compliance (Pass/Fail)** — muzzle, trigger discipline, eye/ear protection, separation of live ammo.
- **Grip integrity (1–5)** — forms and holds an effective grip in the holster before extraction.

- **Index consistency (1–5)** — repeats torso contact points within an acceptable tolerance.
- **Weapon orientation (1–5)** — lifts and orients into retention-ready alignment without excessive arc.
- **Decision integration (Pass/Fail)** — appropriately withholds or initiates presentation based on scenario cues.
- **Re-holstering discipline (Pass/Fail)** — demonstrates correct judgment to secure weapon only when safe.

Include written comments for each criterion; require remediation paths for anything below target.

Common Faults & Coaching Corrections

- **Fault:** "Fishing" for the holster or inconsistent torso contact.
  Coach: Revert to slow, proprioceptive rehearsals and enforce single-motion grip formation.
- **Fault:** Premature outward rotation creating wide arcs.
  Coach: Reinforce vertical lift before orientation through dry walk-throughs and partner observation.
- **Fault:** Late support-hand meeting which forces grip adjustments.
  Coach: Use synchronized two-hand dry repetitions focusing on timing cues.

Safety, Legal & Ethical Considerations

All demonstrations shall use properly cleared and inspected pistols, inert training pistols or distinctly marked trainers; **no live ammunition in the dry area.**

- Emphasize legal doctrine and use-of-force policy at every lesson start. Students must be able to articulate when they would and would not present.

- Instructors are responsible for the environment, range officers, documentation of qualifications, and medical contingency planning.

Sample Instructor Script

- Opening: "The draw-stroke is a four-position program. We train positions, not panic. Each position has a decision and a mechanical consequence."
- For Position 1: "Grip and clear — make the contact points repeatable. That contact is your map when stress narrows the senses."
- For Position 3: "Meet and drive — when your support hand finds the pistol, you are either stabilizing to fire or repositioning to de-escalate. Don't defer the choice."

Instructor Responsibilities

An instructor's professionalism shows in two things: a relentless commitment to safety, and an uncompromising insistence on repeatability. The four-position model is a teaching framework — not a shortcut to force. Use it to diagnose, to correct, and to scale complexity only when students demonstrate documented competence.

Humility drives you back to the basics

Presentation of the Weapon

The pistol must travel so the muzzle remains flat throughout the draw and presentation. A flat muzzle provides the most efficient path to the target and reduces rotational or vertical path errors. If the muzzle rotates up or down during the draw, the shooter has likely introduced a rotation error or a vertical path deviation — correct immediately and repeat the drill until the muzzle stays flat every repetition.

Instructor cue: "Keep the muzzle flat — no tilting."
Correction drill: draw slowly to a ready position and stop at checkpoints to verify muzzle attitude; increase speed only after consistent, flat presentations.

Keep both eyes open and focus on the target (the adversary) while bringing the pistol into the sight picture. As the gun comes up, the sight package should come into alignment naturally; the pistol is pressed toward the target as the trigger begins its initial rearward movement. The ideal sequence is:

1. Weapon pushes forward toward the threat while the trigger finger begins to move rearward.
2. The sight package aligns and the wrists lock.
3. Sight alignment is confirmed.
4. The shot breaks.

Training emphasis: teach students to hold the sights aligned by feel (kinesthetic awareness) when shooting at speed, and to process visual information peripherally rather than forcing a hard, tunnel focus on the sights. This allows for faster, more accurate follow-up shots under stress.

Instructor Commentary — Timing, Standards, and the Draw-Stroke

As a long-time instructor I accept the "sky is blue" theory — some fundamentals are obvious; but experience shows the draw-stroke is the gatekeeper skill: students who cannot present a pistol under time pressure generally fail everything that follows. Put bluntly: the draw-stroke is a performance bottleneck. If a shooter requires more than about **1.5 seconds** from holster to full presentation, defined as the sight package aligned, trigger pre-travel taken up, and the weapon ready to fire they will struggle to deliver timely, accurate shots in realistic scenarios. For novices, a sensible progressive benchmark is to first master the pattern at a slower, consistent cadence (≤ 2.5 seconds) and then compress toward the 1.5-second standard as technique, indexing, and kinesthetic awareness improve.

Too many instructors (the journeyman approach) teach the draw in endless slow motion and never stress the time variable. That well-meaning habit produces technically pretty but tactically useless shooters. I use a pro-timer from the first live-fire introduction and as a constant coaching tool throughout the curriculum. Timed presentations expose hidden inefficiencies — late indexing, premature rotation, weak chest indexing, low clears, or poor hand meeting — better and faster than description alone.

Instructor language:
• "Holster to ready: 1.5 seconds is the target — we tighten to speed only after your muzzle stays flat and your sights are predictable."
• "If you need more than 1.5s, we fix the pattern — not the speed. Repeat perfect. Speed is a byproduct of flawless repetition."

Diagnostics & common failure modes (and what to tell students):
• Late indexing: "You're not finding the holster — feel the pectoral, keep contact." —

drill: slow indexing with eyes closed until the hand consistently hits the holster reference.

• Low clear / premature rotation: "Lift high on the chest, then rotate." — drill: lift-pause-rotate dry-fires to the sight line.

• Muzzle tilt: "Flat muzzle — no banking." — drill: slow draws with coach or video feedback stopping at checkpoints.

• Hands meet late / weak meeting: "Meet and greet sooner — fight for the grip." — drill: partner resistance or one-handed grabs to force earlier lockup.

• Trigger anticipation: "Index finger stays out until picture on target — take up slack on the approach." — drill: dry-fire with weak hand cover, focus on taking up the slack only when the slide is in the sight plane.

Progressive drill plan (use the pro-timer or a metronome):

1. Static dry-fire: split positions 1–4, hold every checkpoint for a 3–5 count.
2. Rhythm dry-fire with metronome: one-two-three-four cadence at a slow tempo; ensure muzzle flat and consistent meeting point.
3. Timed dry-fire with pro-timer: set allowance to 2.5s, repeat 10 reps; record failures and correct patterns.
4. Timed compression: move to 2.0s for 10 reps; then 1.75s; then goal 1.5s — only advance when 9/10 reps are within standard and safe.
5. Live transition: replicate the same cadence on the range with strict safety oversight — continue using the pro-timer and log times.

Coaching ethos: challenge your students and they will rise to the standard, but only if challenge is paired with precise, repeatable corrective feedback. Time pressure should never replace technique; it must expose flaws that you then fix with targeted repetition. Finally, always prioritize safety: finger discipline, muzzle awareness, and a controlled range environment are non-negotiable while compressing speed.

Presentation from the Holster

Teach the draw-stroke as a four-count, rhythm-based sequence. Use a metronome cadence during early drills (one-two-three-four) to build consistency. Maintain body contact with the firing hand during the initial indexing phase to provide a reliable reference under stress.

Position 1 — Indexing and Grip Establishment

On the count of one, move both hands simultaneously.

• Strong-hand (SH) motion: move the SH back along the torso, contacting high on the rib cage (use the stretched upper pectoral as a tactile reference). Maintain contact with the body to locate the holster reliably under stress.
• Elbow and path: the SH elbow moves rearward — think of a high elbow strike to the rear — then the SH hand moves straight down to the holster while maintaining body contact.
• Grip: establish a high tang grip. Keep the SH thumb horizontal (not wrapped tightly around the frame and not pressed alongside the slide). A high-thumb grip increases strong-hand contact and creates beneficial tendon tension that aids recoil management during one-handed or CQB work.
• Support-hand (SuH) motion: move the SuH toward the centerline, rotate the thumb forward, and open the palm to accept the drawn weapon and form the two-hand grip.

Instructor cues: "Index high — feel the pectoral. Maintain contact. High thumb, high tang."

Position 2 — Clear and Raise

On the count of two, clear the holster and raise the weapon.

- Clear the holster and lift the pistol as high as comfortable on the pectoral/armpit area before rotating toward the threat. Lifting high first allows the weapon to break the shooter's sight plane more efficiently as it is extended.
- Safety/disengagement: with the SH thumb, disengage the manual safety if applicable (or prepare to disengage with the SuH at Position 3 if that is safer/required by equipment or training).
- Rationale: rotating immediately after the draw forces an additional lift to break the sight plane; a high draw stroke minimizes unnecessary motion and speeds presentation.

Instructor cue: "Clear high — lift on the chest, then rotate."

Position 3 — Close Quarters / Ready Position

On the count of three, establish the two-hand grip and drive to eye level.

- Meet-and-greet: bring both hands together near the centerline to form a two-hand grip. The exact meeting point varies by shooter anatomy, holster location, dominant eye, and equipment; the overriding principles remain economy of motion and rapid, stable presentation.
- Thumb placement: the SH thumb rests behind the SuH thumb without applying downward pressure that would defeat support-hand grip tension.
- Safety handling: if unable to disengage the safety on the draw, do so now with the non-firing hand.
- Trigger preparation: as the weapon breaks the sight line (slide parallel to the ground, muzzle downrange), begin to take up trigger slack — press the trigger on the way to Position 4. Position 3 should allow for emergency, one-shot opportunities and serve as a two-hand retention position when necessary.

Instructor cue: "Meet centerline — hands together, thumbs stacked — prepare the trigger."

Position 4 — Extension and Fire

On the count of four, extend and deliver the shot.

• Transition: extend the arms into the natural point of extension while the shooter's weight moves slightly forward. The trigger begins to be depressed as the sight picture is verified.
• Shot execution: break the shot, immediately reset the trigger, re-establish the sights, and prepare for subsequent shots as required.
• Follow-up: practice immediate sight re-acquisition drills to reduce recovery time between rounds.

Instructor cue: "Extend to your natural point, verify the picture, then break the shot. Reset and recover."

Loading (and Weapon Handling Posture)

All weapons-handling skills — loading, reloading, immediate action drills (IADs), and clearing procedures — should be trained, rehearsed, and imprinted in a working area directly in front of the chest and chin. Use the phrase **"eye–muzzle–threat"** as a constant reference check: the head stays up so the shooter can simultaneously see the threat area and the weapon.

Why the chest/chin working area?

• Keeps the shooter's head up and sight line unobstructed.
• Allows simultaneous monitoring of the threat and the weapon.

• Simplifies motor patterns — identical indexing position for many manipulations reduces cognitive load under stress.

Instructor directive for drills

1. Begin slow: perform all load/unload and IADs slowly in the chest/chin working area until they are flawless.
2. Increase speed incrementally: add a metronome or count cadence, then progress to dynamic transitions and drawing under time constraints.
3. Integrate visual checks: include target recognition and threat assessment cues while performing manipulations to train cognitive multitasking.
4. Safety posture: ensure muzzle awareness and positive finger discipline (finger indexed along the frame until the sights are on target) during all manipulations.

Instructor note: Reinforce muscle memory by standardizing the working area across all drills. Consistency of position reduces failure modes in high-stress encounters.

Instructor Addenda

Teaching progression:

1. Static dry-fire (split the draw-stroke into positions 1–4; perfect each position).
2. Dynamic dry-fire with a metronome (one-two-three-four cadence).
3. Live transition drills at reduced speed (ensure safety and range rules).
4. Stress inoculation (time pressure, decision-making, malfunction drills).

Common errors & corrections:
• Muzzle tilt during draw — slow the draw, check body contact, and repeat Position 1 indexing drills.
• Premature rotation — emphasize the high clear (Position 2) and practice lift-then-rotate

drills.

• Poor sight alignment at extension — drill slow push-toward-target repetitions focusing solely on sight break.

Range safety reminder: Always follow your range and legal safety rules. Keep the finger indexed until the sights are on the target; verify the backstop and consider training with inert/blue-gun options for early repetitions.

Step-by-Step Framework for *Teaching the Draw-stroke*

Step	*Instructional Focus*	*Drills / Key Points*
1. Introduce the Four Positions	Explain biomechanical reasoning	Dry practice each position slowly and in isolation
2. Position 1 to 2	Focus on consistent grip and high draw	Wall drill, mirror drill, slow reps with eyes closed
3. Position 2 to 3	Train high orientation and meeting of hands	Partner mirror work, step-by-step verbal callouts
4. Position 3 to 4	Work on press out, sight acquisition, trigger press	Presentation drills to different ranges (3/7/15 yd)
5. Full Draw-stroke Reps	Combine all into fluid draw	1/4 speed, 1/2 speed, then full speed (dry/live)
6. Add Stress and Variability	Introduce time pressure and movement	Shot timer drills, CQB retention shooting, target transitions
7. Diagnose & Refine	Evaluate grip formation, hand timing, angle	Video feedback, grip audits, hand isolation drills

Additional considerations for Criminal Investigators or those not in Uniform

Criminal Investigators or other Armed Professionals that are not in Uniform will have the additional consideration of drawing from concealment. The draw-stroke does not change, just the addition of a garment sweep.

OWB Concealed Draw-stroke (Covered by Over-garment)

For LE & CCW Applications

Context-Specific Considerations

LE	CCW
Duty belt w/ retention, OWB holster covered by a softshell, windbreaker, or raid jacket	OWB concealment holster under flannel shirt, jacket, or vest
May transition from uniformed to plainclothes role	Must blend concealment with rapid access in reactive self-defense
Training must simulate both overt draw and concealed access	Speed of access under pressure is critical due to defensive posture

Core Instructional Objectives

- Enable the shooter to defeat the garment efficiently **under duress**
- Maintain **body mechanics** and high-quality grip during garment clearance
- Ensure the shooter can fire from **any point in the draw** if needed (CQB context)
- Preserve concealment techniques **without sacrificing access time**

Modified 4-Position Draw-stroke with Garment Clearance

Pre-Draw – Garment Management Setup

Before Position 1, the shooter must **clear the garment** to access the weapon.

Garment Clearing Techniques:

1. **Strong-Side Rip (Standard Method)**
    - Shooter uses strong hand to sweep the outer garment **up and rearward**, clearing it above the holster line.
    - **Elbow flares out** slightly as hand grabs fabric around the hip or hemline.
    - **Anchor the garment** high on the rib cage or armpit momentarily.
    - Then continue into **Position 1** (grip establishment).
2. **Two-Handed Sweep (Alternate or Tucked Garment)**
    - Both hands rip the shirt/jacket hem **upward** simultaneously.
    - Support hand **holds the garment high on the sternum or chest** while the strong hand transitions to the holster.
3. **Breakaway or Tear-away Access (for LE raid vests or specialized jackets)**
    - Emphasis on using **one gross motor motion** to open jacket and immediately access weapon.
    - Practice this **one-handed or in movement**.

Position 1 (Grip Establishment under Concealment)

- **Critical point**: Ensure the shooter doesn't compromise grip in haste after clearing the garment.
- Many shooters develop the bad habit of **gripping too low or angled** when rushing from concealment.

Instructor Cues:

- "Clear high, grip high."
- "Anchor the garment, don't fight it on the draw."
- "The garment clearance is part of the drawstroke, not before it."

Position 2 (Vertical Lift & Orientation)

- Same principles apply: lift to armpit/pectoral area before rotating.
- **Common mistake** from concealment: rotating the gun **too early** due to rushing.

Instructor Adjustments:

- Drill vertical lift as a standalone component: "Lift first, rotate second."
- Use mirrored dry fire or camera feedback to spot premature muzzle orientation.

Position 3 (Grip Completion & Retention Ready)

- Especially relevant in **close-contact civilian self-defense** or **LE CQB** scenarios.
- At this stage:
  - Jacket may be bunched or flared—ensure shooter keeps **garment out of ejection port and slide path**.
  - **Muzzle awareness** is paramount during movement.

Instructor Drills:

- Dry reps in front of mirror or partner to build garment control muscle memory.
- "Garment up, gun out" cadence training.

Position 4 (Full Presentation & Fire)

- Ensure support-hand thumb is properly placed after garment clearance.
- Many shooters will "rush" into extension without stabilizing the grip—especially after garment delay.

Instructor Cue:

- "Grip and drive, not slap and extend."

Teaching Framework for OWB Concealed Draw-stroke

Step	Focus Area	Key Drill	Instructor Notes
1	Garment Clearing Mechanics	Garment Rip Drill (5 reps per method)	Use timer to compare strong-hand rip vs. two-handed
2	Grip Integrity	Dry Draw to Position 1 w/ garment	Check for grip slippage or angle misalignment
3	Full 4-Count Drawstroke	Step-by-step draw with par timer	Add verbal cues for each position
4	Movement Integration	Draw while stepping offline	Reinforces reactive CCW/LE movement
5	Retention Fire Drills	Fire from Position 3 (1-handed)	Integrate safety disengagement timing
6	Concealment to Fire Under Stress	Timer, concealment garment, lateral targets	Introduce "failure to clear" problem solving

LE & CCW Specific Training Adjustments

For LE:

- Train with full gear, jacket/raid vest **buttoned/zipped** as in patrol/undercover mode.
- Practice **weapon retention scenarios** after draw from OWB under concealment.
- Conduct **weapon access in vehicle/seatbelted** positions (common for surveillance, off-duty work).

For CCW:

- Reps from **typical everyday clothing** (hoodies, flannels, windbreakers).
- Emphasize **garment management in public (e.g., seated at restaurant, driving, carrying bags)**.
- Dry practice in **mirrored environments** to see garment-handling mechanics.

Summary: Key Teaching Cues

- "Clear High, Grip High"
- "Vertical First, Rotate Second"
- "Meet and Greet for Control"
- "Drive Straight, Break Clean"
- "Grip Before Go"

Drawing from an **Inside the Waistband (IWB)** or **Appendix Inside the Waistband (AIWB)** holster requires **adjustments in technique, biomechanics, and safety protocols** compared to OWB carry. The fundamentals of the four-position draw-stroke still apply, but **access mechanics, garment clearance, angles of draw, and muzzle management** must be tailored for these concealment-specific carry positions.

Instructor-Level Overview: Differences in IWB & AIWB Drawstrokes

Aspect	IWB (Strong Side Hip/4–5 o'clock)	AIWB (12–1 o'clock)
Holster Position	Behind the hip bone, under belt line	In front of pelvis, under navel/hip
Draw Angle	Rearward and vertical	Forward and vertical
Garment Clearance	Requires rear sweep or lift	Straight vertical lift
Grip Access	Limited by elbow angle and torso twist	Faster access, shorter motion
Safety Considerations	Muzzle crosses leg/hip during draw	Muzzle crosses **femoral artery/genital area**
Reholstering Risk	Less acute, but still serious	**Highest risk** – must be deliberate and conscious
Advantages	Deep concealment, comfort when seated	Fastest draw time from concealment
Challenges	Slower access, arm entanglement	High reholster danger, must train for safe draw angle

1. Pre-Draw: Garment Clearance

IWB at 4–5 o'clock

- **Garment Rip Style:**
  - Strong hand performs a **rearward sweep** or upward rip of outer garment (shirt, jacket).
  - Support hand may anchor the shirt high on the chest.
- **Watch-points:**
  - Ensure garment clears **over the hip**—instructors must emphasize **not catching the pistol butt** on the way up.
  - Arm must **rotate rearward** to access the grip—requires torso movement.

AIWB (12–1 o'clock)

- **Garment Rip Style:**
  - Strong or support hand grabs **the front hem** and lifts the garment **straight up**, high over the beltline.
  - Often done with **support hand anchoring** garment on the chest while strong hand draws.
- **Watch-points:**
  - Ensure **strong hand stays vertical**; no fishing under shirt.
  - Create a **clear visual pathway** to the grip to reduce chance of ND.

2. Position 1: Grip Establishment

IWB:

- Arm may need to **flare slightly** to reach rearward holster position.

- Ensure **full grip** is achieved before drawing—many shooters compromise grip under pressure due to concealment.

Instructor Emphasis:

- "Rotate, reach, and lock the grip."
- "No fishing, no adjusting mid-draw."

AIWB:

- Grip is acquired by **driving hand straight down** from high chest to belt line.
- Shorter travel makes this **faster**, but must maintain **trigger discipline** even more strictly.

Instructor Emphasis:

- "Grip high, thumb high, elbow to rear."
- "No trigger contact until gun clears belt line and is rotated."

3. Position 2: Lift & Orientation

IWB:

- Weapon is lifted **up and out**, clearing any belt tension or holster retention.
- Rotate muzzle toward target at chest/armpit level to avoid **"muzzle sweep of the hip/thigh."**

Instructor Adjustment:

- Teach a **deliberate upward draw path**, don't let student arc forward immediately.

AIWB:

- Weapon is lifted **vertically** to the sternum line.
- Muzzle must rotate **forward and away from the body**, never angling backward or downward.

Instructor Warning:

- AIWB draws are **fast** but require absolute control and discipline.
- Use **dry fire reps** extensively to prevent premature muzzle rotation or poor indexing.

4. Position 3: Close Quarters Grip Completion

IWB & AIWB:

- Both techniques converge here:
    - **Hands meet at the midline**
    - Establish a two-handed grip
    - Begin prepping the trigger if threat engagement is imminent

Instructor Note:

- With IWB, there may be **more delay** in getting the support hand on due to garment tangle.
- With AIWB, this happens **faster**, but ensure full support-hand purchase before extending.

5. Position 4: Presentation & Fire

- This is largely **identical** across all carry types.
- Weapon is pressed to eye level, with final sight picture and trigger press occurring in sync.

Instructor Cue:

- "Don't race to full extension before building the shot platform."

Reholstering Specifics – Critical for AIWB and IWB

This is the **most dangerous moment** of the entire process due to **muzzle proximity to the body**.

Safe Reholstering Protocols:

1. **Remove distractions** – no multitasking or movement.
2. **Scan, breathe, and slow down.**
3. **Visually confirm** the reholster path is clear.
4. **Index the trigger finger high**, well away from trigger guard.
5. **Reholster deliberately**—never force the gun into the holster.

For AIWB:

- **Lean the hips backward** while reholstering to create space between muzzle and femoral triangle.
- Optionally, **remove the holster from waistband**, holster the gun outside of pants, then replace holster (common safety step in training).

Instructor Mandate:

- Reholster slowly, always with visual confirmation.
- **"Speed on the draw, caution on the holster."**

Instructor-Level Training Progression

Level	Skill	Focus	Drills
Beginner	IWB/AIWB draw isolation	Garment clearing, grip indexing	Dry draw with mirror feedback
Intermediate	4-position integration	Timing, grip integrity, muzzle orientation	Live fire draw to shot (par timer)
Advanced	Movement & stress	Off-line movement, contact shots	AIWB retention fire, IWB lateral draws
Instructor	Diagnostics & safety	Error correction, reholster protocol	Video feedback, emergency stoppage drills

Final Key Teaching Cues

- "Grip deep, clear clean."
- "Lift vertical before you rotate."
- "Eyes lead, muzzle follows."
- "Holster slow, eyes on."
- "AIWB is fast—but only with discipline."

Shooter Performance Objective Triangle

Core Elements: Speed – Accuracy – Consistency

Beginner Level – Learning to Control the Gun

Key Objective: Build foundational ability to hit what you're aiming at safely and predictably.

- **Speed:** Introduced only after safe, consistent weapon handling is achieved. Emphasis is on **deliberate mechanics**, not rapid fire.
- **Accuracy:** Priority #1. Shooters must learn to achieve reliable hits using proper grip, sight alignment, and trigger control.
- **Consistency:** Introduced through **repetitive dry fire**, focusing on stance, draw, and follow-through.

Technique Integration at this level:

- Isolated drills (dry fire, single shot live fire)
- High repetition with **low complexity**
- Reinforce gross motor patterns (grip, presentation, trigger press)

Stress Response Consideration:

- Begin teaching about stress effects on fine motor skills.
- Emphasize relaxed performance. No stress inoculation needed yet.

Intermediate Level – Beginning to Perform Under Pressure

Key Objective: Blend skills and begin to manage cognitive load (e.g., decision-making, transitions, shot cadence).

- **Speed:** Introduced in bursts. Par times and drills like draw-to-first-shot start to matter.
- **Accuracy:** Must still be maintained as speed increases. Hits on zone-specific targets (A-zone or 4" circles).
- **Consistency:** Focus on reproducibility under slight fatigue or movement (multiple reps, compressed time, etc.)

Technique Integration:

- Shooters begin to combine learned techniques (e.g., movement + draw + multiple rounds)
- Performance **may dip temporarily** (Model Baseline 2–3) as new skill layers are added.
- Instructor must help student push through frustration.

Stress Concepts Introduced:

- Gross vs. fine motor skill degradation
- Performance under elevated heart rate (drills w/ burpees, timers)
- Teach visual narrowing and auditory exclusion effects

Advanced Level – Subconscious Execution and Efficiency Under Duress

Key Objective: Execute tasks with unconscious competence and transition seamlessly across complex demands.

- **Speed:** Becomes reactive and natural. Visual processing drives shooting tempo.
- **Accuracy:** Maintained even during transitions, movement, and compressed timelines. *"Fast is fine, but accurate is final."*
- **Consistency:** Bullet performance reflects training depth. Hits are no longer lucky; they're *expected*.

Technique Integration:

- Technique is now subconsciously integrated (Model Baseline 3–4).
- Drills include low-light, stress, simulated injury, decision-making.
- Focus shifts from mechanics to **problem-solving under stress**.

Stress Mitigation & Motor Skills:

- Train under **elevated heart rate** (>140 bpm) to preserve performance
- Practice complex motor tasks (e.g., reloads, transitions) during SNS activation drills
- Visualization and self-talk actively coached ("breathe, see it, say it, do it")

Instructor-Level Understanding – Teaching Under Pressure and Across Progressions

Key Objective: Understand the science of stress, performance, and motor learning so you can build shooters, not just pass quals.

1. Teaching Through the Triangle

- **Speed, Accuracy, and Consistency** are *not* separate goals — they are interdependent.

Speed, Accuracy, and Consistency Are Not Separate Goals

Balance
Target
Threat
Time

- Instructors must show shooters how to balance the triangle based on target type, threat, and time.
- Example:
    - *Close threat, low risk = Speed & Predictive Shooting (Confirmation 1 / Slap trigger).*
    - *Partially obscured target = Accuracy + Deep Trigger Prep(Confirmation 3)*

2. Technique Integration Curve

- **Model Baseline 1–2:** Early wins when student focuses on one thing (e.g., grip refinement).
- **Model Baseline 2–3:** Dip in performance as new technique is integrated into real drills. *Instructor MUST push student past frustration here.*
- **Model Baseline 3–4:** True subconscious competence. "I don't think about it anymore — I just do it right."

Instructor Note: Don't overload new shooters with technique stacking too early. Introduce new layers only once the previous is consistent under mild pressure.

3. Managing the Stress Curve (SNS Activation)

- Teach how the **Autonomic Nervous System** influences decision-making and performance:
    - Fine motor degradation (~115 bpm)
    - Complex motor loss (~145 bpm)
    - Auditory exclusion, tunnel vision, and depth perception loss (>150 bpm)
- **Goal:** Train students to operate in the 115–145 bpm window — the "performance zone."

Instructor Objective: Use drills (e.g., time pressure, physical stress, unexpected commands) to raise heart rate while preserving *form under fire*.

4. Inoculate to Stress Through Repetition and Simulation

- Use **Simunitions / Airsoft / Role-Play** to introduce real consequences
- Short drills → Complex strings → Decision drills

- **Repetition builds prediction** → Prediction builds confidence → Confidence reduces panic

Example:

"Tap-Rack-Ready" becomes automatic only when:

- The movement is rehearsed under **controlled and stressed conditions**,
- The shooter **understands the context** (malfunction vs. dry gun),
- The instructor has reinforced correct movement with **corrective feedback at speed**.

5. Build the Warrior Mindset, Not Just the Skillset

- Teach visualization, mental rehearsal, and performance scripting
- Use instructor-led "talk-throughs" to reinforce self-coaching
- Encourage aggressive, proactive posture in drills (*Dominate weapon → Dominate opponent → Dominate environment*)

Instructor Cue:

"Don't let the fight surprise you. You've already been there a hundred times — in your reps, in your mind, in your training."

Summary Table: Progressive Triangle Breakdown

Level	Speed	Accuracy	Consistency	Technique Focus	Stress Handling
Beginner	Slow/Measured	High Priority	Repetitive Form	Isolated reps	Intro to fine motor control
Intermediate	Controlled	Sustained	Timed drills	Skill stacking begins	Elevated heart rate exposure
Advanced	Reactive	Maintained	Subconscious	Real-world application	Inoculated via realistic sims
Instructor	Diagnostic	Target-specific	Taught to others	Teaching + performance	Teaches stress inoculation

Shooter Performance Objective Triangle Instructor Framework

Goal: Train shooters through the progressive development of **Speed, Accuracy, and Consistency**, while integrating techniques, inoculating to stress, and building mindset.

Phase 1: Establish the Foundation (Beginner to Early Intermediate)

Objective: Build safe, repeatable mechanics with strong fundamentals under low/no pressure.

Step 1: Introduce the Triangle Concept

- Use visual aids or draw the triangle: Speed – Accuracy – Consistency.

- Explain the relationship: **Speed without Accuracy is irrelevant, Accuracy without Speed is insufficient, and Consistency makes both reliable**.

Step 2: Drill Basic Marksmanship

- Teach grip, stance, sight picture, and trigger press.
- Run basic drills (e.g., single-shot accuracy from ready and from holster).
- Emphasize **repeatable grip** and **sight tracking** over time.

Step 3: Dry Fire & Diagnostic Reinforcement

- Introduce *Live Trigger Dry Fire* with wall drills, trigger preps, and reset training.
- Begin dry-fire **trigger isolation** under your supervision.

Step 4: Teach Technique Integration Model (Baseline 1–2)

- Introduce one performance-enhancing technique at a time (e.g., prepping the trigger, high thumbs-forward grip).
- Let shooters experience the **initial performance bump** from focused execution.

Phase 2: Controlled Complexity (Mid-Level Intermediate)

Objective: Begin stacking techniques and introducing pressure/decision-making.

Step 5: Reinforce Triangle Under Pressure

- Use **simple timer-based drills** (e.g., draw-to-first-shot with par times).
- Add *accountability* through scoring zones or pass/fail standards.

Step 6: Apply Technique Integration (Baseline 2–3)

- Add movement, multiple targets, or transitions.
- Expect a **temporary dip in performance**—coach through frustration.
- Teach that **this dip is a normal and necessary step** in learning.

Step 7: Introduce Stress Physiology

- Use basic physical stressors: e.g., jumping jacks before drills, loud commands, short time limits.
- Teach students how **fine/complex motor skills degrade under SNS activation** (visual narrowing, trigger errors, misreads).

Step 8: Start Building Stress Inoculation

- Use controlled scenario training or SimFX/Airsoft.
- Observe changes in form under pressure and debrief student perception vs. performance.
- Encourage brief instructor-led **post-drill self-assessment** ("What did you see? What worked? What didn't?").

Phase 3: Advanced Integration (Advanced Shooters)

Objective: Perform with subconscious competence under increasing levels of stress and complexity.

Step 9: Push for High-Speed Accuracy

- Use confirmation-based shooting drills (e.g., 1-dot = speed only, 2-dot = color confirmation, 3-dot = full visual confirmation).

- Run timed headshot drills, obscured targets, or hostage offset drills under time pressure.

Step 10: Reinforce Baseline 3–4 Performance

- Coach students into subconscious integration:
    - "You don't think about your grip anymore—you just fix it before the beep."
    - "Your body's doing it. Now your eyes and brain need to lead it."

Step 11: Apply Realistic, Tactical Context

- Run multi-phase problem-solving drills (e.g., move to cover, verbal commands, threat ID).
- Start teaching *in-structure stress*—unknown start commands, light/noise changes, judgment calls.
- Push cognitive decision-making inside complex motor tasks.

Step 12: Teach Visualization and Self-Coaching

- Assign *daily mental rehearsal* exercises.
- Guide them to use *positive task-oriented self-talk* before and during complex drills.
- Encourage reflection: "What do I need to see next time? What do I fix next run?"

Phase 4: Instructor-Level Concepts

Objective: Prepare instructors to diagnose performance, manage stress inoculation, and teach skill progression across all levels.

Step 13: Teach the Triangle from a Coaching Lens

- Show instructors how to **evaluate performance breakdowns**:
    - Misses? = Accuracy
    - Hesitation? = Confidence or technique confusion
    - Sloppy performance? = Inconsistent execution or lack of integration

Step 14: Teach the Technique Integration Curve

- Help instructors spot where students are in the curve:
    - Excited (new skill, working well)
    - Frustrated (too many moving parts)
    - Confident (subconscious control returning)

Step 15: Plan Training Based on Motor Skill Science

- Apply **SNS heart rate zones** (115–145 bpm) when planning intensity.
- Teach instructors to use **gross motor drills under high stress, complex motor skills under controlled conditions**.
- Train them to "scale" drills: task complexity + stressor = desired skill exposure.

Step 16: Reinforce Warrior Mindset Building

- Embed visualization, mindset lectures, and mental walk-throughs in every advanced course.
- Use layered scenario immersion to build **emotional and physiological inoculation**.
- Teach instructors to lead not just technical development, but **mental performance preparation**.

Bonus: Sample Daily Progression Template

Example 1-Day Block (Intermediate Level)

Time	Focus Area	Objective	Drill Example
09:00–09:30	Dry Fire Isolation	Reinforce technique + trigger control	Wall drill, press/reset cadence
09:30–10:30	Warm-Up Accuracy	Group-focused live fire + precision tracking	5-shot dot drill, 3x5 cards
10:30–11:30	Speed Injection	Controlled speed via timer-based drills	Draw-to-A zone @ 7yds
11:30–12:00	Technique Stack + Transitions	Stack reload or movement under pressure	2 targets + mag change
13:00–14:00	Stress Performance	Elevate heart rate + accuracy retention	Sprint + 3-target drill @ 10yds
14:00–15:00	Decision-Making Under Pressure	Shoot/no shoot + accuracy standards	Photo targets, hostage offset drills
15:00–16:00	Scenario Integration	Apply skills in uncertain scenario	Low light, unknown commands, verbal drills

INSTRUCTOR MODULE: SHOOTER PERFORMANCE OBJECTIVE TRIANGLE

Module Title: Shooter Performance Objective Triangle and Integrated Performance Training

Training Level: Beginner to Instructor

Objective: Equip instructors with a structured method for developing shooter performance through the triad of Speed, Accuracy, and Consistency, integrated with technique adoption, stress exposure, and cognitive preparation.

OVERVIEW

The Shooter Performance Objective Triangle consists of three critical elements:

- **Speed:** The shooter's ability to deliver rounds rapidly from a ready or holstered position.
- **Accuracy:** The shooter's ability to place rounds in vital zones under varying conditions.
- **Consistency:** The shooter's ability to repeatedly demonstrate both speed and accuracy across multiple reps, scenarios, and environments.

This model works in conjunction with the Technique Integration Curve, Stress Performance Science, and the shooter's physical/mental capacity to deliver under pressure.

PHASED DEVELOPMENT MODEL

Phase 1: Foundational Control (Beginner to Early Intermediate)

Instructor Goals:

- Instill safe weapon handling and mechanical repetition.
- Emphasize deliberate accuracy over speed.

Key Concepts:

- Dry fire fundamentals (grip, trigger press, sight alignment).
- Simple live fire accuracy drills.
- Repetition under low stress.

Drills:

- Wall Drill (Trigger Isolation)
- One-Round Accuracy from Ready
- 5-Round B8 Slow Fire (7yd)

Phase 2: Controlled Complexity (Mid-Level Intermediate)

Instructor Goals:

- Introduce the interplay of the triangle elements.
- Begin integration of multiple techniques.
- Train under mild stress or time.

Key Concepts:

- Technique stacking: movement, reloads, transitions.
- Performance dip awareness (Baseline 2–3).
- Heart-rate elevation and basic stress response.

Drills:

- Draw to First Shot (Par Time)
- 1–2–3 Target Transition
- Tap-Rack-Ready under Timer

Phase 3: Advanced Integration (Advanced Shooters)

Instructor Goals:

- Solidify unconscious competence under dynamic stress.
- Maintain triangle balance under time and environmental pressure.

Key Concepts:

- Complex scenarios with movement, decision, and stress.
- Performance consistency under time and fatigue.
- Transition to confirmation-based shooting (1-2-3 visual confirmation levels).

Drills:

- Shoot/No-Shoot Visual ID Drills
- Movement to Cover + Fire
- 2-Round Headbox Timed Standards

INSTRUCTOR APPLICATION

Teaching Through the Triangle:

- Diagnose breakdowns via triangle imbalance.
- Reinforce triangle adjustments depending on target, distance, and scenario.

Technique Integration Curve:

1. Initial Performance Boost
2. Temporary Dip (Due to Conscious Integration)
3. Subconscious Mastery

Performance Under Stress:

- Teach ANS response: SNS/PNS roles
- Motor skills: Fine (degrades ~115 bpm), Complex (~145 bpm), Gross (>150 bpm)
- Use stress inoculation tools (Simunitions, Airsoft, timer, elevated HR drills)

MENTAL PERFORMANCE

Visualization & Self-Talk:

- Coach shooters to mentally rehearse drills, visualize success, and use instructional self-talk.
- Integrate warrior mindset: aggressive, prepared, and deliberate.

Mindset Goals:

- Dominate the weapon.
- Dominate the situation.

- Dominate the visual field.

Instructor Note: This module is designed to be scalable. Increase or decrease complexity and pressure based on shooter maturity and course duration. Always link technical training back to

Instructor Module Expansion: OODA Loop – Boyd's Cycle

Overview

The **OODA Loop** is a decision-making and action-execution cycle developed by U.S. Air Force Colonel John Boyd. Originally designed for air-to-air combat, its principles now widely apply to **tactical, competitive, and combative shooting** and **defensive decision-making**.

The acronym stands for:

1. **Observe**
2. **Orient**
3. **Decide**
4. **Act**

This is not a linear process—it's a **cyclical, recursive model** that helps shooters process and dominate rapidly changing situations.

Breakdown of the OODA Loop in a Shooting Context

1. Observe

- **Gather information through all sensory channels**: eyes, ears, touch, and proprioception.

- Environmental scan: Identify threats, positions, lighting, bystanders, and cover.
- On the range: Identify target type, distance, position, and movement.

Instructor Focus:

- Train students to see more than just the target (target ID, environment, and movement).
- Reinforce scanning before and after engagements.
- Use multiple stimulus inputs in drills (visual, audible cues).

2. Orient

- **Process and analyze the data** gathered in the Observe phase.
- Involves interpretation based on:
    - Past experience
    - Training and doctrine
    - Cultural and psychological factors
    - Physical ability
    - Gear and weapon setup

Instructor Focus:

- Teach shooters how **bias and expectation** can delay this step.
- Use scenario drills to challenge assumptions.
- Emphasize the importance of proper gear setup and muscle memory to minimize *processing time.*

3. Decide

- Choose a course of action based on orientation.

- Example decisions: Engage or not, single shot or controlled pair, move to cover or hold position.

Instructor Focus:

- Develop decisiveness under pressure.
- Use drills that create **micro-decisions**: target priority, type of engagement, movement choice.
- Teach decision-making under compressed time with visual/mental stress.

4. Act

- Execute the decided course of action with **speed and precision**.
- This is where **motor programs and muscle memory** play a major role.

Instructor Focus:

- Actions must be trained until subconscious.
- Use repetitions that are high quality, consistent, and correct.
- Emphasize **execution without hesitation** once a decision is made.

Loop Restarts

Every action causes a new change in the environment. That change feeds back into **new observation**, and the cycle begins again.

Train students to **loop faster and more effectively** than their opponent or the situation—this is known as "**getting inside the enemy's OODA Loop.**"

OODA Loop & Shooter Performance Triangle Integration

- **Speed** applies to **Act** and the loop time itself.
- **Accuracy** is critical during the **Act** phase—ineffective or errant actions must be avoided.
- **Consistency** is developed through drilling the loop—until action selection and execution are reliable under stress.

Practical Instructor Drills

OODA Stimulus Reaction Drill

- Targets face away. Instructor gives a visual or verbal cue.
- Shooter must observe, orient to target type (threat/no threat), decide and act accordingly.
- Use multiple target types (handgun drawn, no weapon, hostage, etc.).

OODA Loop Walk-Through Scenarios

- Use shoot/no-shoot drills with added complexity: environmental audio, moving targets, low light.
- Force students to walk through their loop afterward in AAR (After Action Review).

Instructor Takeaway

"The goal is not just to shoot fast. It's to **decide and act faster** than the threat—**without compromising judgment or control.** That's the difference between reacting and dominating."

In my second book *"A Green Berets Guide to Enhanced Pistol Shooting Skills (ISBN 979821640354)"*, I introduced the structural components; that I believe through observation and teaching tens of thousands of students, which a shooter must learn to incorporate to be successful. In my third book **"Green Beret Instructor's Guide to Everyday Carry (ISBN 979-8-218-78586-4)** I introduced a more robust version of this concept.

Since this book is being written at an instructor level for those that will be elevating armed professionals to their peak performance and beyond it is time to provide a more detailed breakdown of this concept.

The Anatomically Detailed Breakdown of Pistol Shooting Structure: Why It Matters

As an Instructor of the Armed Professional, it is your duty to understand pistol shooting at a level beyond rote mechanics. True marksmanship is rooted in anatomy, physics, and human biomechanics. Each structural element—grip, stance, sight alignment, sight picture, trigger control, and follow-through—relies on specific anatomical structures working in concert. Failure to understand these connections reduces your ability to teach, diagnose, and correct deficiencies on the spot.

1. Grip: The Foundation of Control

The grip is far more than "holding the gun." It is the fulcrum from which control, recoil management, and shot consistency originate. Anatomically, it engages:

- **Forearm flexors and extensors**: stabilize the wrist and control muzzle rise.
- **Thenar and hypothenar eminences**: provide fine motor control and distribute recoil forces evenly.

- **Intrinsic hand muscles**: ensure a non-dominant hand supports without over-gripping, preventing tremor or fatigue.

Why it matters: A poor grip shifts the point of impact unpredictably, particularly in rapid fire. For instructors, observing micro-movements in the wrist or hand can immediately reveal tension, overcompensation, or improper alignment. Without understanding the underlying anatomy, corrections become generic and often ineffective.

2. Stance: The Engine of Stability

Stance is the skeletal and muscular platform from which the gun is delivered. Key structures:

- **Lower extremities (quadriceps, hamstrings, calves)**: absorb recoil and maintain center of gravity.
- **Core musculature (rectus abdominis, obliques, erector spinae)**: stabilizes the torso, preventing lateral sway.
- **Hip alignment**: directs energy line from shoulders to feet, maintaining balance and control under stress.

Why it matters: POA vs. POI deviations often trace directly to poor stance. A shooter leaning, shifting weight incorrectly, or failing to engage core muscles will show consistent errors in elevation or horizontal placement. Instructors who understand the biomechanics of stance can anticipate errors before shots stray.

3. Sight Alignment and Sight Picture: Fine Motor Coordination

Sight alignment is the precise orientation of the front and rear sights, while sight picture is the integration of sights onto the target. Anatomical involvement:

- **Ocular muscles (extraocular muscles)**: track and fixate on front sight.

- **Neck and upper trapezius**: stabilize the head to prevent vertical or horizontal sway.
- **Shoulder muscles (deltoids, rotator cuff)**: maintain arm elevation and support alignment.

Why it matters: Even minute head tilt or improper sight alignment can shift POI by inches at close range. Understanding the musculoskeletal contributors allows instructors to spot micro-errors: for example, a high POI may be traced to slight forward head tilt, not trigger flinch.

4. Trigger Control: The Neuro-Muscular Interface

Trigger press is not simply "squeeze." It is the controlled release of stored energy through precise neuromuscular coordination. Anatomical structures:

- **Finger flexor muscles**: provide consistent pressure on the trigger.
- **Wrist stabilizers**: prevent lateral movement during press.
- **Central nervous system (motor cortex)**: governs timing, rate of fire, and inhibition of reflexive flinch.

Why it matters: Mismanaged trigger press is the leading cause of POA vs. POI shift. An instructor must understand that jerking the trigger is often a neurological habit amplified by tension, rather than a conscious error. Diagnosing this requires anatomical insight to instruct proper finger placement, controlled flexion, and nervous system retraining.

5. Follow-Through: Reinforcing Consistency

Follow-through ensures that the shot delivers consistent results and that immediate feedback is accurately perceived. Key anatomical structures:

- **Forearm and wrist extensors**: maintain grip pressure after the shot.

- **Shoulders and upper back**: control recoil and realign the gun.
- **Eyes and visual system**: track shot impact and prepare for next engagement.

Why it matters: Instructors must recognize that sloppy follow-through is not a minor detail—it masks structural deficiencies in grip, stance, and trigger control. A shooter who immediately drops the gun or shifts posture post-shot may unknowingly disrupt POI, and failure to correct this at the anatomical level leads to chronic inconsistencies.

The Instructor Imperative

An instructor who understands these anatomical connections does more than teach techniques—they diagnose, correct, and engineer success under live-fire conditions. Every deviation in shot placement can be traced back to a biomechanical failure, whether in the fingers, wrists, shoulders, core, or eyes. Teaching without this understanding is guesswork.

In practice:

- Recognize tension in the thenar eminence and adjust grip.
- Observe core engagement failures and adjust stance or weight distribution.

- Detect neck or ocular misalignment to correct sight picture.
- Identify neuromuscular firing errors to fix trigger control.

Without anatomical comprehension, instructors rely on arbitrary corrections. With it, every adjustment is surgical, deliberate, and instantly effective. For the Armed Professional, this is not academic—it is the difference between predictable marksmanship under stress and deadly uncertainty in the field.

Shooting Structure: Anatomical and Mechanical Breakdown

A shooter must create a **solid, repeatable skeletal and muscular structure** that both supports recoil management and promotes visual efficiency. Breakdowns at any level—from **posture to grip pressure** create disruptions in POA vs. POI.

1. **Head Up, Eyes Up**

Instruction: *Look where you want to shoot. Bring the gun to your line of sight.*

- **Cervical spine** should remain vertical and neutral (not compressed or flexed).
- The **orbital axis** (eyes) must align with target-level focus.
- Eyes should drive the movement: the **hand–eye connection** ensures fast target acquisition.

Why it matters: Lowering the head introduces **neck tension** and creates downward pressure that can cause the front sight to dip, especially under recoil.

2. **Nose Over Toes**

Instruction: *Weight forward over the balls of the feet.*

- Promotes **anterior weight distribution** and forward engagement of the **center of mass (COM)**.
- Shoulders, hips, and knees aligned to form a **forward-ready fighting stance**.
- Engages the **hip flexors, gluteus medius**, and **tibialis anterior** for balance.

Why it matters: A backward or upright posture will shift recoil force into the lumbar spine and heels, resulting in muzzle rise or shooter instability.

3. Shoulders Relaxed, Not Raised

Instruction: *No unnecessary tension. Raise your head to relieve shoulder tightness.*

- Relaxes **upper trapezius, levator scapulae**, and **sternocleidomastoid** muscles.
- Promotes clean scapular function, prevents shoulder fatigue.

Why it matters: Tense shoulders disrupt natural arm movement, affect fine motor control, and reduce endurance.

4. Chest–Arm Triangle High and Even

Instruction: *Elbows out, triceps above nipples, form a triangle from arms to chest.*

- Forms an equal triangle between both **humeri (upper arms)** and the **sternum**.
- Shoulders slightly rolled forward for consistent elbow alignment.
- **Triceps brachii** are engaged and stabilize the shooting platform.

Why it matters: Uneven arms shift the gun laterally or vertically, leading to irregular recoil paths and lateral POI shifts.

5. Forearm Tension from Elbows to Wrists

Instruction: *Tension begins at the elbow and carries through to the wrist joint.*

- Engages **brachioradialis, flexor carpi radialis**, and **extensor carpi radialis longus**.
- Both arms should feel equally firm and "alive" from elbow to grip.

Why it matters: Inconsistent forearm tension compromises stability during recoil impulse and may affect sight recovery.

6. Engage Both Wrist Tendons ("Locked Forward")

Instruction: *Wrist flexor tendons should be evenly tensed in a forward-locked position.*

- **Flexor carpi ulnaris** and **flexor carpi radialis** keep the wrist angled forward.
- Prevents upward recoil and keeps muzzle level post-shot.
- **Isometric tension** applied equally on both hands.

Why it matters: A "broken" or "limp" wrist causes the muzzle to lift erratically, delaying target reacquisition.

7. Thumbs High—Within Mechanical Limits

Instruction: *Thumbs as high as possible without interfering with the slide.*

- Activates **thenar eminence** (thumb pad group) for leverage.
- Strong-side thumb slightly forward; support-side thumb forward and slightly higher.

Why it matters: High thumbs aid in recoil tracking and muzzle indexing but must not ride the slide or block ejection.

8. Palm Pressure Drives Grip

Instruction: *Both palms push into the frame—support hand applies more pressure.*

- Use **hypothenar eminence** and **thenar pad** to apply inward and forward pressure.
- Support hand provides **60–70% of grip tension**, strong hand ~30–40%.

Why it matters: Dominant-hand overpressure leads to trigger jerk; support-hand dominance gives stability and steering.

9. Do Not Adjust Fingers After Initial Grip

Instruction: *Set the grip during the draw. No fidgeting afterward.*

- Involves **intrinsic hand muscles: lumbricals, interossei, flexor digitorum profundus**.
- Changing pressure mid-string destabilizes the recoil control loop.

Why it matters: Re-gripping creates movement of the muzzle and interrupts neural pathways for consistency.

10. Support Index Finger Indexes Trigger Guard

Instruction: *Support index finger should drive into the underside of the trigger guard.*

- Creates **tactile feedback** and establishes indexing reference.
- Activates **flexor digitorum superficialis** for firm engagement.

Why it matters: Builds reference and consistency in grip—helps in low light or under stress to reinforce hand alignment.

11. Support Fingers Fit Knuckle Notches of Strong Hand

Instruction: *Index and middle fingers nest into the strong-hand finger grooves.*

- Achieves **interlocking grip geometry**
- Maximizes skin-to-frame contact and mechanical advantage

Why it matters: Inconsistent finger placement allows the gun to shift in the hand under recoil.

12. Strong-Hand Fingers Pull Rearward

Instruction: *Middle, ring, and pinky fingers apply rearward pressure into the backstrap.*

- Uses **flexor digitorum profundus** and **flexor digitorum superficialis**
- Anchors the gun into the palm for better muzzle control

Why it matters: Lack of rearward pressure lets the gun torque or roll upward under recoil.

13. Strong-Hand Thumb Applies Forward Pressure

Instruction: *Thumb and palm push forward, opposing the pull of the fingers.*

- Creates **isometric tension** along the longitudinal axis
- Engages **opponens pollicis** and **abductor pollicis brevis**

Why it matters: Completes the front-to-back tension loop and stabilizes the gun longitudinally.

14. Trigger Finger Moves Independently

Instruction: *Trigger finger isolates movement—no sympathetic movement with other fingers.*

- Requires neural independence via **motor cortex training**
- Only **flexor digitorum profundus** of the index finger should activate

Why it matters: If other fingers move with the trigger finger, POI shifts laterally—classic trigger jerk or milking.

15. 360° Vise Grip

Instruction: *Hands provide all-direction pressure: side-to-side, front-to-back, diagonal.*

- Form an **isometric tension net** around the gun
- Prevents any shift during recoil impulse
- Arms, hands, and tendons create a cohesive recoil control system

Why it matters: Anything less than full circumferential tension = movement of the muzzle = variable POI.

Summary for Instructors

Structure Element	Anatomical Focus	Diagnostic Error When Missing
Head/Eyes Up	Cervical spine, eye axis	Muzzle dips, poor indexing
Weight Forward	Hips, knees, ankles	Recoil pushes shooter off balance
Wrist Locked	Flexor/extensor carpi	Muzzle flip or delay in sight recovery
360° Grip	Intrinsics + forearm flexors	Gun shifts in hand, delayed follow-ups
Isolated Trigger Finger	FDS/hand proprioception	Group shift, lateral POI errors

Instructors need to understand and also be able to relate the same information to various students in various shooting disciplines.

I spend most of my days training Law Enforcement Agents/Officers, so with that in mind, as an instructor I must get a "buy in" from my students. To accomplish this a good instructor needs to understand the why.

Combat-Ready Shooting Structure for LE & CCW

"Structure drives consistency, consistency drives survivability."

A solid structure underpins accuracy, recoil control, and speed. For LE and CCW, structure must remain **stable under pressure**, **agile under movement**, and **repeatable under stress**—whether from a duty rig or concealment.

1. Head Up, Eyes Up – "See to Solve"

- **Context:** You don't draw unless you've identified a threat. Head and eye position dictate awareness and speed of response.
- **Instruction:** Look directly at the target. Bring the gun up to your line of sight, don't lower your head to the gun.
- **Anatomy:** Neutral cervical spine; engage **levator scapulae** and **superior trapezius** gently to hold posture.
- **Failure Result:** Head forward/down causes poor indexing and increased sympathetic shoulder tension, slowing response.

2. Nose Over Toes – Combat Posture

- **Context:** Forward balance enables explosive movement, stable recoil control, and force projection.
- **Instruction:** Slight forward lean from the **ankles**. Nose over your toes. Weight over **balls of the feet**.
- **Anatomy:** Engages **glutes**, **hip flexors**, **quadriceps**, **gastrocnemius**, and **tibialis anterior**.
- **Failure Result:** Leaning back = muzzle rise, disrupted recoil control, and delayed follow-up shots.

3. Relaxed Shoulders, Head Lifts You

- **Context:** Muscle tension adds inconsistency and fatigue, especially during prolonged incidents.
- **Instruction:** Shoulders down and relaxed. Lift your head tall—don't pull it forward.

- **Anatomy:** Minimize activation of **upper traps**, **sternocleidomastoid**, and **scalenes**.
- **Failure Result:** Tense shoulders raise elbows, tighten grip unconsciously, and reduce endurance.

4. Chest–Arm Triangle (Symmetry = Control)

- **Context:** This structure absorbs and redirects recoil across both arms evenly.
- **Instruction:** Elbows slightly out, triceps above nipple line. Arms form an isosceles triangle.
- **Anatomy:** Engage **deltoids, triceps, pectoralis major**, and **latissimus dorsi**.
- **Failure Result:** Uneven triangle leads to lateral muzzle jump and slower sight tracking.

5. Forearm Tension Elbow to Wrist

- **Context:** Consistent forearm tone stabilizes the gun during movement and recoil.
- **Instruction:** Keep both arms "alive" from the elbow forward. Not stiff, but firm.
- **Anatomy:** Active **brachioradialis, flexor carpi radialis, extensor carpi radialis longus**.
- **Failure Result:** Slack forearms = shock absorbed in the wrists = delayed return to target.

6. Wrist Tendons Locked Forward

- **Context:** Forward wrists reduce muzzle rise and keep the gun on target during rapid strings.
- **Instruction:** Flex wrists slightly forward (isometric lock), keep even tension on both sides.

- **Anatomy: Flexor carpi ulnaris**, **flexor carpi radialis**, **extensors** stabilize the wrist.
- **Failure Result:** Weak wrist = muzzle flip + poor shot placement during stress fire.

7. High Thumbs, Slide-Clear

- **Context:** Thumbs help track recoil and improve control without interfering with slide or controls.
- **Instruction:** Support-side thumb rides high and forward; strong-side thumb just under it.
- **Anatomy:** Uses **thenar eminence**, **opponens pollicis**, and **adductor pollicis**.
- **Failure Result:** Low or wrapped thumbs delay sight return and decrease lateral control.

8. Palm Pressure = Gun Control

- **Context:** Under recoil, grip pressure must be 360° and centered.
- **Instruction:** Strong hand pulls rearward, support palm drives inward and forward.
- **Anatomy:** Pressure from **thenar/hypothenar pads**, and **interossei** stabilize the grip.
- **Failure Result:** Gripping too hard with the gun hand = flinching, trigger jerk, poor POI.

9. No Finger Adjustment After Draw

- **Context:** Fidgeting with grip during a draw can shift POA and slow the shot.
- **Instruction:** Set it and forget it—your draw must end in your shooting grip.

- **Anatomy:** Intrinsic finger control from **lumbricals, flexor digitorum profundus**.
- **Failure Result:** Loss of grip geometry and shot timing under stress.

10. Support Index on Trigger Guard (Index Point)

- **Context:** Tactile contact under the trigger guard builds hand alignment memory under concealment stress.
- **Instruction:** Push index finger up under the trigger guard as a mechanical stop.
- **Failure Result:** Poor grip reference increases rotational error and gun shift.

11. Support Fingers Fit into Strong Hand Knuckles

- **Context:** Interlocking geometry maximizes surface contact and recoil direction.
- **Instruction:** Index and middle fingers nest into strong hand grooves naturally.
- **Failure Result:** Gaps = gun shift = inconsistent point of impact on follow-up shots.

12. Strong Hand Fingers Pull Rearward

- **Context:** Anchoring the gun rearward fights muzzle lift and roll.
- **Instruction:** Middle, ring, and pinky fingers pull straight back into the backstrap.
- **Anatomy:** Uses **flexor digitorum profundus** and palm flexors.
- **Failure Result:** Gun lifts out

13. Strong Side Thumb Pushes Forward

- **Context:** Creates isometric tension from front to back.

- **Instruction:** Apply counter-pressure with the thumb web and pad forward.
- **Failure Result:** Inconsistent recoil path without this balancing force.

14. Trigger Finger Must Move Independently

- **Context:** Trigger control is the #1 accuracy driver in close-range defensive shooting.
- **Instruction:** Isolate trigger finger movement—no sympathy from other fingers.
- **Failure Result:** If grip fingers move with the trigger = lateral group shifts, classic milking.

15. 360° Vise-Like Grip

- **Context:** Defensive and law enforcement shootings demand recoil control under duress.
- **Instruction:** Apply full, circular pressure—front to back, side to side, diagonal.
- **Failure Result:** Incomplete pressure leads to twist, lift, or lateral muzzle movement.

Summary for LE & CCW: Combat Relevance

Structural Element	Why It Matters in the Real World
Head Up, Eyes Up	Improves threat ID, maintains visual control
Nose Over Toes	Helps fight during recoil or physical contact
Shoulders Relaxed	Reduces fatigue, maintains fine motor skill
Triangle Structure	Keeps gun level and recoil consistent
Wrist Lockout	Reduces rise, improves follow-ups
Thumb & Palm Positioning	Affects both slide reliability and recoil tracking
Grip Geometry	Prevents gun shift under stress
Trigger Finger Isolation	Preserves accuracy when it matters most

Instructor Training Guide: Combat-Ready Shooting Structure for LE & CCW

Purpose:

To equip instructors with the anatomical understanding and instructional cues necessary to teach consistent, high-performance shooting structure tailored for Law Enforcement (LE) and Concealed Carry (CCW) contexts.

1. Head Up, Eyes Up – "See to Solve"

Objective: Maintain threat focus and target clarity.

- Instruct: "Look directly at what you need to shoot. Bring the gun to your eyes, not your head to the gun."
- Anatomy: Neutral cervical spine, eyes level.

- Common Errors: Head forward/down, creates downward muzzle angle and shoulder tension.
- Fix: Mirror drills, dry fire with visual focus on a point.

2. Nose Over Toes

Objective: Promote combat stance and recoil control.

- Instruct: "Lean forward from the ankles. Nose over toes."
- Anatomy: Engages hips, glutes, and anterior chain.
- Common Errors: Leaning back, heel loading.
- Fix: Wall lean drills, recoil control while moving.

3. Shoulders Relaxed

Objective: Reduce fatigue and maintain range of motion.

- Instruct: "Lift the head, let the shoulders fall."
- Anatomy: Upper traps, SCM, levator scapulae.
- Common Errors: Raised shoulders under stress.
- Fix: Relaxation drills, emphasize breathing cadence.

4. Chest-Arm Triangle

Objective: Symmetry in support and recoil management.

- Instruct: "Elbows out, triceps above the nipple line."
- Anatomy: Triceps, deltoids, pecs.
- Common Errors: Uneven extension, dropped elbows.
- Fix: Mirror stance drills, triangle with laser training.

5. Forearm Tension

Objective: Stabilize pistol platform.

- Instruct: "Tension from elbows to wrists, not stiff but engaged."
- Anatomy: Brachioradialis, forearm flexors/extensors.
- Common Errors: Limp wrists or stiff arms.
- Fix: Elastic band tension drills, shot recovery timing.

6. Wrist Tendons Locked Forward

Objective: Minimize muzzle rise.

- Instruct: "Lock both wrists slightly forward."
- Anatomy: Flexor carpi ulnaris/radialis.
- Common Errors: Collapsing wrists on recoil.
- Fix: Recoil tracking drills, laser dot control.

7. High Thumbs

Objective: Guide and manage recoil.

- Instruct: "Thumbs high and forward, but clear of the slide."
- Anatomy: Thenar eminence, opponens pollicis.
- Common Errors: Wrapped thumbs, riding the slide.
- Fix: Re-grip drills, dry fire press with high thumbs.

8. Palm Pressure

Objective: Stabilize grip structure.

- Instruct: "Press palms inward, support hand stronger."
- Anatomy: Thenar/hypothenar pads.
- Common Errors: Overgripping strong hand.
- Fix: Pressure pad drills, strong vs. support hand analysis.

9. Grip Consistency

Objective: Avoid shifting under stress.

- Instruct: "Establish grip on the draw. Don't fidget."
- Anatomy: Flexor digitorum profundus/superficialis.
- Common Errors: Readjusting grip after draw.
- Fix: Draw-to-shot timer drills, concealment reps.

10. Support Indexing on Trigger Guard

Objective: Create tactile reference point.

- Instruct: "Drive the support index under the trigger guard."
- Anatomy: Finger flexors and proprioceptive nerves.
- Common Errors: Low or floating support hand.
- Fix: Indexing drills, reference point pressure checks.

11. Interlocked Fingers

Objective: Maximize surface contact.

- Instruct: "Nest support fingers into the strong hand notches."
- Anatomy: Interossei, lumbricals.
- Common Errors: Gaps in grip geometry.
- Fix: Interlock drills, pressure mapping.

12. Rearward Pressure with Strong Hand Fingers

Objective: Anchor gun into the backstrap.

- Instruct: "Pull back with middle, ring, and pinky."
- Anatomy: Finger flexors.
- Common Errors: Floating pinky or uneven pull.
- Fix: Pressure squeeze drills, one-hand isolation checks.

13. Forward Pressure with Thumb

Objective: Counterbalance rearward pull.

- Instruct: "Drive strong side thumb forward."
- Anatomy: Opponens pollicis, adductor pollicis.
- Common Errors: Thumb not engaged.
- Fix: Isometric thumb-push drills.

14. Trigger Finger Isolation

Objective: Maintain shot precision.

- Instruct: "Only the trigger finger moves."
- Anatomy: Index flexors (FDP), motor isolation pathways.
- Common Errors: Milking or sympathetic grip.
- Fix: Finger isolation drills, trigger reset training.

15. 360° Vise Grip

Objective: Create full grip enclosure.

- Instruct: "Grip front to back, side to side, top to bottom."
- Anatomy: Full hand musculature.
- Common Errors: One-directional pressure only.
- Fix: Grip ring drills, live fire follow-up shot analysis.

Final Coaching Tip:

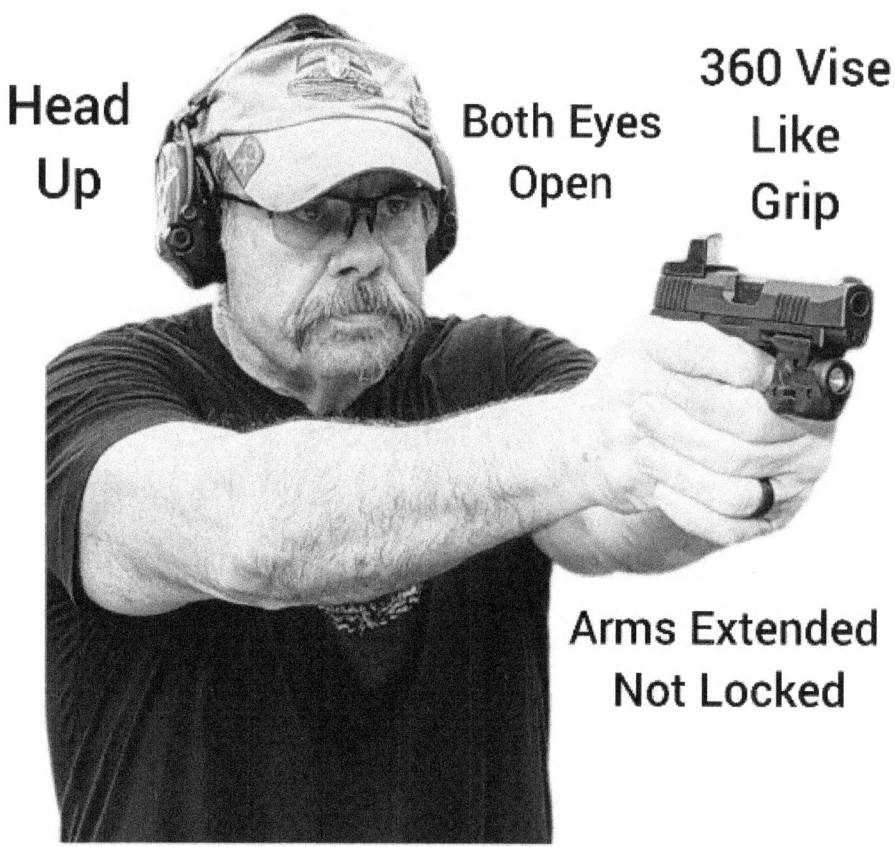

"Structure is subconscious control of recoil under conscious decision-making."

LE context: Train for structure under movement, barricades, low light.

CCW context: Emphasize structure from concealment, in confined space, or crowd environment.

Quick Structure Checklist for LE & CCW

1. Use this during instruction, dry fire evaluation, or live fire assessment.

2. Head up, eyes on threat – bring sights to eye level

3. Nose over toes – aggressive forward stance

4. Shoulders relaxed – eliminate unnecessary tension

5. Chest–arm triangle – elbows out, triceps above nipples

6. Forearms alive – tension from elbow to wrist

7. Wrists locked forward – resist muzzle rise

8. Thumbs high – forward, clear of slide

9. Palm pressure – support hand applies more pressure

10. Grip set on draw – no re-adjusting under stress

Index finger of support hand under trigger guard

11. Support fingers locked into strong hand notches

12. Strong hand fingers (middle, ring, pinky) pull rearward

13. Strong hand thumb drives forward into grip

14. Trigger finger moves independently

15. 360° vise grip – pressure in all directions

Building the Shooting Structure from the Ground Up

Mastering the foundational elements of a solid shooting structure—encompassing stance, posture, and grip—stands as a cornerstone of proficient pistol handling, directly influencing accuracy, recoil control, and overall safety in high-stakes situations. For individuals who conceal carry a pistol, this knowledge empowers them to respond swiftly and effectively to threats, minimizing errors under stress while enhancing their confidence and legal defensibility through precise, controlled actions that prioritize de-escalation and precision over panic. Instructors, meanwhile, must cultivate a profound grasp of these principles to impart not just mechanical skills but also the nuanced rationale behind them, enabling them to tailor instruction to diverse body types, scenarios, and skill levels, ultimately fostering safer, more competent shooters who can adapt and excel in real-world applications.

A solid shooting structure is fundamental to effective pistol handling, providing the foundation for accuracy, recoil management, and safety. This chapter outlines the key elements of stance and posture, starting from the feet and progressing upward. By establishing a stable, aligned, and tension-free structure, shooters can achieve consistent performance across various scenarios. We will then explore popular stances, their advantages and drawbacks, and recommendations for specific applications, before transitioning to grip techniques.

Establishing the Foundation: From Feet to Shoulders

Begin with the lower body to create a balanced platform that supports the entire shooting posture. The goal is to ensure stability, mobility, and natural alignment with the target while minimizing unnecessary tension.

1. **Feet: Flat and Positioned for Balance**

   The feet should remain flat on the ground, with the possible exception of the toes digging slightly into the surface for enhanced grip.
   - The strong-side foot (gun side) is generally positioned about halfway back relative to the instep of the support-side foot.
   - Smaller shooters may prefer a slightly more aggressive stance, aligning the toes of the strong-side foot with the heel of the support-side foot.
   - The toes of both feet should point toward the target to promote proper hip alignment.
   - Feet should be spaced approximately shoulder-width apart.
   - Key contributions of the feet:
     - **Stability**: A solid platform that minimizes unnecessary movement, with balanced weight distribution (typically shifted slightly forward onto the balls of the feet). Feet positioned shoulder-width apart or slightly wider help resist recoil and maintain control.
     - **Mobility**: The ability to move quickly in any direction as needed, facilitated by slightly bent knees that keep the shooter agile.

2. **Knees: Unlocked for Flexibility**

   Keep the knees unlocked and slightly bent to lower the center of gravity, enhancing balance and readiness for movement.

3. **Hips: Squared to the Target**

   Present the hips straight toward the target, avoiding an open or rotated position to maintain natural alignment.

4. **Chest: Aligned and Relaxed**

   The chest should face the target squarely, in harmony with the hips. Avoid using muscle tension to "force" the pistol toward the target; the structure should guide alignment naturally.

5. **Shoulders: Relaxed and Tension-Free**

Maintain relaxed shoulders without shrugging, rolling, or dropping the chin. Ensure no tension originates from the shoulders, as this can disrupt the overall posture.

6. **Elbows: Unlocked and Elevated**

Keep the elbows unlocked and positioned above the chest (with triceps aligned above the nipple line). Extend the pistol as far from the face as possible without locking the elbows to optimize sight alignment and recoil absorption.

7. **Chin: Neutral and Slightly Forward**

Hold the chin in a neutral, upright position, slightly forward so the nose is even with or just ahead of the toes. This promotes a subtle "nose over toes" posture without aggressive leaning.

8. **Eyes: Focused Straight Ahead**

Direct the eyes straight toward the target, selecting a small, specific spot for precision focus.

A well-constructed stance from the feet to the shoulders, as described, delivers stability and mobility. It also provides additional benefits essential for effective shooting:

1. **Recoil Management**
    - A forward lean in the torso, combined with extended arms, enables the body to absorb and manage recoil more efficiently.
    - This setup facilitates quicker sight recovery and return to target after each shot.
2. **Consistency and Repeatability**
    - A stance that is straightforward to replicate across shots and environments.
    - It fosters muscle memory, enhancing accuracy through uniform positioning.
3. **Comfort and Endurance**
    - The posture must be sustainable for extended periods without inducing fatigue.
    - It minimizes tension, which could otherwise compromise grip and trigger control.
4. **Alignment with the Target**
    - Naturally directs the pistol toward the target.
    - Supports proper sight alignment and sight picture with minimal adjustments.

Popular Shooting Stances

Several established stances meet these criteria, each with strengths and limitations tailored to the shooter's experience, physique, and operational requirements. The Isosceles, Weaver, and Modified Isosceles are among the most common.

1. Isosceles Stance

Description:

- The shooter faces the target squarely.
- Arms are extended straight forward, forming an isosceles triangle with the body.
- Feet are shoulder-width apart, with weight shifted slightly forward.

Pros:

- Simple and intuitive, making it easy for beginners to learn.
- Effective recoil management, as body mass directly absorbs the force.
- Ideal for body armor, presenting the full plate toward the threat.
- Facilitates faster target transitions due to symmetrical posture.
- Well-suited for red dot sights, maintaining natural dot alignment in the window.

Cons:

- May feel stiff or less flexible for some users.
- Results in more perceived recoil in the arms compared to stances with greater muscular involvement.
- Potentially less stable under stress, particularly if balance is compromised.

2. Weaver Stance

Description:

- A bladed posture with the support-side foot forward.
- The strong arm is extended straight, while the support arm is bent.
- Employs push-pull tension between the hands for control.

Pros:

- Superior recoil control through muscular tension, effectively managing muzzle rise.
- Natural for those familiar with rifle shooting due to similar positioning.
- Enhances agility, resembling a fighter's stance for close-quarters maneuvers.
- Reduces the shoulder profile, offering potential advantages in cover or concealment.

Cons:

- More complex to teach, requiring coordination and developed muscle memory.
- Suboptimal for body armor, as the side profile exposes vulnerabilities.
- Less effective with red dot sights, as the head may not align squarely behind the optic.
- Can lead to muscle fatigue during prolonged use, especially in the support arm.

3. Modified Isosceles Stance

Description:

- A hybrid combining elements of Isosceles and Weaver.
- Feet are slightly staggered for improved balance.

- Arms are nearly straight like in Isosceles, but the body is subtly bladed.

Pros:

- Balanced recoil control, leveraging both body mass and muscular tension.
- Enhanced mobility from the staggered foot placement.
- Greater stability under recoil, with forward weight bias supporting rapid follow-up shots.
- Excellent for tactical applications, blending armor compatibility with readiness for movement.

Cons:

- Demands practice and may not feel intuitive for beginners.
- Risk of inconsistency if shooters inadvertently shift toward pure Isosceles or Weaver.
- Lacks standardization, with minor variations potentially impacting repeatability.

Shooters construct a robust shooting structure by prioritizing stability from the feet upward, positioning them flat and shoulder-width apart with toes aimed at the target, unlocking knees for agility, squaring hips and chest forward, relaxing shoulders, elevating unlocked elbows, maintaining a neutral chin slightly advanced, and focusing eyes intently on a precise spot. This deliberate alignment delivers superior recoil absorption through forward lean and extended arms, ensures repeatable consistency via muscle memory, sustains comfort during prolonged sessions by eliminating tension, and naturally orients the pistol toward the target for effortless sight alignment. Among popular stances, the Isosceles offers simplicity and symmetry ideal for beginners and armored users but may amplify perceived recoil; the Weaver excels in muscular control and mobility for dynamic environments yet risks fatigue and suboptimal optic alignment;

while the Modified Isosceles balances both, providing tactical versatility though demanding practice for mastery. Instructors who deeply comprehend and dynamically teach these elements empower concealed carriers to wield pistols with precision and poise, underscoring the subject's vital role in elevating personal defense from reactive instinct to disciplined expertise.

Over the years, I have come to believe that the essence of effective recoil management lies in its profound importance yet inherent simplicity, transforming what could be a daunting challenge into a seamless extension of the shooter's form. By adopting a forward lean in the torso paired with extended arms, the body absorbs and dissipates recoil forces with remarkable efficiency, allowing for rapid sight recovery and a swift return to target after each discharge. This foundation not only promotes consistency and repeatability—enabling effortless replication across varied shots and environments while building muscle memory for enhanced accuracy through uniform positioning—but also prioritizes comfort and endurance, ensuring the posture remains sustainable over prolonged sessions without inducing fatigue or excess tension that might impair grip and trigger control. Ultimately, such alignment naturally orients the pistol toward the target, facilitating impeccable sight alignment and picture with minimal adjustments, empowering shooters to achieve precision, control, and confidence in every engagement.

The Difference between Reacting and Dominating

Decide and Act Faster. Without Compromising Judgment or control

Weapon Reloads: A Layered Breakdown

Foundational Principles (Applicable to All Reloads)

- **Control Zone**: Perform all reloads in front of the upper chest and chin, maintaining an "eye-muzzle-threat" alignment.
- **Two Hands in Motion**: Ensure both hands move simultaneously to minimize time.
- **Visual Discipline**: Shift eyes to the magwell only as necessary, then immediately return focus to the threat.
- **Finger off Trigger**: Keep the trigger finger indexed outside the trigger guard throughout the manipulation.
- **Efficiency under Pressure**: Prioritize consistent, simple, and resilient movements that withstand stress.

Emergency Reload (Slide-Lock Reload)

An emergency reload addresses a shooter-induced malfunction, such as running out of ammunition. Concealed carry permit holders should always carry at least one spare magazine for potential tactical reloads following expended rounds.

"The slide is locked to the rear. The pistol is empty. You are out of ammunition—this is an emergency."

Step-by-Step Instructor Breakdown

1. **Stoppage Recognition**
   - The shooter presses the trigger, experiences no discharge, feels a dead trigger, and observes the locked slide.

- Remove finger from trigger and bring the weapon to the control zone.

2. **Magazine Ejection**
    - Keep the pistol vertical.
    - Depress the magazine release using the strong-hand thumb or support-hand thumb.
    - Allow the empty magazine to drop freely (no retention).
    - *Instructor Note*: Position the strong-hand thumb above the slide stop lever to prevent premature activation if employing the slide release method.

3. **Index and Insert New Magazine**
    - The support hand draws a fresh magazine from the pouch using proper indexing.
    - Shift visual focus to the magwell as required.
    - Insert the magazine firmly and deliberately.

4. **Chamber a Round**
    - Select one of the following techniques:
        - Slingshot method.
        - Overhand/power stroke.
        - Slide release (only if trained and the slide stop is accessible).
    - Release the slide fully—do not ride it forward.

5. **Rebuild Grip and Reassess Threat**
    - Reestablish a two-handed grip.
    - Extend the pistol and acquire a fresh sight picture.
    - Continue engagement or reassess the situation.

Layered Learning Progression

Level	Focus	Instructor Cues	Common Errors
Beginner	Simple topping off	"Mag in, grip on, back out."	Watching mag fall; fumbled draw.
Intermediate	Smooth transitions	"Eyes threat → eyes magwell → eyes threat."	Poor grip re-establishment.
Advanced	Speed and awareness	"Topped off and back in the fight."	Premature ejection of magazine; incorrect mag selection.

Magazine Exchange (Tactical Reload with Retention)

Ammunition remains in the firearm, but a reload is necessary while retaining the partially spent magazine.

Two Primary Methods

Method 1: Catch First, Then Insert

1. Bring the pistol to the control zone.
2. Kant inboard to view the magwell.
3. Eject the magazine into the support hand.
4. Secure the magazine in a pocket or pouch.
5. Index a fresh magazine and insert it.
6. Reacquire the grip and reassess.

Method 2: Fresh Mag First (Preferred for Speed)

1. The support hand draws a fresh magazine.
2. Position it at the base of the pistol.

3. Eject the old magazine while retaining it between the index finger and thumb.
4. Insert the new magazine immediately.
5. Secure the retained magazine in a pocket.
6. Reacquire the grip and reassess.

Instructor Module: Loading, Press Check, and Unloading Procedures

Core Principle

All firearm handling must occur within the control zone—the area directly in front of the shooter's chest and chin. This approach reinforces alignment among the eyes, firearm, and threat, promoting safe and efficient manipulations even under stress.

Layered Skill Progression

Layer	Focus	Goal	Instructor Note
Beginner	Safety, familiarity, repetition	Develop clean procedural habits	Prioritize clarity and coach each repetition
Intermediate	Efficiency, pressure-tested handling	Improve speed without sacrificing control	Introduce dynamic drills (e.g., timed repetitions)
Advanced	Economy of motion, context adaptation	Perform consistently under simulated stress	Integrate into scenario-based training
Instructor	Diagnose errors, correct technique	Build skills in others, ensure doctrinal consistency	Use demonstration, error induction, and layered feedback

Checklist Framework

Loading (Slide Forward / Slide Locked)

Control Zone Position (Working Area)

- Draw the firearm and position it in the chest-level workspace.
- Orient the muzzle in a safe direction (e.g., toward the range or a downed threat).
- Keep the finger off the trigger, indexed in a high register.

Magazine Indexing and Insertion

- Use the support hand to retrieve the magazine via an indexing method.
- Insert the magazine with deliberate pressure, avoiding aggression.
- Adhere to the Soft Hands Principle: Refrain from slapping the magazine to prevent premature slide release.

Chambering a Round

Power Stroke / Overhand Slide Manipulation Method

Purpose

The Power Stroke, also known as the Overhand Method, is a robust and reliable technique for manipulating the slide of a semi-automatic pistol. It facilitates chambering a round, conducting a press check, clearing malfunctions, or performing slide-lock reloads.

Mechanics of the Power Stroke

This method maximizes leverage and mechanical advantage, ensuring reliability under stress, adverse conditions, or diminished fine motor skills.

Step-by-Step Breakdown

1. **Position the Firearm**:
   - Bring the pistol into the control zone (chest-height workspace in front of the face).
   - Orient the pistol inboard (tilted slightly inward toward the body) or vertically upright (slide facing upward).

2. **Establish Grip**:
   - Strong hand: Maintain the firing grip.
   - Support hand: Reach over the top of the slide with the entire palm—fingers angled forward, palm covering the rear serrations.
   - Grip pressure: Firmly wrap fingers over the top and around the sides, akin to grasping a hammer or heavy tool.

3. **Manipulate the Slide**:
   - Pull the slide straight to the rear with the support hand (avoid upward or diagonal motion).
   - Simultaneously push forward with the strong hand to create push-pull tension for enhanced reliability and control.
   - Release the slide cleanly once it reaches full rearward travel—do not ride it forward.

4. **Recovery**:
   - As the slide drives forward and chambers the round, immediately re-establish a two-handed grip.
   - Extend the pistol and acquire a fresh sight picture.

- Recover to Position 3 (high ready) or compressed ready, with the finger off the trigger.

Why the Power Stroke Is Preferred

Purpose

The Power Stroke, also known as the Overhand Method, is a robust and reliable technique for manipulating the slide of a semi-automatic pistol. It facilitates chambering a round, conducting a press check, clearing malfunctions, or performing slide-lock reloads.

Mechanics of the Power Stroke

This method maximizes leverage and mechanical advantage, ensuring reliability under stress, adverse conditions, or diminished fine motor skills.

Step-by-Step Breakdown

1. **Position the Firearm**:
   - Bring the pistol into the control zone (chest-height workspace in front of the face).
   - Orient the pistol inboard (tilted slightly inward toward the body) or vertically upright (slide facing upward).
2. **Establish Grip**:
   - Strong hand: Maintain the firing grip.
   - Support hand: Reach over the top of the slide with the entire palm—fingers angled forward, palm covering the rear serrations.
   - Grip pressure: Firmly wrap fingers over the top and around the sides, akin to grasping a hammer or heavy tool.

3. **Manipulate the Slide**:
    - Pull the slide straight to the rear with the support hand (avoid upward or diagonal motion).
    - Simultaneously push forward with the strong hand to create push-pull tension for enhanced reliability and control.
    - Release the slide cleanly once it reaches full rearward travel—do not ride it forward.
4. **Recovery**:
    - As the slide drives forward and chambers the round, immediately re-establish a two-handed grip.
    - Extend the pistol and acquire a fresh sight picture.
    - Recover to Position 3 (high ready) or compressed ready, with the finger off the trigger.

Why the Power Stroke Is Preferred

Factor	Benefit
Gross motor skills	Requires less dexterity under stress (sympathetic nervous system-dominant)
Mechanical leverage	Engages large muscle groups in the back and shoulders
Versatility	Effective for clearing malfunctions, press checks, and slide-lock reloads
Symmetry	Easier to teach and perform with either hand or in off-hand scenarios
Tactile consistency	Ideal for gloved hands or wet, bloody, or gritty conditions

Factor	Benefit
Factor	Benefit
Gross motor skills	Requires less dexterity under stress (sympathetic nervous system-dominant)
Mechanical leverage	Engages large muscle groups in the back and shoulders
Versatility	Effective for clearing malfunctions, press checks, and slide-lock reloads
Symmetry	Easier to teach and perform with either hand or in off-hand scenarios
Tactile consistency	Ideal for gloved hands or wet, bloody, or gritty conditions

Slingshot Method (Inboard Rotation) – Detailed Expansion

Purpose

The Slingshot Method is a fundamental technique for chambering a round or clearing malfunctions by pulling the slide fully to the rear and releasing it under spring tension. It is simple, effective, and relies on gross motor skills.

Mechanics of the Slingshot Method

This method enhances tactile feedback, ensures consistent chambering, and minimizes the need for fine motor skills—making it ideal under stress.

Step-by-Step Breakdown

1. **Bring the Firearm to the Control Zone**

   - Draw or return the pistol to the working area (chest-high, in front of the face).

- Rotate the firearm slightly inboard (about 30–45 degrees inward) so the ejection port faces outward and the top of the slide is exposed to the support hand.

2. Grip the Slide:

- Strong hand: Maintain the firing grip, finger off the trigger.
- Support hand: Reach up and grasp the rear of the slide from both sides using the thumb and fingers, like pinching the back of a slingshot.
- Grip placement: Use the rear serrations or traction area—avoid grabbing over the top of the ejection port.
- Engage all fingers for control, emphasizing the thumb and index/middle fingers for strength.

3. Rack the Slide:

- Push forward with the strong hand while pulling back firmly with the support hand.
- This simultaneous motion generates the push-pull tension required for a full slide cycle.
- Release the slide cleanly at full rearward travel—do not ride it forward.
- Allow the recoil spring to chamber the round under full tension.

4. Post-Action Grip Recovery:

- Immediately re-establish a two-handed grip.
- Extend the pistol.
- Acquire a fresh sight picture or return to Position 3 (close-quarters ready), depending on context.

Technical Benefits of the Slingshot Method

Attribute	Value
Gross motor based	Easy to retain under stress
No reliance on slide stop	Ideal if motor skills deteriorate or the slide stop malfunctions
Ambidextrous	Works for left- or right-handed shooters without hardware dependence
Consistent slide velocity	Enhances reliability for chambering a round
Clean mechanical operation	No interference with internal parts or ejection port

Slide Release Method (Slide Locked Only)

(Also known as: Slide Lock Lever, Slide Stop, Slide Catch)

Purpose
The Slide Release Method chambers a round from slide lock by depressing the slide stop lever, allowing the slide to drive forward under full spring tension. It is fast and efficient but demands greater dexterity, hand strength, and platform familiarity.

Mechanics of the Slide Release Method
Slide release is the quickest way to restore functionality after slide lock—if executed correctly, deliberately, and under control.

Step-by-Step Breakdown

1. **Position the Firearm in the Working Area**:

   - Bring the pistol into the control zone (chest-level, in front of the face).
   - Maintain alignment among eyes, muzzle, and threat.

2. **Confirm Slide Locked to the Rear**:

   - Verify the slide is held open, typically after emptying the magazine or manual locking during administrative handling.

3. **Insert Magazine**:

   - Support hand indexes and inserts a fresh magazine firmly into the mag well.
   - Avoid over-slamming the magazine, which may cause premature slide drop (inconsistent across platforms and users).

4. **Depress the Slide Release Lever**:

   - • Use the strong-hand thumb to press down firmly on the slide release lever.
   - Alternatively, use the support-hand thumb (common with Glock-style pistols or shorter thumbs) immediately after seating the magazine.
   - The slide will advance, chambering a round.

5. **Grip and Recover**:

   - Establish a proper two-handed grip.
   - Extend the pistol and acquire a fresh sight picture.
   - Keep the finger off the trigger until the decision to fire is made.

Technical Notes

Factor	Explanation
Spring tension	Modern pistols feature stiff recoil springs—requires strong, deliberate thumb pressure
Platform-specific	Lever size, position, and mechanical advantage vary (e.g., Glock, SIG, Smith & Wesson)
Ambidexterity	Many levers are non-ambidextrous—left-handed shooters may encounter challenges
Fine vs. gross motor	A fine motor action, less reliable under stress compared to overhand or slingshot methods

Post-Load Actions

- Reacquire a solid two-handed grip.
- Extend the firearm and obtain a sight picture.
- Keep the finger indexed.
- Recover to Position 3 or close-quarters ready.

Neurological Imprinting Concept

1. Repetition within the same spatial context accelerates recall under stress.
2. Maintaining eye-muzzle-threat alignment keeps the shooter head-up and aware of threats.

Press Check (Verifying a Chambered Round)

Grip and Control

- Maintain the strong-hand grip; position the thumb high on the tang or slide.
- Use the support hand to manipulate the slide—index and middle fingers in front of the rear sight.
- Pull the slide just enough to observe the casing or feel it with the pinky (in low-light conditions).

Confirm Battery

- Allow the slide to return forward under tension.
- Tap the rear of the slide to verify full battery.
- Never rely solely on loaded chamber indicators.

Post-Check Actions

- De-cock if using a double-action/single-action pistol (where applicable).
- Return to the holster only after a full control check.

Unloading Procedure

- Draw the firearm to the control zone.
- Point the muzzle downrange or in a safe direction.
- Keep the finger off the trigger.

Magazine Removal

- Remove the magazine and retain it.

Clear the Chamber

- Rack the slide three times—observe the ejection of any round.
- Lock the slide to the rear.
- Visually and physically inspect the chamber and mag well.
- Check it twice: Look away and re-confirm (Check It Twice principle).

Final Actions

- Release the slide (if transitioning to dry-fire training).
- De-cock (if applicable).
- Holster safely, performing a thumb check to verify battery or de-cocked status.

Instructor Tips for Delivery

Phase	Cue Words	Corrections
Loading	"Two hands in motion," "Soft hands," "Control zone"	Correct over-forceful magazine insertions or failure to use slingshot
Press Check	"Verify visually or by touch," "Battery check"	Address over-racking or failure to verify slide closure
Unloading	"CIT: Check It Twice"	Reinforce visual and tactile confirmation

Weapons Malfunction Clearance: Type 1 & Type 2

"Stoppages are fought and cleared from the chest, not the waist. All manipulations occur in the control zone—eye, muzzle, threat."

INSTRUCTOR OVERVIEW: Understanding Stoppages

- A **malfunction** or **stoppage** is an unintended interruption in the pistol's cycle of operation.
- All shooters must be able to:
    1. **Identify** what the weapon is doing (or not doing),
    2. **Diagnose** the likely cause based on visual and tactile feedback,
    3. **Apply the correct corrective action** in the fewest steps necessary.

TYPE 1 MALFUNCTION

AKA: *Failure to Fire / Click No Bang*

Symptoms:

- "Dead trigger" — you press the trigger, and nothing happens
- Slide is in **battery** (fully forward)
- No felt recoil
- Possible failure to seat magazine, bad primer, or misfeed

CLEARING A TYPE 1 MALFUNCTION: IMMEDIATE ACTION DRILL

"Tap – Rack – Reassess"

Step-by-Step Process

1. **Stoppage Stimulus Detected**
    - Pistol is in the aimed-in position
    - Trigger pressed → **No bang**
    - Shooter senses a "dead trigger" (no resistance or audible reset)
    - Shooter **removes finger from trigger**

2. **Weapon Diagnosis**
    - Shooter **breaks the wrist up** (elbows remain in)
    - Looks at the ejection port without coming off target
    - Slide appears fully forward → Type 1 likely

3. **Immediate Action**
    - **TAP**
        - Strike the base of the magazine with support hand palm to ensure its fully seated
        - Use enough pressure to lock it in but not enough to damage feed lips
    - **RACK**
        - Use slingshot or power stroke method to rack the slide
        - Ejects any bad round and loads a new one
    - **REASSESS**
        - Reacquire grip and push back out
        - Obtain sight picture and evaluate the threat condition

Instructor Teaching Notes: Type 1

Area	Insight
Control zone	Ensure manipulations happen chest-high for visibility and consistency
Trigger discipline	Reinforce immediate trigger finger removal
Pressure	Too little tap may not seat mag; too hard may misalign feed lips
Corrections	Don't allow students to tilt gun too far or sweep others while racking
Cue Words	"Tap it, rack it, send it." or "Fix it like you mean it."

Drills for Type 1 Training

Drill	Purpose
Induced Type 1 (dummy round)	Insert inert round in mag to simulate failure to fire
Dry Fire Tap-Rack	Repetition of proper hand movement
1-Round + Dummy Reps	Builds recognition of click/no bang reaction

AKA: *Failure to Eject / "Stovepipe" / Slide Out of Battery*

Symptoms:

- Slide is slightly out of battery (not fully forward)
- Brass visible in ejection port, often sticking out at an angle
- "Soft click" or mushy trigger
- Caused by limp-wristing, dirty extractor, or faulty ejection

CLEARING A TYPE 2 MALFUNCTION: AGGRESSIVE RACKING

"Don't pick the brass out—violence of action clears it faster."

Step-by-Step Process

1. **Stoppage Stimulus Detected**
    - Dead trigger or weak trigger pull
    - Pistol in the aimed-in position
    - Shooter removes finger from trigger
2. **Weapon Diagnosis**
    - Shooter breaks the wrist up
    - **Brass is visibly stuck in the ejection port**
    - Slide is visibly **out of battery**
    - Shooter **identifies a Type 2 malfunction**
3. **Immediate Action**
    - **Support hand performs aggressive rack** using:
        - **Overhand power stroke**
        - OR **slingshot method**
    - Do not try to pick the brass out; force it out via full slide cycle
    - **Do not induce double-feed** by short-stroking
4. **Reassess and Fire**
    - Rebuild grip
    - Push back out
    - Acquire sight picture
    - Decide to re-engage threat or scan

Instructor Teaching Notes: Type 2

Area	Insight
Action = Aggression	Clearing must be **fast and violent**, not finessed
Control zone = visibility	Keep manipulations at chest level for rapid feedback
Cue Words	"See brass? Rack fast." or "Don't baby the slide—send it flying."
Training Aid	Use spent brass to simulate stovepipe manually for reps
Common Mistakes	Picking brass, riding the slide, weak rack, or pressing trigger before resolving issue

DIFFERENTIATING TYPE 1 VS TYPE 2 – INSTRUCTOR GUIDE

Feature	Type 1	Type 2
Slide position	Fully in battery	Slightly out of battery
Brass visible	No	Yes – in ejection port
Trigger feel	Dead trigger	Soft or no reset
Correction	Tap-Rack-Reassess	Immediate aggressive rack
Primary cause	Mag not seated, bad primer	Failure to eject, limp wristing

The 3Ps of Pistol Presentation

1. Presentation

This refers to the **mechanics of bringing the pistol from the holster to the target** in a controlled and consistent manner.

- **Biomechanical efficiency**: The movement should be straight, minimizing wasted motion. The pistol should travel on a predictable line, not an arcing or scooping path.
- **Consistency**: Every repetition must look the same—whether in training or under stress. Presentation is not just about speed, but about delivering the pistol to the eye-target line with repeatable precision.
- **Grip integrity**: Proper grip must be established in the holster and maintained through the presentation. A poor initial grip compromises everything that follows.

Instructor Point: Stress that shooters "fight from the holster they train with." Presentation is only as good as the grip, stance, and indexing built at the start.

2. Pressure

Pressure refers to the **applied grip force and trigger control** during the draw and extension.

- **Grip Pressure**: Must be firm enough to manage recoil but not so tense that it causes tremors or anticipatory movement. The support hand applies inward and forward pressure, locking the pistol into the shooter's frame.

- **Trigger Pressure**: As the pistol joins the eye-target line, pressure on the trigger should be **staged and controlled**. The shooter must avoid "snatching" the trigger at full extension. Instead, pressure is applied smoothly as the sights settle.
- **Mental Pressure**: This also extends to the psychological component—keeping composure under time stress, close-distance threat, or high heart rate.

Instructor Point: Pressure is not just physical. It is the balance between **controlling the pistol and controlling yourself.**

3. Pathway

Pathway is the **trajectory of the pistol to the target**—the invisible line along which the pistol travels.

- **Straight-line Pathway**: The pistol should travel in a direct line from the holster to the target, moving efficiently into the shooter's line of sight. Scooping, fishing, or lateral "wandering" of the muzzle wastes time and consistency.
- **Visual Pathway**: The eyes lead the pathway. The shooter must pick up the sight picture early and bring the gun to the line of vision—not dip their head to the gun.
- **Retractable Pathway**: Pathway works both ways. Just as the pistol travels outward efficiently, it must be retracted smoothly for reholstering, reloads, or post-engagement scanning.

Instructor Point: Emphasize that pathway is about **economy of motion**. The shortest, cleanest path reduces decision time (Hick's Law) and improves speed without loss of accuracy

Pulling It Together

The **3Ps—Presentation, Pressure, Pathway—work as a system**:

- **Presentation** ensures the pistol is delivered correctly.
- **Pressure** ensures control of both the firearm and the shooter.
- **Pathway** ensures efficiency and repeatability of movement.

When trained together, these Ps create a biomechanically sound, stress-proof draw stroke that holds under both competition and combat conditions.

The 3Ps of Pistol Presentation

The Process

Presentation
Pressure
Pathway

Create Biomechanical Efficiency

Training Module: The 3Ps of Pistol Presentation

(Presentation · Pressure · Pathway)

Beginner Level (Fundamentals)

Objective: Build awareness of the 3Ps and establish consistent mechanics.

Key Points

1. **Presentation**
   - Establish a correct grip in the holster.
   - Draw the pistol directly toward the eye-target line.
   - Keep movements smooth and consistent—speed comes later.
2. **Pressure**
   - Apply a firm, even grip with both hands (no gaps or uneven tension).

- Avoid "crushing" the grip—use consistent forward and inward pressure.
- Trigger finger indexed until the pistol is on target.

3. **Pathway**
    - Move the pistol in a straight, efficient line from holster to target.
    - Lead with the eyes: lock onto the target first, then bring pistol to line of sight.
    - Avoid "scooping" or over-extending.

Drills

- **Dry Fire Presentation Drill**: 10–20 slow reps focusing on grip and straight-line draw.
- **Wall Drill**: Stand close to a wall, present the pistol without the muzzle drifting sideways—teaches clean pathway.
- **3P Verbal Reinforcement**: Instructor calls "Presentation / Pressure / Pathway" as students execute each step.

Intermediate Level (Performance)

Objective: Apply the 3Ps at speed under realistic conditions.

Key Points

1. **Presentation**
    - Consistency at speed—draw stroke looks the same every time.
    - Focus on first-round hit accuracy while increasing pace.
2. **Pressure**
    - Adjust grip pressure dynamically: tight enough for recoil control, relaxed enough for precision.

- Begin applying trigger pressure ("prep") as sights approach target.
3. **Pathway**
    - Efficient movement at speed—no wasted arcs or scoops.
    - Pathway consistency during multiple target transitions.

Drills

- **Draw to First Shot Drill**: Timed draws at 3–7 yards with strict accuracy requirement.
- **Trigger Prep Drill**: Present the pistol and stage the trigger smoothly—breaking only when sight picture stabilizes.
- **Target Transition Drill**: Engage two targets using the same clean pathway each time.

Advanced Level (Stress-Proofing)

Objective: Harden the 3Ps against stress, movement, and adverse conditions.

Key Points

1. **Presentation**
    - Adapt presentation from seated, moving, or compromised positions.
    - Maintain mechanics even when using concealment or barriers.
2. **Pressure**
    - Manage grip and trigger under stress (shot timer, low light, heart rate).
    - Emphasize mental pressure management: breathing, calm execution.
3. **Pathway**
    - Maintain pathway efficiency when moving off-line or using lateral footwork.

- o Retract pathway into low ready or compressed ready as needed for multiple threats.

Drills

- **Stress Timer Drill**: Students draw and fire under par times to test mechanics.
- **Movement Presentation Drill**: Draw while moving laterally or stepping off line.
- **Low-Light 3Ps Drill**: Apply same principles using handheld or WML illumination.

Instructor Level (Teaching & Diagnostics)

Objective: Teach instructors how to evaluate, correct, and refine the 3Ps in students.

Instructor Checklist

- **Presentation**:
    - o Is the grip correct before the pistol leaves the holster?
    - o Is the pistol delivered to the eye-target line without wasted motion?
- **Pressure**:
    - o Is grip pressure balanced between hands?
    - o Is trigger press staged smoothly instead of snapped?
    - o Is student showing mental control under pressure?
- **Pathway**:
    - o Does the pistol move in a straight line, or is there scooping/curving?
    - o Are eyes leading the pistol to the target?
    - o Is the pathway retractable and repeatable?

Instructor Drills

- **Error Identification Drill**: Students deliberately exaggerate poor Presentation, Pressure, or Pathway; instructors diagnose and correct.
- **3P Breakdown Teaching**: Instructors explain and demo each P separately, then integrate them for the full draw stroke.
- **Progressive Overload Drill**: Add variables (timer, multiple targets, concealment) while ensuring students maintain the 3Ps.

Summary

The **3Ps—Presentation, Pressure, Pathway—create a biomechanical and mental framework for a stress-proof pistol draw.**

- Beginners learn clean fundamentals.
- Intermediate shooters build speed and accuracy.
- Advanced shooters stress-proof mechanics in real-world conditions.
- Instructors use the 3Ps as diagnostic tools to correct errors and reinforce consistency.

The 3Ps of Pistol Presentation

Presentation · Pressure · Pathway

Beginner Level: Foundation

Goal: Build consistent mechanics and awareness of the 3Ps.

1. **Presentation**
    - Grip formed in the holster.
    - Pistol lifted and driven in a straight line toward the eyes.
    - Movement is smooth, not rushed.
2. **Pressure**
    - Firm, balanced grip from both hands.
    - No over-crushing—just enough to manage recoil.
    - Trigger finger straight until the pistol is on target.
3. **Pathway**
    - Pistol moves on a straight track—no fishing, scooping, or arcing.
    - Eyes lock on the target first; pistol follows into vision.
    - Return path (reholstering) mirrors the draw.

Drill: *Dry-fire presentation.* 10 slow reps, calling out each P as you move.

Intermediate Level: Performance

Goal: Execute the 3Ps with speed and accuracy.

1. **Presentation**
    - Draw is identical every time, regardless of speed.
    - First-round hit accuracy is non-negotiable.
2. **Pressure**
    - Grip is consistent across multiple strings of fire.
    - Trigger is prepped during extension—breaking only as sights settle.
3. **Pathway**
    - Pathway remains straight at full speed.
    - Efficient transitions—muzzle tracks cleanly between targets.

Drill: *Draw to First Shot on timer.* Must balance accuracy and speed while maintaining 3Ps.

Advanced Level: Stress-Proofing

Goal: Maintain the 3Ps under stress, movement, and real-world variables.

1. **Presentation**
    - Works from concealment, seated, or moving positions.
    - Same mechanics regardless of starting point.
2. **Pressure**
    - Grip and trigger control hold under timer, low light, and elevated heart rate.
    - Mental pressure is managed—shooter executes, not overthinks.
3. **Pathway**
    - Muzzle stays efficient even when stepping off-line or engaging multiple threats.
    - Retraction pathway is just as clean for scanning, reloading, or reholstering.

Drill: *Movement + Timer Drill.* Step laterally, draw, and engage. Check for clean 3Ps under stress.

Instructor Level: Teaching & Diagnostics

Goal: Use the 3Ps to evaluate, coach, and correct.

- **Presentation** → Look for wasted motion, scooping draw, or poor initial grip.
- **Pressure** → Check hand tension balance; watch for trigger snatch or grip collapse.

- **Pathway** → Observe muzzle travel; correct "fishing" or inconsistent lines.

Instructor Drill: *Error Demo.* Have students exaggerate mistakes in each P. Diagnose and correct using the 3Ps as the framework.

Summary

The **3Ps** create a framework for a **biomechanically efficient, stress-resistant draw stroke**:

- **Presentation** delivers the pistol consistently.
- **Pressure** controls the pistol and the shooter.
- **Pathway** keeps the draw efficient and repeatable.

Train slow, build consistent 3Ps, then add speed and stress.

The 3Ps of Pistol Presentation

Presentation · Pressure · Pathway
Instructor Quick Reference

1. Presentation

- Grip formed correctly in holster.
- Draw stroke is direct, efficient, and repeatable.
- Pistol delivered to eye–target line (eyes lead, pistol follows).

Common Errors:

- Scooping or arcing draw.

- Poor grip established in holster.
- Head drops to meet pistol.

2. Pressure

- Firm, balanced grip pressure (support hand drives inward/forward).
- Trigger prep during extension—smooth press as sights settle.
- Control **both** pistol and mental pressure.

Common Errors:

- Over-crushing grip, causing tremor.
- Trigger slap/snatch at full extension.
- Grip collapse after first shot.

3. Pathway

- Straight-line draw, no wasted motion.
- Muzzle tracks cleanly between targets on transitions.
- Retract pathway is controlled (low ready, reholster, reload).

Common Errors:

- "Fishing" or scooping upward.
- Muzzle wandering during transitions.
- Sloppy reholstering pathway.

Instructor Diagnostic Checklist

- Grip correct before pistol leaves holster.
- Pistol moves on straight pathway to eye–target line.
- Trigger press staged smoothly, not snapped.
- Grip and pressure remain consistent under speed/stress.
- Pathway is clean both outward (draw) and inward (reholster/retract).

Key Teaching Points

- **All things Fast must be accomplished by being Efficient!**
- Speed builds only after consistent 3Ps.
- Use the 3Ps to diagnose and correct any draw error.

Authors Note: Super Dave Harrington was a very good friend and one of my true shooting mentors, Dave passed away in August of 2025 while I was in the process of writing this book. I feel that is only fitting to include some of the concepts that he taught me. Until the Last Rally Point, my Brother.

Holding, Aiming, Firing, and Timing, Do not over do it!

Super Dave Harrington's point about *not overdoing* the principles of marksmanship gets at something many shooters—especially those in the defensive, tactical, or practical shooting worlds—struggle with: the balance between technical mastery and real-world application.

When he breaks it down to **holding, aiming, firing, and timing**, he is distilling the fundamentals into a simplified framework that is easy to remember and apply under stress. Let's unpack this further:

1. Holding (Grip and Stability)

- The way the shooter physically controls the weapon.
- A correct grip ensures recoil management, consistency, and efficiency of follow-up shots.
- Many shooters overcomplicate grip by constantly tweaking hand angles and pressure points instead of finding a *repeatable, biomechanically strong hold*.
- Harrington's emphasis suggests: **establish a grip that lets you manage the pistol and then stop overthinking it.** Trust your training.

2. Aiming (Sight Alignment & Sight Picture)

- The act of directing the firearm where it needs to go.
- Whether iron sights, red dot, or point shooting, the essential principle is aligning the gun in relation to the target.
- Shooters often "over-aim"—spending too much time perfecting the sight picture, when in reality a *good enough* sight picture is sufficient for most defensive and practical contexts.
- Harrington's simplicity reminds us: **aiming isn't art—it's alignment. Don't stall progress by demanding perfection when combat accuracy suffices.**

3. Firing (Trigger Control)

- Where the bullet's path is truly decided.
- Smooth, consistent trigger press without disturbing the sights is the heart of accuracy.
- This is another area shooters tend to overanalyze, often inducing anticipation, jerking, or hesitation.
- Harrington's perspective: **you don't need mystical techniques—you just need to break the shot cleanly.**

4. Timing (Efficiency & Decision-Making)

- Perhaps the most overlooked principle.
- It is not just about *when* to fire, but *how long to spend on each element of the process*.
- Shooters can overdo fundamentals by being too slow, trying to make everything "perfect," which wastes precious time.
- Conversely, rushing timing without control leads to misses.

- Harrington's concept here: **know when to accept the shot and when to move on. Accuracy balanced with speed is key.**

The Core Message

Harrington is saying that the *principles of marksmanship are not complicated*. They should serve the shooter, not become a mental prison. Many overanalyze every micro-movement, creating paralysis by analysis. His breakdown reminds us:

- **Hold the gun right.**
- **Aim it at the target.**
- **Press the trigger correctly.**
- **Do all this in time with the situation.**

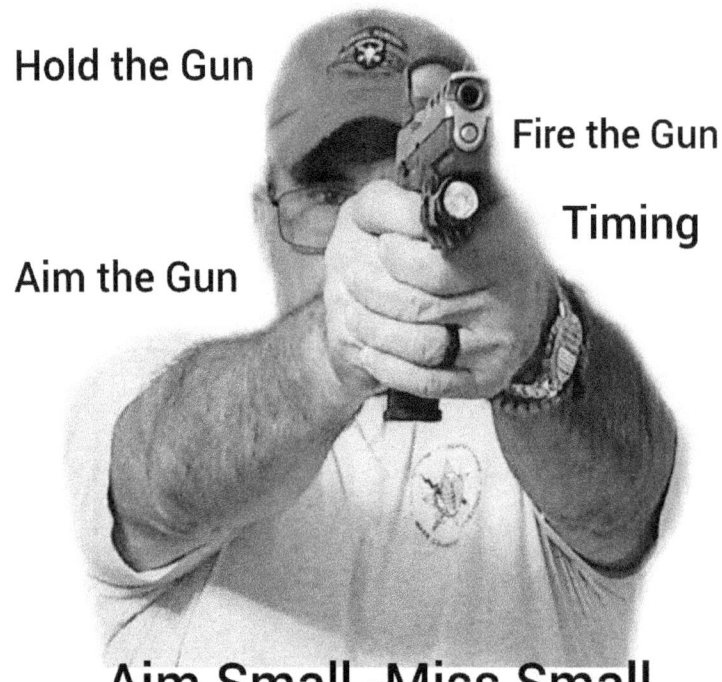

That's it. The rest is refinement, not reinvention.

Instructor Module: The Simplified Principles of Marksmanship

(Based on Harrington's "Hold, Aim, Fire, Time")

Introduction for Students

Marksmanship can become unnecessarily complicated when shooters obsess over every small detail. The truth is simpler: success comes from mastering and applying the essentials—**holding, aiming, firing, and timing.** These principles, when understood and applied consistently, form the backbone of every accurate and efficient shot.

As your instructor, my goal is to strip away the excess and reinforce what matters most.

1. Holding (Grip and Stability)

Concept: How the shooter physically controls the firearm.

- **Checkpoints for Students:**
    - Establish a high, firm grip with both hands.
    - Apply even pressure—support hand drives the majority of recoil management.
    - Keep wrists locked in a natural forward position.
    - Maintain consistent grip from the holster to follow-through.

Training Cue: *"Grip it once, grip it right, and leave it alone."*

Instructor Note:

Correct the habit of over-adjusting grip between shots. Reinforce consistency over constant tinkering.

2. Aiming (Sight Alignment & Sight Picture)

Concept: Aligning the firearm to hit the intended target.

- **Checkpoints for Students:**
    - Understand the relationship between sights (or dot) and target.
    - For close-range defensive shooting: accept a coarse sight picture ("good enough" accuracy).
    - For precision: refine alignment without over-holding.
    - Eyes lead the gun; don't "hunt" with the pistol.

Training Cue: *"Find it, trust it, and press."*

Instructor Note:

Stress that *perfect sight pictures* are not always required. Teach shooters to evaluate the shot's context—speed vs precision.

3. Firing (Trigger Control)

Concept: Where accuracy is truly decided.

- **Checkpoints for Students:**
    - Place finger pad consistently on the trigger.
    - Press straight to the rear—no jerking, slapping, or anticipation.
    - Maintain sight stability through the break.
    - Reset during recoil; don't pin or slap excessively.

Training Cue: *"Press the trigger—don't fight it."*

Instructor Note:
Remind shooters that poor trigger management ruins good aiming. Build confidence with dry fire and ball-and-dummy drills.

4. Timing (Efficiency & Decision-Making)

Concept: Balancing speed, accuracy, and situational necessity.

- **Checkpoints for Students:**
    - Learn to accept an *adequate* sight picture—avoid over-confirmation.
    - Break shots as soon as the gun returns to alignment.
    - Understand the context:
        - Close & fast = speed matters most.
        - Far & precise = accuracy matters most.
    - Train rhythm: grip, sight, press, recover, repeat.

Training Cue: *"Shoot as fast as you can hit—no faster, no slower."*

Instructor Note:
This is the principle that ties everything together. Teach shooters to trust their ability, avoid hesitation, and let training dictate timing instead of overthinking under stress.

Summary for Students

Marksmanship does not need to be complicated. If you can:

1. **Hold** the gun firmly and consistently,
2. **Aim** it at the target,

3. **Fire** with a clean trigger press,
4. **Time** your shots according to the situation—

—you have mastered the foundation of pistol shooting. Everything else is refinement and efficiency.

Drill Progression: Hold – Aim – Fire – Time

Phase 1: Dry Fire (No Ammunition)

Purpose: Build mechanics without recoil or noise distraction.

Drill 1: Grip & Presentation Check (Holding)

- **Setup:** Unloaded pistol, safe area.
- **Execution:**
    1. Draw from holster.
    2. Build two-hand grip and press to extension.
    3. Freeze and self-check (hand placement, wrist lock, pressure).
- **Reps:** 10–15 perfect reps.
- **Instructor Cue:** *"Consistency, not speed."*

Drill 2: Wall Drill (Aiming + Firing)

- **Setup:** Unloaded pistol, muzzle 1 inch from blank wall.
- **Execution:**
    1. Establish grip.
    2. Aim at an imaginary target point.
    3. Press trigger smoothly—sights must not move.
- **Reps:** 10–20 presses.

- **Instructor Cue:** *"Sight still—trigger straight."*

Drill 3: Cadence Count (Timing)

- **Setup:** Unloaded pistol, safe area.
- **Execution:**
    1. Present pistol on target.
    2. Instructor calls cadence ("1…2…3…").
    3. Student presses trigger in rhythm with command.
- **Reps:** 3 sets of 5 reps.
- **Instructor Cue:** *"Match the beat, don't rush the press."*

Phase 2: Live Fire – Fundamentals

Purpose: Apply mechanics under recoil.

Drill 4: Five Shot Slow Fire (Holding & Aiming)

- **Setup:** 5-yard target.
- **Execution:**
    1. Perfect grip and sight alignment.
    2. Fire 5 deliberate shots, focus on *hold and sight picture stability*.
- **Scoring:** All hits inside 3-inch circle.
- **Instructor Cue:** *"Accuracy first. Recoil is proof you're working."*

Drill 5: Ball and Dummy (Firing)

- **Setup:** Partner loads magazine with random snap caps.
- **Execution:**
    1. Fire controlled strings.

2. Observe sight movement when trigger is pressed on dummy round.
- **Focus:** Diagnoses anticipation and poor trigger mechanics.
- **Instructor Cue:** *"The gun should not know the difference."*

Drill 6: Controlled Pair Cadence (Timing)

- **Setup:** 7-yard target.
- **Execution:**
    1. On signal, fire 2 rounds.
    2. First round: sight picture.
    3. Second round: break shot as sights return.
- **Scoring:** Both inside 6-inch circle.
- **Instructor Cue:** *"Shoot as fast as you can confirm the gun."*

Phase 3: Live Fire – Integration

Purpose: Blend all four principles under realistic conditions.

Drill 7: 1–R–1 Drill (Hold, Fire, Timing Under Pressure)

- **Setup:** 7–10 yards, 3 targets or 1 target with multiple scoring zones.
- **Execution:**
    1. Fire 1 round → reload → fire 1 round.
    2. Maintain grip consistency, aim quickly, manage trigger under stress.
- **Scoring:** Both hits inside 6-inch circle.
- **Instructor Cue:** *"Grip never changes, sights always return."*

Drill 8: 3–2–1 Drill (Timing & Transitions)

- **Setup:** 3 targets, spaced 1–2 yards apart, 7-yard line.

- **Execution:**
    1. Fire 3 rounds on target 1.
    2. Transition, fire 2 rounds on target 2.
    3. Transition, fire 1 round on target 3.
- **Focus:** Rhythm and efficiency.
- **Scoring:** All hits in scoring zones.
- **Instructor Cue:** *"See enough to shoot—no more, no less."*

Drill 9: The Test (Final Integration)

- **Setup:** B8 bullseye, 10 yards, 10 rounds, 10 seconds.
- **Execution:**
    1. On signal, fire 10 rounds freestyle.
    2. Goal: blend *hold, aim, fire, time* under a measurable standard.
- **Scoring:** 90/100 or better.
- **Instructor Cue:** *"The clock doesn't lie—the sights don't either."*

Progression Summary

1. **Dry Fire**: Build mechanics without stress.
2. **Live Fire Fundamentals**: Reinforce principles with accuracy drills.
3. **Integration Drills**: Add speed, decision-making, and pressure.

When taught progressively, students internalize Harrington's message: **marksmanship is simple—hold, aim, fire, and time. Don't overcomplicate it.**

Additional Training Considerations

Armed professionals wear body armor with plates

When an armed professional wears body armor with plates—particularly hard rifle-rated plates—the standard pistol draw stroke from a duty belt is affected in ways that require deliberate adjustment. The armor adds bulk, changes body mechanics, and alters the way the pistol must be accessed under pressure.

1. Interference with Grip Acquisition

- **Problem:** The bulk and overlap of body armor plates often extend downward over the top of the duty belt and holster. This can block or restrict the natural path of the dominant hand when reaching for the pistol.
- **Adjustment:** Professionals must drive the elbow outward slightly and approach the pistol from a more lateral angle, rather than a straight downward "textbook" draw. This ensures the web of the hand establishes a full firing grip without dragging across the vest.

2. Elbow and Shoulder Position

- **Problem:** With plates covering the torso, a standard "elbow back" motion in the draw stroke can result in the forearm striking the armor, impeding speed and efficiency.
- **Adjustment:** Instead of flaring the elbow backward, the draw should emphasize a more **outward and upward sweep**, using shoulder rotation to clear the armor and smoothly index the pistol to the centerline.

3. Presentation Pathway

- **Problem:** Armor can interfere with the close-to-body upward lift of the pistol, particularly if the shooter uses a high-ride holster. The gun can snag or bump against the carrier during the transition from holster to presentation.
- **Adjustment:** Modify the draw into more of a **"J-curve" motion**—the pistol clears the holster straight up, then moves slightly outboard before driving forward. This arc clears the vest and ensures a clean, direct path into extension.

4. Retention Holsters and Armor

- **Problem:** Duty holsters with active retention systems (e.g., ALS, SLS, or thumb release) require precise hand placement. Armor bulk can cause incomplete or misaligned access under stress.
- **Adjustment:** Train to rotate the wrist outward slightly during the release motion, ensuring the retention devices are reliably defeated even with the vest restricting wrist angles.

5. Seated and Vehicle Considerations

- **Problem:** Plates limit torso flexion, making it harder to bend or rotate at the waist to access the pistol, especially when seated in a patrol car or armored vehicle.
- **Adjustment:** Officers and soldiers must integrate **hip rotation** rather than upper-body bending when drawing, training the body to pivot at the legs and hips instead of trying to force torso flexion blocked by plates.

6. Biomechanical Efficiency

- **Problem:** Wearing armor changes the natural center of gravity and shoulder mobility. If the professional uses the same "unarmored" draw stroke, friction points will slow movement.
- **Adjustment:** The draw stroke must remain biomechanically consistent with armor in place. That means training repetitions with plates on, developing a modified movement pattern that still follows economy of motion but accounts for the changed geometry of the body.

7. Training Considerations

- Dry-fire practice and live-fire drills **must be conducted in full kit**. Training in uniform or soft armor only, then assuming the draw will remain identical with rifle plates, sets the shooter up for failure under stress.
- Instructors should emphasize **individual adjustment**—plate cut (SAPI, swimmer, shooter), holster ride height, and body type all affect the ideal draw modification.

Bottom Line:
Body armor with plates creates real-world interference with a duty belt pistol draw. Professionals must adapt by widening their access angle, modifying the elbow/shoulder path, and ensuring the pistol clears the vest cleanly. These adjustments must be trained until they become subconscious, ensuring a smooth, and reliable draw stroke under the pressure of real engagements.

Instructor-ready drill sequence

Instructor-ready drill sequence for teaching and ingraining the modified pistol draw stroke while wearing body armor with plates. This progression moves from controlled dry-fire to dynamic live-fire, reinforcing biomechanics, economy of motion, and stress inoculation.

Instructor Drill Progression: Pistol Draw Stroke with Plates

Phase 1: Dry-Fire Mechanics (Armor Familiarization)

Objective: Build awareness of armor interference points and engrain biomechanical adjustments.

1. **Armor Check Drill**
    - Students stand in front of a mirror or partner.
    - Slowly perform the draw stroke while wearing full armor.
    - Identify contact points (grip interference, elbow bumping plate, gun snagging vest).
    - Instructor correction: adjust elbow outward, wrist angle, and draw arc.
2. **Grip Acquisition Reps**
    - From a duty holster, practice establishing a full firing grip without drawing the pistol.
    - Repeat 25–50 times, focusing on hand angle and clearing vest overlap.
3. **"J-Curve" Draw Path Reps**
    - Students perform partial draws: clear the holster, arc pistol slightly outward, then return to holster.

- Instructor ensures path clears the armor without "scraping" the pistol against the plate carrier.

Phase 2: Dry-Fire Draw to Presentation

Objective: Link the modified access with a clean extension.

1. **Elbow & Shoulder Isolation Drill**
   - Students draw in slow motion.
   - Instructor watches for elbow contact with armor—corrects with outward rotation.
2. **Wall Index Drill**
   - Stand 2–3 feet from a wall.
   - Draw pistol and extend without striking the wall (forces outward clearance, not chest drag).
3. **Clear to Sight Picture Drill**
   - Full dry-fire draw stroke to a sight picture on a safe target.
   - Emphasize consistency of modified motion.
   - 10 sets of 10 repetitions (100 total).

Phase 3: Live-Fire Fundamentals

Objective: Transfer modified draw into controlled fire under minimal stress.

1. **Single Shot Draw**
   - From duty holster with armor, draw and fire one accurate shot at 7 yards.
   - Focus: clean access, no plate interference.
   - 5 strings of 5 repetitions (25 total).
2. **Two-Shot Cadence Drill**

- Same draw, but fire two shots.
- Emphasis: maintain pistol stability despite slightly altered grip path.

3. **Failure-to-Clear Drill**
    - If pistol bumps armor or snag occurs, shooter must reset, fix body mechanics, and re-engage.
    - This reinforces adapting under pressure rather than forcing bad reps.

Phase 4: Stress and Movement Integration

Objective: Build subconscious competence under real-world conditions.

1. **Shot Timer Drill**
    - Random start beep, draw and fire one accurate shot at 7 yards.
    - Goal: consistent sub-1.5s draw with plates (goal adjusted per skill level).
2. **Movement Integration**
    - Add step left/right on draw to simulate real-world engagement with body armor weight shift.
    - Reinforces hip-driven movement instead of blocked torso bending.
3. **Seated Vehicle Drill**
    - Student seated in mock patrol car / armored vehicle seat.
    - Practice accessing pistol with armor bulk restricting torso flexion.
    - Instructor cue: emphasize hip rotation and lateral hand entry.

Phase 5: Force-on-Force / Scenario

Objective: Validate under tactical pressure.

- **Force-on-Force Scenario (Simunition / UTM)**

- Role-player threat emerges, officer must draw and engage from holster while wearing armor.
- Evaluated on speed, clean access, and weapon retention integrity.
- Debrief after each scenario for correction.

Instructor Notes

- Require **all training in full armor**—otherwise, students revert to their unarmored draw habits.
- Vary **plate carrier types** (SAPI, shooter cut, swimmer cut) for adaptability.
- Emphasize **biomechanical economy**: the modified stroke should not be a "workaround," but a repeatable, efficient motion.
- Use **video playback** so students can see where their draw collides with armor.

Modified Pistol Draw Stroke with Body Armor and Plates

Instructor Training Module

Introduction

When wearing body armor with rifle plates, armed professionals must make specific adjustments to their pistol draw stroke. The armor adds bulk, limits range of motion, and alters natural access to the duty belt holster. If these adjustments are not trained until automatic, the draw stroke will be slowed, snagged, or incomplete under stress.

This module provides instructors with a structured progression—from dry-fire to scenario training—that builds efficient, biomechanical consistency for drawing and presenting a pistol while wearing plates.

Key Adjustments

1. **Grip Access:** Widen hand angle to avoid armor overlap and establish a full grip.
2. **Elbow & Shoulder Path:** Drive elbow outward, not back into the plate.
3. **Draw Arc:** Use a slight outward "J-curve" to clear vest bulk.
4. **Retention Systems:** Rotate wrist outward slightly to reliably defeat holster locks.
5. **Hip Rotation:** Move from the hips instead of trying to bend or twist against plate restriction.

Drill Progression

Phase 1: Dry-Fire Mechanics

Objective: Build awareness of armor interference and ingrain the modified stroke.

- **Armor Check Drill** – Slow draw in front of mirror/partner to identify snag points.
- **Grip Acquisition Reps** – 25–50 reps of establishing firing grip without full draw.
- **J-Curve Path Reps** – Draw halfway, clear vest, return to holster.

Coaching Cues:

- "Elbow out, not back."
- "Clear the vest, don't scrape it."
- "Full firing grip every time."

Phase 2: Dry-Fire Presentation

Objective: Link modified access to a smooth extension.

- **Elbow & Shoulder Isolation Drill** – Focus on outward elbow rotation.

- **Wall Index Drill** – 2–3 feet from wall, extend without striking it.
- **Sight Picture Reps** – 100 total dry-fire draws to target focus.

Phase 3: Live-Fire Fundamentals

Objective: Confirm clean, reliable access under live conditions.

- **Single Shot Draw (7 yds)** – 25 reps focusing on clearing armor.
- **Two-Shot Cadence Drill** – Reinforce grip stability after modified draw.
- **Failure-to-Clear Reset Drill** – If snag occurs, reset immediately and correct mechanics.

Phase 4: Stress & Movement Integration

Objective: Build subconscious competence under pressure.

- **Timer Drill** – Draw & fire 1 shot on beep, goal <1.5s with plates.
- **Lateral Step Drill** – Draw while stepping left/right to simulate engagement.
- **Seated Draw Drill** – Practice from patrol car/vehicle seat, emphasizing hip rotation.

Phase 5: Force-on-Force Scenarios

Objective: Validate under tactical pressure.

- **Simunitions / UTM Engagements** – Student must draw and engage role-player while wearing armor.
- **Evaluation:** Speed, clean access, retention integrity.
- **Debrief:** Immediate correction and reinforcement.

Instructor Notes

- Train **only in full armor**—students revert to unarmored habits otherwise.
- Demonstrate with **different plate cuts** (SAPI, shooter, swimmer) to show variation.
- Record **video playback** for feedback on snag points and wasted motion.
- Stress **biomechanical economy**—the modified draw must remain efficient, not clumsy.

Performance Standards

- **Consistency:** 90% clean draws without snagging.
- **Speed:** Sub-1.5 seconds to first shot (adjust for agency standard).
- **Accuracy:** First-round hit within an 8-inch circle at 7 yards.
- **Adaptability:** Ability to draw effectively while standing, moving, and seated.

Summary:
Drawing a pistol from a duty belt while wearing plates requires deliberate modifications. The professional must adjust grip angle, elbow path, and presentation arc while training the body to move from the hips, not the restricted torso. With structured, progressive training, the modified draw stroke becomes natural and reliable, ensuring the armed professional remains combat-effective under real-world conditions.

The dynamics change significantly

The dynamics **change significantly** when the pistol is the secondary weapon and a slung rifle hangs in front of the shooter. The body armor plates are only part of the interference; the rifle creates an additional obstacle that must be managed **without losing control of the**

primary weapon. I'll add this as an additional **section of modifications and drills** that integrates seamlessly with the above module

Additional Modifications: Drawing Pistol with a Slung Rifle

When the pistol is the **secondary weapon**, the shooter must draw around an empty (or malfunctioned) rifle hanging across the front of the plate carrier. This introduces added complications in **body mechanics, sling management, and muzzle awareness**.

Key Modifications

1. **Rifle Control Before Draw**
    - **Problem:** If the rifle is not managed first, it can block holster access, tangle with the pistol, or swing dangerously during the draw.
    - **Adjustment:** Establish a consistent method to control or stow the rifle before initiating the draw. Common options:
        - **Support Hand Control:** Drive the rifle to the support-side hip or thigh with the support hand.
        - **Sling Tension Drop:** Let the sling pull the rifle down and outward, creating clearance.
        - **Hand Trap Method:** Trap the rifle against the body with the support forearm while drawing with the strong hand.

2. **Clearance Path Adjustment**
    - **Problem:** Rifle hangs directly in front of the torso, narrowing the pistol's draw pathway and presentation.
    - **Adjustment:** Modify the pistol's presentation into a slightly **wider, outward arc** to avoid colliding with the rifle's receiver, optic, or sling hardware.

3. **Support Hand Availability**
   - **Problem:** Support hand may be occupied with rifle control, limiting the ability to establish a two-handed pistol grip immediately.
   - **Adjustment:** Accept an initial **strong-hand-only presentation**, then transition to two hands once the pistol is clear and the rifle is stabilized.

4. **Sling Management**
   - **Problem:** Slings can snag on pistol grip, holster, or shooter's arm during the draw.
   - **Adjustment:**
     - Ensure sling is properly adjusted before training (tensioned to allow rifle to drop but not hang excessively).
     - Practice sweeping or rolling the strong arm under/over sling material during the draw until fluid.

5. **Retention Awareness**
   - **Problem:** During high stress, focus may shift entirely to the pistol, causing the rifle to dangle or swing into unsafe positions.
   - **Adjustment:** Reinforce **positive muzzle awareness** of the slung rifle. Students must keep the muzzle down and away from legs and feet at all times.

Drill Additions for Rifle + Pistol Transition

Dry-Fire Transition Mechanics

- Begin with rifle in shoulder, simulate malfunction or empty mag.
- Support hand drives rifle to support-side hip/thigh.
- Strong hand executes modified pistol draw while rifle is controlled.
- Reholster sequence must also include rifle management.

Live-Fire Transition Drills

1. **Primary-to-Secondary Transition Drill**
    - Start with rifle, fire 2–3 rounds, simulate empty.
    - Rifle controlled to side → pistol drawn → engage with 2–3 rounds.
    - Reset and repeat, focusing on clean rifle control.
2. **Strong-Hand Only to Two-Hand Transition Drill**
    - Begin transition with rifle control in support hand.
    - Draw and fire pistol strong-hand only for 1–2 rounds.
    - Once stable, bring support hand to pistol grip and continue engagement.
3. **Movement Integration**
    - Perform transition while stepping laterally or rearward.
    - Emphasize maintaining rifle muzzle down, pistol presentation clear.

Instructor Notes

- Enforce **consistency of rifle management method**—random or sloppy transitions cause snags and wasted time.
- Correct students who try to "fight" the rifle instead of controlling it with sling or support hand.

- Stress **strong-hand-only competency**—a realistic requirement when support hand is occupied.
- Time standard: Sub-2.5 seconds from simulated rifle stoppage to first accurate pistol shot at 7 yards.

Summary:

When the pistol serves as a secondary weapon, the draw stroke must be modified not only for body armor but also for the presence of a slung rifle. Controlling the rifle, managing sling tension, and accepting an initial one-handed pistol presentation are critical skills. With deliberate practice, the transition becomes smooth, safe, and reliable in real-world conditions.

Aggressive Shooting with High Accountability

Over the years I have learned that aggressive, effective shooting is not about recklessness, it is about speed with control, decisiveness with accountability. The two critical elements that allow this balance are **absolute grip control** and **visual confirmation.** When mastered, these foundations give the shooter the ability to shoot sooner, move with purpose, and maintain precision under stress.

The Foundation: Grip and Vision

Every advanced skill in shooting rests on grip and vision. A shooter must lock down an uncompromising grip—**consistent, predictable, and durable**—that does not change under stress, fatigue, or movement. Grip is the anchor that allows recoil management, rapid sight recovery, and the confidence to shoot aggressively without loss of control.

Vision is the governor. It dictates *when* a shot can be fired, and whether it will be accountable. The eyes must stay connected to the exact point of impact. The gun follows the eyes, and the trigger breaks only when the visual confirmation is present.

Movement: A Separate Skill Set

Movement must first be trained as an independent skill before it is paired with live fire. Once shooters understand how to move efficiently, they can begin integrating it with shooting. Movement takes two primary forms:

- **Shooting while moving**
- **Moving into and out of positions** (entries and exits)

The principle is simple but profound: *you want to shoot sooner so that you don't have to shoot faster.* By setting up earlier or maintaining accountability while moving, the shooter eliminates the need to artificially compress split times or push beyond controllable speed.

Shooting Sooner vs. Shooting Faster

This concept represents a decisive advantage in nearly every domain of shooting, whether in combat, law enforcement, or competition. Shooting sooner ensures that accuracy is preserved, accountability is maintained, and time is gained without sacrificing control.

Rushing to shoot faster without the foundation of grip and vision results in missed shots, poor accountability, and diminished confidence. By contrast, shooting sooner is about efficiency: **arrive visually, confirm grip stability, and break the shot at the first accountable opportunity.**

The Standard for Professionals

For instructors, the message is clear: train fundamentals at the highest level. Grip and vision must be overdeveloped—far beyond casual competence—because these skills do not degrade under pressure, they sustain performance. Movement, speed, and dynamic applications are only effective when they are supported by those core fundamentals.

Aggressive shooting is not about reckless speed. It is about **controlled aggression, disciplined fundamentals, and uncompromising accountability.** Grip and vision unlock that potential, and movement, when layered on top, makes the shooter faster without being careless.

The Message is Clear Train the Fundamentals To the Highest Level

Grip and Vision Must Be Overdelevoped

Instructor Training Checklist: Aggressive Shooting with Accountability

1. Grip Fundamentals

- Grip is **consistent, predictable, and durable**
- Establish full hand contact with no shifting under recoil
- Pressure is even, with support hand locking the gun into the dominant hand
- Test grip under fatigue, stress, and during movement
-

2. Vision Control

- Stay visually connected to the exact point of intended impact
- Do not break the shot until a **clear visual confirmation** is present
- Eyes lead, gun follows
- Reinforce that **vision dictates when to shoot**

3. Movement Training (Without Shooting)

- Train entries and exits separately before combining with fire
- Keep body low and stable—avoid bouncing vision off the target
- Maintain grip integrity while moving
- Build efficiency: shortest path, minimal wasted motion

4. Movement with Shooting

- Two applications:
    - Shooting **while moving**
    - Shooting **into/out of positions**
- Principle: *shoot sooner so you don't have to shoot faster*
- Emphasize accountability—no rushed shots, only early accurate ones

5. Performance Standard

- Shots must remain accurate and accountable at speed
- No loss of grip during movement
- Visual confirmation achieved before every trigger press
- Shooter demonstrates ability to arrive, stabilize, and shoot sooner without artificial speed

- ## The B-8 Speed Bull Standard: Instructor Proficiency and Performance
- I just came off the range working a pre-qualification with HSI students, assisted by Firearms Instructor Training Program candidates. Our post-shoot discussion turned to the difference between being able to **shoot** and being able to **instruct**. My position is clear: in any field, and especially in firearms, instructors must maintain a performance level above their students. Competence is not enough—credibility demands proficiency.
- To demonstrate that proficiency, I set a standard. Any instructor should be able to fire **10 rounds in 10 seconds at 25 yards on a B-8 target** and score a minimum of **70 points**. This drill reflects a foundational understanding of sights, structure, and trigger control under the pressure of time. Shooting at 5 and 7 yards can make anyone look like a hero, but distance exposes flaws. The **25-yard line tells no lies**—it reveals whether the fundamentals are intact or if bad habits are hidden behind close-range speed.
- This benchmark is not universally popular, particularly among so-called instructors who rely on rudimentary skills and self-identify as "trigger pullers." But once speed enters the equation, the truth emerges: **grip outweighs trigger in importance.** A locked-in vision on the sight package, supported by a rock-solid grip, provides the consistent, predictable, and durable platform required for rapid trigger manipulations. Without that grip, the best trigger press in the world falls apart under time stress.
- The B-8 speed bull drill is not just a test of marksmanship—it is a litmus test for instruction. If you cannot execute at this standard, you have little business standing in front of students as a credible authority.
- At the instructor level, performance must consistently reflect mastery of the fundamentals executed with precision. The instructor's grip must demonstrate the correct balance of tension and friction, making recoil predictable and repeatable

across distance and speed. This example reinforces for students that a properly established grip is the foundation of consistent shooting performance and far outweighs trigger manipulation in importance. Achieving and maintaining 90% accuracy or better provides clear evidence that speed and accuracy are not incompatible goals. This is not an advanced technique—it is simply the application of basic fundamentals performed to a higher, instructor-level standard.

- Speed and accuracy are not mutually exclusive and any instructor that is able to demonstrate a 90 or better on a Speed Bull has firmly established to students the ability to place very accurate fire (90/100 on a B-8) in under 10 seconds (sub second splits) should be their goal!

-

No Light/Low Light

No Light/Low Light an analysis of **law enforcement officer (LEO) shooting accuracy**, focusing on hit/miss percentages, lighting conditions, and officer positioning—based on available studies. Unfortunately, detailed data on lightning (i.e. weather/electrical) conditions during shootings isn't publicly available. However, we do have relevant insights regarding visibility (like daylight vs. nighttime) and positional contexts when officers fired.

Hit-Miss Statistics

Dallas PD (2003–2017)

- **Incident-level accuracy**: In single-officer, single-suspect shootings, officers hit the suspect **at least once** in about **54%** of incidents.
- **Bullet-level accuracy**: Out of **354 total rounds**, only **~35%** of rounds struck the target—meaning **65%** missed. A separate literature review corroborates this: incident hit rate ~54%, bullet hit rate ~35%.

New York Police Department (NYPD)

- In situations where **gunfire was not returned**, average hit rate was around **30%**.
- In **active gunfights**, the hit rate dropped to **18%**.

Older Studies & Broad Trends

- Hit rates across various U.S. jurisdictions "**rarely exceed 50%**"—officers miss targets as often or more often than they hit them.
- Specific older data:
    - Michigan (1976–81): **27%** hit rate.

- NYPD (1987): **26%**; (1988): **31%**; (1990): **23%**.
  - Los Angeles: in the 1970s **56%**, but dropped to **28%** in the 1980s.
  - Metro-Dade, Florida (1984–88): **31%**
- A PolitiFact assessment concluded that while "less than 30%" as a general statement is only partially accurate, hit rates can indeed be below 30% depending on the agency and context.

Lighting Conditions (Daylight vs. Night)

Dallas PD study:

- **Daylight shooting incidents** were significantly more likely to result in a hit than those occurring during evening or overnight hours. This suggests visibility plays a critical role in accuracy.

Officer Position & Context of Shooting

Although there's limited data explicitly detailing officer stance or posture during shootings, some relevant factors emerge:

- **Gunfire return**: When officers are under fire, accuracy drops significantly (e.g., NYPD's 18% hit rate in gunfight versus 30% when not under fire). This implies stress and positioning adjustments under threat degrade precision.
- **Stress and movement**: High-stress, time-pressured situations impair marksmanship. A review noted that probable inaccuracies stem from anxiety, the rarity of firearm use, and the inherently stressful nature of real-world shootings.
- **Positional movement complexities**: Although not LEO-specific, research covering human dynamics emphasizes that shooter and target movement—especially of hands and arms—occurs faster than an officer's ability to respond accurately, making accurate hits in dynamic scenarios especially difficult.

Aspect	Key Insights
Hit Rate	Incident-level: ~54% (Dallas PD); Bullet-level: ~35%—many misses in real situations.
Cross-Agency Variation	Older data: Michigan ~27%, NYPD ~23–31%, LAPD ~28–56%, Metro-Dade ~31–100%. Overall, rarely above 50%.
Under Fire	Accuracy drops—NYPD: ~30% when not shot at, ~18% during gunfire.
Lighting	Daylight incidents more likely to result in hits than night.
Movement & Stress	Movement and stress significantly impair precision; realistic training needed.

Additional Instructor Knowledge

Real-world data consistently shows that law enforcement shooting accuracy is frequently modest, with hit rates often below 50% and individual round hit rates often in the 18–35% range depending on context. **Daylight and absence of return fire yield better outcomes**, while stress, movement, and low visibility degrade precision. However, **data**

on lighting anomalies (like storms or flashes) and officer body positioning remains largely undocumented.

No-Light, Low-Light, and Weapon-Mounted Light Employment for Law Enforcement Officers

Training Progression, Employment Considerations, and Lessons from Military Applications

1. Why Low-Light Training Is Non-Negotiable

Statistics and real-world encounters consistently reveal that a significant percentage of officer-involved shootings occur in diminished light conditions. Darkness conceals threats, degrades situational awareness, and magnifies stress. Many officers instinctively rely on technology (weapon-mounted lights or optics) without first mastering the fundamentals of sight alignment and target identification in no-light and low-light conditions. This is a critical gap. Technology is a force multiplier, not a substitute for skill.

Before introducing weapon-mounted lights, officers must understand how to effectively operate with iron sights in reduced visibility. If a light fails or conditions make light use tactically or legally inappropriate, the officer must still be able to deliver accurate fire.

2. Training Plan Progression: No Light → Low Light → Weapon-Mounted Lights

A structured progression builds both competence and confidence. Training should be layered and scenario-driven.

Phase 1: No-Light Fundamentals

- **Objective:** Teach officers to maintain sight alignment and trigger control with degraded visual cues.
- **Training Elements:**
    - Dry fire in a darkened environment to build proprioception and kinesthetic alignment.
    - Indexing and presenting the pistol without over-reliance on visual feedback.
    - Flash-sight picture techniques and front sight focus under minimal visual references.
    - Target discrimination drills using silhouettes or shapes that require identification by shape and movement rather than detail.

Phase 2: Low-Light Training

- **Objective:** Introduce external light sources and develop the ability to leverage available light.
- **Training Elements:**
    - Using ambient light sources (streetlights, headlights, windows) for target identification.
    - Drills on adjusting vision and adapting to changing light conditions.
    - Integration of handheld light techniques (Harries, FBI, neck index, etc.) to separate illumination from muzzle direction, minimizing the risk of flagging non-threats.
    - Movement drills emphasizing light discipline and minimizing silhouetting.

Phase 3: Weapon-Mounted Light (WML) Employment

- **Objective:** Teach officers to employ weapon-mounted lights responsibly and tactically.
- **Training Elements:**
    - Mechanics: momentary vs. constant-on activation, switch manipulation under stress.
    - Target identification and positive threat verification before engaging.
    - Integrating WML with sight picture and recoil control.
    - Avoiding over-reliance on WML; reinforcing that muzzle should not be used as a flashlight indiscriminately.
    - Scenario-based force-on-force emphasizing shoot/no-shoot decisions under dynamic lighting.

Instructor's Note: The progression should incorporate decision-making stress. The ultimate goal is *target identification first, shooting second*. Every round fired in low light must meet legal and moral standards for deadly force.

One Light is No Light!

Run a weapons Light But always have a Handheld backup light

Be Prepared

3. Legal Considerations in Light Employment

Law enforcement officers face significant legal and civil liability in low-light encounters. Key points include:

- **Muzzle Discipline:** Weapon-mounted lights should not be used as a general-purpose flashlight. Pointing a firearm at an unidentified person simply to illuminate them may constitute aggravated assault or brandishing in some jurisdictions.
- **Target Identification:** Every shot must be justifiable. Failure to properly identify a target due to inadequate training can lead to tragic mistakes and legal consequences.
- **Documentation and Training:** Agencies should ensure officers receive documented low-light/WML training to defend their actions in court. Policies must explicitly define acceptable uses of light.

4. Military vs. Law Enforcement Applications: Lessons and Differences

Military units typically operate with a **rifle as the primary weapon**, transitioning to a handgun only as a secondary. Military rules of engagement often allow for broader use of weapon lights as part of offensive maneuvers in combat zones. Law enforcement encounters, however, are governed by constitutional use-of-force standards and the need to protect civilians in populated environments.

Key distinctions:

- **Mission Focus:** Military operations are generally offensive; law enforcement is defensive and reactive.
- **Collateral Risk:** LE engagements often occur around innocent bystanders; the need for target discrimination is higher.
- **Weapon Transition:** Military personnel typically transition from rifle to pistol when the primary is unavailable (malfunction, confined spaces). LE officers may only have a handgun as their primary, making low-light pistol proficiency non-negotiable.

5. Practical Recommendations for Agencies

- **Policy Development:** Clear guidelines on WML and handheld light usage.
- **Scenario-Based Training:** Include building searches, traffic stops, and domestic encounters in no-light/low-light.
- **Instructor Development:** Train-the-trainer programs to ensure department-wide competency.
- **Periodic Requalification:** Incorporate low-light modules into annual or semi-annual firearms qualification.

Conclusion

Mastering no-light and low-light engagements is not a luxury—it is a duty. Officers who cannot see, identify, and engage threats ethically and tactically in diminished light conditions risk mission failure, injury, and liability. By progressing from iron sight fundamentals in no light, to ambient light exploitation, to disciplined weapon-mounted light use, officers develop layered competence that aligns with both tactical necessity and legal responsibility.

I have tried to create a comprehensive, professional-level breakdown of efficient flashlight techniques for law enforcement officers (LEOs), I have structured separate **search techniques** from **shooting techniques**, while also addressing the integration of **weapon-mounted lights (WMLs)** and the legal and tactical considerations unique to law enforcement.

The Role of Flashlights in Law Enforcement

For law enforcement officers, flashlights are more than illumination tools—they're essential for target identification, officer safety, and legal justification in use-of-force encounters. Proper training ensures officers understand when and how to use handheld and weapon-mounted lights without compromising safety or escalating legal risk.

I. Search Techniques (Handheld Flashlights)

When searching with a flashlight, the officer's primary goal is **to gather information and identify threats without unnecessarily revealing their position or telegraphing intent.** Effective search techniques minimize exposure and maximize control over the light beam.

1. Harries Search Technique

- **Method:** Flashlight is held in the support hand under the firing hand, back of the hands pressed together.
- **Advantages:** Creates a stable platform if a shot is needed; allows tight beam control; keeps the beam aligned with potential threats.
- **Search Use:** While often taught for shooting, Harries can be adapted for deliberate searching when moving tactically in confined spaces.

2. FBI Technique

- **Method:** Flashlight held away from the body at head height or above; not directly in front of the officer.
- **Advantages:** Disassociates light from officer's center mass, reducing risk of drawing fire; allows quick light-on/light-off "painting" of areas.
- **Search Use:** Excellent for scanning rooms or open spaces; light can be flashed intermittently to reduce exposure.

3. Neck Index / Jaw Index Technique

- **Method:** Flashlight held tight against jawline or neck with support hand; beam follows line of sight.
- **Advantages:** Intuitive; allows easy movement and scanning; keeps beam aligned with eyes.
- **Search Use:** Works well indoors, provides strong control and quick transition to firearm use.

4. Modified FBI / Low-Ready Search

- **Method:** Flashlight angled downward toward the floor or ground, illuminating an area indirectly.
- **Advantages:** Minimizes backscatter when used near walls; prevents light from blinding the officer; reduces silhouetting.
- **Search Use:** Ideal for moving through unknown areas; indirect lighting preserves night vision and surprise.

5. Strobe and Momentary-On Usage

- **Method:** Using momentary-on switches for brief bursts or strobing to disorient threats.
- **Advantages:** Prevents constant beacon effect; preserves officer's tactical advantage.
- **Search Use:** Use intermittently, not as a constant mode, to avoid telegraphing movement.

II. Shooting Techniques (Handheld Flashlights)

When shots may need to be fired, flashlight technique must allow **sight alignment, trigger control, and recoil management** while also enabling positive threat identification.

1. Harries Shooting Technique

- **Application:** Same position as for search; creates an isometric tension between hands for stability.
- **Use Case:** Works best in confined spaces; aligns light with firearm bore.
- **Considerations:** Requires training to avoid sweeping hands across muzzle.

2. Rogers / SureFire Technique

- **Method:** Flashlight is held between index and middle finger of support hand; pressed against firearm with tailcap activated.
- **Advantages:** Allows nearly full two-handed grip; ideal with small handheld lights with tail switches.
- **Considerations:** Requires proper hand fit and dexterity; not ideal with larger flashlights.

3. Neck Index Shooting

- **Method:** Same as search version; beam aligns naturally with line of sight.
- **Advantages:** Natural, quick to deploy under stress; less fatiguing than Harries.
- **Considerations:** Not as stable for extended shooting as Rogers or Harries.

4. Chapman / Ayoob Technique

- **Method:** Light held like a syringe in support hand, thumb operating switch; allows two-handed support on gun.
- **Advantages:** Works well with larger flashlights; comfortable grip.
- **Considerations:** Requires practice to maintain alignment and control.

Training Emphasis for Shooting with Handhelds:

- Light should be used sparingly and momentarily; **positive identification is mandatory before trigger press.**
- Officers must avoid "light fixation" (keeping light constantly on target), which creates a predictable aiming point for threats.

III. Weapon-Mounted Light (WML) Integration

Weapon-mounted lights are increasingly common for duty pistols and patrol rifles. They enhance control but introduce **unique training and legal considerations** for law enforcement.

1. Benefits:

- Allows full two-handed grip on firearm.
- Provides constant alignment of bore and light.

- Superior for dynamic or high-stress engagements.

2. Drawbacks and Legal Concerns:

- **Muzzle Discipline:** A WML points wherever the muzzle points; searching with a WML risks flagging non-threats.
- **Legal Implications:** Courts have scrutinized officers who illuminate persons or property with a firearm-mounted light without legal justification.
  - **Best Practice:** Search with handheld light; transition to WML only when lawful deadly force is reasonably anticipated.

3. Training Integration:

- Teach **handheld-first, WML-second** sequence: search with handheld light, transition to WML only when weapon presentation is justified.
- Practice **low-ready WML scanning:** muzzle angled downward, illuminating via spill light to avoid unnecessary muzzling.
- Drills should include transitioning between handheld and WML under stress, including malfunction clearance and reloads.

IV. Operational and Policy Considerations

- **Light Discipline:** Officers should train to use light in short, controlled bursts—never as a constant beacon unless needed.
- **Equipment Selection:** Lights should have sufficient lumens (modern standard: 500–1000+) with momentary switches and durable mounts.
- **Policy Alignment:** Agency policies should specify when and how handheld vs. WMLs may be used for searching and illumination.

Weapon Mounted Lights

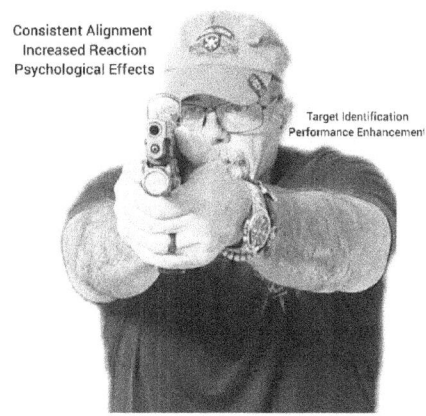

Conclusion: Training Builds Confidence and Legal Safety

Flashlight proficiency is not just about tactics—it's about survivability and liability. Officers who train extensively with both handheld and weapon-mounted lights can **identify threats accurately, reduce risk to bystanders, and articulate their actions clearly in court.**

Properly separating search and shooting techniques, and understanding when to integrate WMLs, ensures that officers can make legally defensible, tactically sound decisions under stress.

Lesson Plan: Low-Light Flashlight Techniques for Law Enforcement Officers

Course Title:

Low-Light Flashlight Employment for Law Enforcement

Duration:

4–6 hours (classroom + live-fire practical)

Target Audience:

Sworn law enforcement officers; adaptable for academy recruits or in-service training.

Instructor:

[Instructor Name, Credentials]

1. Learning Objectives

Upon completion, students will be able to:

1. Explain the tactical and legal importance of flashlight use in law enforcement.
2. Demonstrate effective **handheld search techniques** and apply proper light discipline.
3. Demonstrate effective **handheld shooting techniques** under low-light conditions.
4. Understand and articulate the **legal considerations** of weapon-mounted light (WML) use.
5. Transition smoothly between handheld and WML during realistic scenarios.
6. Make sound threat identification and use-of-force decisions in low-light environments.

2. Safety Considerations

- Strict adherence to the four firearm safety rules at all times.
- Clear and brief all students on range and scenario safety procedures.
- Use blue guns or inert weapons during dry drills.

- On live-fire range: clearly designate light-on/light-off commands and cease-fire procedures.
- Ensure adequate illumination for emergency medical response on range.

3. Instructional Content Outline

A. Introduction (Classroom – 45 min)

- The role of flashlights in officer safety and legal defense.
- Statistics: % of LE shootings occur in low-light (FBI UCR data).
- Common risks: silhouetting, target misidentification, legal exposure.
- Light discipline principles: *momentary vs constant-on*, backscatter, cover and movement.

B. Search Techniques (Dry Demo – 45 min)

- **FBI technique**: offset light for officer survivability.
- **Neck/Jaw Index**: intuitive scanning and fast transitions.
- **Modified low-angle search**: indirect lighting to minimize exposure.
- **Momentary vs strobe use**; avoiding "flashlight fixation."

C. Shooting Techniques (Dry Demo – 45 min)

- Harries, Rogers/SureFire, Neck Index, Chapman/Ayoob.
- Pros/cons, ergonomics, and application in different environments.
- Dry practice with inert guns: light activation + trigger press alignment.

D. Weapon-Mounted Light (WML) Considerations (Classroom/Demo – 30 min)

- Benefits: two-handed control, bore/light alignment.
- Drawbacks: legal risks, muzzle discipline.
- Agency policy discussion; when to transition from handheld to WML.

4. Practical Exercises & Drills (Range – 2.5–3 hours)

Drill 1: Search Patterns (Dry & Live)

- Dim/no-light environment; handheld light only.
- Search a room or lane using each technique.
- Identify threat/non-threat targets; no shots fired initially.
- **Objective:** Light discipline, positive identification.

Drill 2: Search-to-Shoot Transitions

- Targets include threats (armed photo silhouettes) and no-shoots.
- Begin with handheld light in search mode; transition to shooting if justified.
- Use Harries and Rogers techniques with live fire.
- **Objective:** Decision-making under low light, correct technique.

Drill 3: Light & Move

- On command, illuminate briefly, fire, move laterally.
- Repeat using momentary light only.
- **Objective:** Break habit of being stationary; integrates movement + light.

Drill 4: WML Integration

- Search with handheld light.
- Upon threat cue, transition to WML (holster or activate mounted light).
- Engage target; practice reloading and malfunction drills with WML.
- **Objective:** Smooth transition, muzzle discipline with WML.

Drill 5: Force-on-Force (Optional, if resources available)

- Use marking rounds or Simunitions.
- Role players in darkened rooms.
- Student must use light to ID threats; legally articulate decision after.
- **Objective:** Scenario-based judgment training.

5. Evaluation Criteria

Students will be evaluated on:

- **Knowledge:** Participation in discussion; passing a written or oral quiz on legal/tactical considerations.
- **Skills:** Proper light use, safe handling, and ability to demonstrate at least two search and two shooting techniques with 100% safe muzzle discipline.
- **Decision-Making:** Correct threat identification and use-of-force decisions in low-light scenarios.

6. Required Equipment

- Duty pistol and/or rifle with holster/sling.
- Handheld flashlight (500+ lumens recommended) with momentary switch.
- Weapon-mounted light (if issued).

- Inert training gun for dry work.
- Protective gear (eye/ear pro, ballistic vest if required).
- Targets: threat/non-threat photo silhouettes, no-shoot overlays.
- Cones or barricades for cover simulation.

7. Instructor Notes & Tips

- Begin with dry runs; add stress and live fire gradually.
- Emphasize articulation: students should be able to explain why they illuminated and why they fired.
- Use backlighting and barriers on range to replicate real-world low-light conditions.
- Incorporate after-action review: "What did you see? What did you decide?"

The Importance of Dry Fire

Dry fire is non-negotiable — not an optional extra, but the bedrock of competent, repeatable performance. In Special Forces classrooms we finished brutal live-fire days and then went straight to deliberate, unhurried dry-fire work for hours because that intentional repetition forges mechanical consistency, ironclad discipline, and unshakeable confidence. Dry-fire trains the nervous system to do the right thing under stress: refined trigger control, reliable sight alignment, a repeatable presentation from the holster, and the muscle memory that turns hesitation into instinctive action. As an instructor you must understand dry-fire's variants — from dead-trigger diagnostics to cognitive integration drills — so you can accurately diagnose breakdowns, prescribe focused repetitions, and progressively overload students without live rounds. Teach it hard, teach it often, and demand precise execution: when dry-fire is institutionalized in your program, novices stop guessing and start performing — and armed professionals leave your class prepared, composed, and capable when it matters most.

Safety Imperative: When engaging in dry fire, handle your unloaded pistol with the same rigor and protocols as you would a loaded firearm. Compromising on safety—even in the absence of ammunition—invites hazardous habits that could prove catastrophic in live scenarios.

Core Dry Fire Principles for Armed Professionals

Dry-fire is not a warm-up — it is the curriculum. For armed professionals it isolates the essential building blocks of marksmanship so those blocks can be stacked reliably under stress. For instructors it provides the diagnostic microscope: remove the noise of recoil and live ammunition and you see exactly where the motor program, timing, and decision loop are failing. Teach dry-fire first, teach it always, and treat mastery of its fundamentals as the gate through which all competence must pass.

1. **Dry Fire Develops All Fundamentals except Recoil Management**
   This method refines grip, trigger control, presentation, sight alignment and picture, target transitions, draw strokes, and reloads. Its sole limitation resides in the inability to replicate the physical forces of recoil, which necessitates complementary live fire practice.

2. **Leveraging Dead Trigger for Grip Assessment**
   A well-executed dead trigger repetition enables instructors to evaluate pistol stability under simulated stress. Weak or imbalanced grips cause the sight package to shift; a proper grip maintains immobility. This setup fosters an ideal environment for precise diagnostics and corrective feedback.

3. **Consistency, Predictability, and Repeatability (CPR)**
   Transform every action into a reliable pattern:
   - **Consistent:** Deliver identical inputs on each iteration.
   - **Predictable:** Yield the same outcome reliably.
   - **Repeatable:** Sustain performance amid time constraints, fatigue, or elevated stress.

4. **Time and Dedication Yield Proficiency**
   Repetition propels mastery. Neurological research and expert consensus indicate that achieving subconscious execution—transitioning a skill from deliberate thought to automatic response—often demands thousands of deliberate repetitions. Dry fire provides an economical, safe avenue to accumulate this volume.

Teaching Dry Fire to Novice Shooters

Introduce dry fire methodically to novices, prioritizing safety and foundational understanding:

- **Begin with Simplicity:** Initiate dry fire only after thoroughly explaining firearm safety rules, muzzle discipline, and standard range commands.
- **Incorporate Realism Progressively:** Novices often falter during the shift from dry to live fire due to the absence of recoil, muzzle flash, and report in training. Mitigate this by clarifying from the start: "Dry fire hones mechanical precision; live fire cultivates reactions and recoil mastery."
- **Foster Early Confidence:** Commence with straightforward exercises, such as wall drills or trigger presses on large, proximate targets.
- **Employ Precise Terminology:** Adopt clear, accurate language—favor "press" over "pull" for the trigger, and specify "target-focused" or "sight-focused" when discussing visual alignment.
- **Evaluate Grip Pathways:** Guide students to replicate their grip identically each time, encouraging them to decelerate and sense the progressive buildup of pressure before initiating a draw.

Teaching Dry Fire to Intermediate Shooters

For shooters advancing beyond basics, escalate complexity to bridge training toward real-world application:

- **Incorporate Layered Challenges:** Integrate advanced tasks like concealed carry draws, reloads, and multi-target transitions.
- **Apply Pressure Elements:** Introduce timed benchmarks, decision-making drills, and stress inoculation techniques, such as verbal prompts or auditory distractions.

- **Hone Mechanical Precision:** Utilize video recordings or mirrors to verify clean movement trajectories, ensuring pistol presentation aligns with the eye-target line and sight acquisition occurs seamlessly.
- **Implement Dead Trigger Diagnostics:** At this stage, expose shooters to aggressive trigger inputs on a dead trigger. This reveals deficiencies in grip stability, hand positioning, and unintended sympathetic tensions.

Practical Dry Fire Drills for All Proficiency Levels

These versatile drills reinforce key skills across novice, intermediate, and advanced shooters:

1. **Draw to Sight Picture Drill**
    - Cultivate a uniform draw trajectory.
    - Ensure the sight package settles precisely on the target without oscillation or descent.
2. **Dead Trigger Grip Assessment Drill**
    - Employ a dead trigger and execute forceful presses.
    - Instructors monitor for sight disturbances; any dot or sight movement signals grip flaws.
3. **Target Transition Drill**
    - Propel the pistol between targets while preserving a level sight package.
    - Avoid mimicking recoil motions.
4. **Reload Repetitions**
    - Perform repeated magazine exchanges with eyes fixed on the target.
    - Verify consistent magazine indexing and insertion.
5. **Structural and Movement Rehearsals**
    - "Dirt dive" scenarios such as stage navigation, room clearance, or dynamic sequences.

- Dry fire transitions, postural adjustments, and movement efficiencies.

Configuring Dead Trigger Press by Pistol Type

Adapt dead trigger setups to firearm mechanisms for optimal training:

- **Double-Action Pistols:**
  Press through the double-action pull; post-hammer fall, continue pressing without reset.
- **Single-Action Pistols:**
  Following the initial press, refrain from resetting; perform subsequent repetitions on the dead trigger.
- **Striker-Fired Pistols:**
  Inhibit reset by inserting a rubber band or index card into the breech, holding the slide slightly out of battery.

Instructor Advisory: Direct students to press with maximum intensity—the greater the force, the more readily subtle grip weaknesses emerge.

Final Guidance for Instructors

Dry fire does not supplant live fire; it underpins it. As an instructor, you must:

- Articulate precisely what dry fire accomplishes and its limitations.
- Embed dry fire into curricula at every instructional tier.
- Diagnose issues in grip, trigger control, and presentation more expediently than during range sessions.

Reinforce this axiom: "Dry fire programs the skills; live fire tests them." When students deliver flawless, consistent, and resilient dry fire repetitions, they stand prepared to translate those competencies into live environments—with assured confidence, command, and poise.

Comparative Analysis: Live Trigger Dry Fire, Dead Trigger Dry Fire, and Ball and Dummy Drills

This section delineates three pivotal dry fire variants, highlighting their definitions, objectives, distinctions, and applications.

1. **Live Trigger Dry Fire**
   Definition: Involves pressing the trigger to release the striker or hammer, mimicking an actual discharge. The trigger retains "live" resistance and breaks, common in striker- and hammer-fired systems. Slide cycling resets the trigger between repetitions.
   Purpose:
   - Hone trigger press mechanics.
   - Detect and rectify anticipation, flinching, or heeling.
   - Strengthen sight alignment and stability through the break.
   - Develop neuromuscular pathways for fluid, controlled presses.
     Feedback Mechanism: Sight or red dot deviations at the break reveal errors; augment with lasers or dot trackers.

2. **Dead Trigger Dry Fire**
   Definition: Conducted with a spent trigger that offers no break or striker fall, following an initial dry fire without reset. In striker-fired pistols, the trigger remains slack post-press unless racked; DA/SA variants may yield a double-action pull.
   Purpose:
   - Refine mechanics independent of trigger breaks.

- Foster consistency in draw strokes, grip presentation, reloads, target transitions, and recoil follow-through.

    Feedback Mechanism: Focuses on visual and kinematic consistency, excluding trigger dynamics; facilitates high-repetition volumes sans resets.

3. **Ball and Dummy Drills (Live or Simulated)**

    Definition: Intersperses live rounds with inert dummies in a magazine, or simulates via unpredictable outcomes in dry fire. Aims to unmask anticipation under uncertainty; in live fire, dummies expose pre-ignition movements.

    Purpose:
    - Identify and correct flinching or recoil anticipation.
    - Cultivate mental fortitude amid stress.
    - Bolster trigger consistency irrespective of results.

    Feedback Mechanism: Observable reactions—dips, flinches, blinks, or jerks—when no discharge occurs.

Feature	Live Trigger Dry Fire	Dead Trigger Dry Fire	Ball and Dummy Drills
Trigger Status	Functional (breaks)	Non-functional (no break)	Mixed (some break, some don't)
Slide Reset Required	Yes (striker-fired guns)	No	No (dry fire) / Yes (live fire)
Primary Focus	Trigger control, sight stability	Mechanics, grip, transitions	Anticipation, mental discipline
Best For	Precision dry fire drills	Volume reps, reloads, transitions	Diagnosing flinch in live/dry fire
Feedback Type	Visual on sights/dot at break	Visual/motion (not trigger)	Shooter reaction to unexpected result

Feature	Live Trigger Dry Fire	Dead Trigger Dry Fire	Ball and Dummy Drills
Risk of Poor Habit	Low if done slowly and correctly	Medium if repeated with poor form	High if flinch is not corrected immediately
Need for Live Ammo?	No	No	Yes (traditional) / No (simulated)

Instructor-Level Comprehension of Dry Fire

Defining Dry Fire: Dry fire entails deliberate firearm manipulation and marksmanship practice absent live ammunition. It encompasses neuromuscular conditioning, cognitive reinforcement, and procedural ingraining, constructing skills without recoil's interference to pinpoint and rectify subtle errors.

Instructor Objectives:

- Generate impeccable, automated repetitions of core shooting behaviors.
- Eliminate distractions like recoil, noise, and environmental pressures for micro-error diagnosis.
- Perfect sight pictures, trigger control, grips, draws, reloads, and transitions at optimal cadences.
- Condition skills for emergencies, movements, and concealment in a secure, efficient manner.
- Enhance decision-making via dry decision drills or mental simulations.

Dry fire blueprints the gunfighter's capabilities; live fire validates them.

Key Observations for Instructors during Dry Fire

Scrutinize student performance to identify and address deficiencies:

1. **Trigger Press Mechanics**
    - Ensure straight-rearward motion without lateral deviation.
    - Verify finger placement suits the firearm (neither excessive nor insufficient).
    - Monitor for proper prepping and staging in compressed positions.
2. **Sight Stability at Break**
    - Sights or dots must remain static as the trigger breaks.
    - Red dots should hold center in the window through press and follow-through.
3. **Grip Integrity**
    - Maintain isometric tension between hands.
    - Prevent collapse or compensatory adjustments during presses.
    - Secure high tang positioning without slippage down the backstrap.
4. **Visual Discipline**
    - Align focus with the task: target- or dot-oriented.
    - Eliminate glances at the firearm, particularly in reloads or draws.
    - Detect overrides, such as head lifts pre-press.
5. **Efficient Mechanics**
    - Draw strokes: Repeatable, body-proximate, assertive, and linear.
    - Reloads: Consistent magazine indexing without fumbling.
    - Transitions: Snappy muzzle drives, not drags.
6. **Mental Engagement**
    - Confirm active processing and visualization, not rote motions.
    - Assess whether internal monologue supports or hinders performance.

Guiding Novice Shooters in Dry Fire

Commence with this foundational explanation: "Dry fire renders shooting instinctive—free from live ammunition's pressures, costs, and distractions. Here, we achieve perfection; each repetition forges habits that endure under duress."

Distill into three pillars:

1. **Master Fundamentals without Interference**
   "Without recoil or blast, we demand absolute control—unifying grip, sights, and trigger. Mastery here precedes speed in live fire."
   Novice Tip: "Observe your front sight or red dot. Movement during presses signals anticipation; press smoothly to immobilize it."
2. **Program Muscle Memory**
   "View dry fire as coding: repetitions dictate stress responses. Prioritize perfection; velocity follows quality."
   Novice Tip: "Avoid haste; etch flawless repetitions. Your body will accelerate naturally with clean habits."
3. **Employ Realistic, Iterative Scenarios**
   "Rehearse draws, reloads, malfunctions, and transitions as they unfold in confrontations. This is preparation, not pretense."
   Novice Tip: "Treat each draw as a response to genuine peril."

Common Novice Errors and Corrections

Error	Manifestation	Correction Strategy
Rushing Reps	Choppy draws, inconsistent grips	"Slow is smooth. Perfect it first."
Glancing at Gun	Confirming slide or magwell	"Trust your index. Focus on the threat."
Slapping Trigger	Sight/dot shifts at break	"Press to the wall. Control the press."
Overgripping	Trembling sights, excess tension	"Firm grip, relaxed arms. Avoid choking."

Advantages of Dead Trigger Dry Fire for Grip Evaluation

Dead trigger dry fire excels in assessing and enhancing grip architecture, offering uninterrupted repetitions that isolate grip under stress without recoil or reset interruptions.

Key Benefits:

1. **High-Volume Reps without Slide Reset**
   Traditional dry fire demands racking between presses in striker-fired pistols. Dead trigger permits seamless multiples, revealing grip endurance over sequences (e.g., simulated sustained fire).
   Benefit: Assess initial setup alongside long-term durability—detecting collapse, loosening, or fatigue.
2. **Trigger Immobility Enables Pure Grip Scrutiny**
   Absent breaks, shooters avoid anticipation or flinching, eliminating compensatory grip adjustments. Instructors concentrate on pressure balance (support vs. firing

hand), thumb positioning, heel voids, and backstrap migration.

Benefit: Yields unadulterated visuals of grip dynamics, untainted by trigger-related variables.

3. **Facilitates Dynamic Grip Testing in Motion**

   Ideal for draws, transitions, or reloads where trigger action is secondary to retention. Monitor consistency through movements, unnecessary rebuilds, or compensatory over-gripping.

   Benefit: Probes functional resilience under stress, sans artificial pauses.

4. **Red Dot Tracking for Diagnostic Insights**

   Simulate recoil tracking with rapid presses (no racking required). Observe dot centering or drift to uncover imbalances, finger isolation lapses, or hand torque.

   Benefit: Gauges grip's recoil management efficacy, even hypothetically.

5. **Pinpoints Grip Inconsistencies**

   With minimal variables (only hand and pistol motion), isolate issues:

Observation	Potential Grip Deficiency
Muzzle drifts left/right between reps	Uneven support hand tension
Dot vanishes or floats	Inadequate grip pressure or finger curl
Gun descends in hand	Weak backstrap contact / recoil shelf failure
Inconsistent recoil handling	Deficient compression and muscular alignment

Recommended Dry Fire to Live Fire Ratio

For defensive pistol practitioners emphasizing skill development, adopt a 5:1 to 10:1 dry-to-live fire ratio—executing 5 to 10 dry repetitions per live round.

Rationale:

1. **Dry Fire Constructs Skills; Live Fire Validates Them**
   Dry fire isolates essentials (grip, draw, sight picture, trigger) without recoil's disruption. Live fire introduces stressors like noise and pressure—suited for testing, not initial learning. Dry fire resolves issues; live fire uncovers them.
2. **Enables Vast Repetition minus Costs or Exhaustion**
   Sessions yield 100+ repetitions sans ammunition or physical wear. Live fire's recoil curtails volume due to expense, fatigue, and logistics.
3. **Supports Neurological and Motor Development**
   Forging neuromuscular pathways for intricate actions demands hundreds or thousands of accurate repetitions. Dry fire delivers this scale efficiently.

Sample Ratios by Shooter Category:

Shooter Type	Dry:Live Ratio	Example (per 100 Live Rounds)
Civilian CCW / Self-Defense	7:1 to 10:1	700 dry reps
Competitive Shooter	5:1 to 7:1	500 dry reps
Law Enforcement (Qual-Focused)	4:1 to 6:1	400 dry reps
Novice (Early Stages)	10:1+	Heavy dry emphasis

Advanced and Lesser-Known Dry Fire Methodologies

Beyond conventional "stand-and-press" routines, innovative dry fire variants elevate performance for concealed carriers, instructors, and elite shooters by fusing visual acuity, cognitive demands, stress simulation, and realism.

1. **Cognitive/Processing-Oriented Dry Fire**

   Embed decision tasks pre- or mid-engagement.

   Examples: Engage red targets only if green appears; respond to verbal/visual prompts on numbered targets; incorporate cards, dice, or apps for dynamic shifts.

   Purpose: Accelerates OODA loop, sharpens time-constrained decisions, and refines target discrimination beyond rote mechanics.

2. **Visual Acuity and Perception Dry Fire**

   Trains sight clarity, focus shifts, and acquisition velocity.

   Examples: Target minuscule dots (1/4-inch) at eye level for precision; alternate distances/sizes rapidly; occlude red dots with tape for target-centric shooting.

   Purpose: Enhances dot capture, confirmation tiers, and sight processing amid visual clutter.

3. **Compressed-Time/Micro-Drill Dry Fire**

   Isolates singular movements at elevated repetition counts.

   Examples: Mag reloads from belt sans pistol; concealment draws to presentation only; trigger wall preps from ready positions.

   Purpose: Perfects elusive micro-motions too swift for live fire dissection.

4. **Startle-Flinch Override Dry Fire**

   Builds recovery from reflexive disruptions.

   Examples: Initiate from off-balance "startle" postures; draw post-unpredictable "GO!" cues; incorporate coach-induced bumps or motions.

   Purpose: Trains sympathetic nervous system override, restoring focus post-interruption.

5. **Low-Light/No-Light Dry Fire**

   Adapts handling for diminished visibility.

   Examples: Employ flashlight methods (Harries, neck index, weapon-mounted lights); rehearse in dim/red-lit spaces with silhouettes; draw via audio cues alone.

Purpose: Develops orientation, illumination integration, and search-engagement in home defense contexts.

6. **Dynamic Positional Dry Fire**

   Emulates non-static, practical stances.

   Examples: Execute from seated, kneeling, prone, or supine; incorporate offline steps, sidesteps, or pivots; train in vehicles, doorways, or tight quarters.

   Purpose: Conditions mechanics for authentic, variable scenarios.

7. **Unstable Platform Dry Fire**

   Reinforces grip and alignment under disequilibrium.

   Examples: Balance on boards or foam during draws/presses; engage from swaying positions; one-handed shots while supporting an object.

   Purpose: Simulates stress-induced instability for robust control.

8. **Timer-Based Micro-Goal Dry Fire**

   Imposes temporal constraints on discrete actions.

   Examples: Draw to "shot" under 1.50 seconds; reload to press in <2.0 seconds; acquire dot from ready in 0.80 seconds (using timer dry modes).

   Purpose: Fuses explosive speed with disciplined execution, rendering training objective-oriented.

Bonus Integration: Layer into blocks—technical (draw/reload/press), cognitive (ID/decision), disruption (startle/movement/light)—for holistic preparation surpassing rudimentary dry fire.

Dry-fire is where survival becomes habitual — not a hobby, but a training imperative. Through relentless, deliberate repetitions performed without ammunition, armed professionals hard-wire precise grip, economical draw-strokes, consistent sight alignment, and unflinching trigger presses so those responses activate automatically when it matters most. Instructors must teach dry-fire with surgical focus: isolate one variable at a time, employ diagnostics like dead-trigger and press-and-reset drills, layer in dynamic positional work and timed transitions, and progressively add cognitive tasks so decision-making and motor programs synchronize under pressure. Log reps, grade to concrete standards, and remediate immediately — anything less invites guesswork in a lethal encounter. When coached by knowledgeable instructors who insist on measurable mastery, thousands of targeted iterations become neurological imprinting: motor skills recede beneath conscious thought, composure replaces panic, and a carrier's actions in crisis are decisive, lawful, and repeatable. Dry-fire doesn't replace live fire — it guarantees that live fire validates skill, rather than discovers hope.

Instructor responsibilities — be surgical and measurable. Use short, focused diagnostics: one variable per drill, three metrics (consistency, time, and deviation), and immediate corrective feedback. Observe at eye level; cue with precise language ("thumb left 3/8 inch," "push with ball of index finger — not the pad," "stop the draw at chest level for indexing"). Record rep counts and times. Grade to a standard: acceptable reps per minute, 90% hits on a 3-inch front-sight dot at X yards, sub-.8s holster-to-first-shot for the level, etc. If the student can't meet the standard in dry-fire, they do not advance to live fire.

Progression template (easy to implement):

1. **Static isolation** — single element drills (trigger only; draw only; sight alignment only).
2. **Linked micro-skills** — combine two elements (draw + sight; sight + trigger) with slow deliberate reps.
3. **Timed repetitions** — add tempo and small time pressure while maintaining 90–95% quality.
4. **Integrated scenarios** — add movement, decision tasks, and low-stress role play.
5. **Live-fire validation** — once dry-fire standards are repeatedly met, validate with measured live-fire repetitions.

Practical drills instructors should use nightly:

- **Dead-trigger diagnostic** — press to the wall of the trigger, hold steady for 3–5 seconds, look for press-side motion or sight drift.
- **Press-and-reset ladder** — press, reset to the tactile click without releasing finger forward, repeat to ingrain reset feel.
- **Draw-to-sight index** — draw slowly to the point where the front sight first appears, hold, then press; reinforces consistent presentation.
- **Transition cadence** — two-target slow transitions emphasizing support-hand lead and sight recovery.
- **Speed-precision pairing** — alternate fast, controlled pairs with single deliberate precision shots to teach tempo control.

Safety and culture — treat dry-fire with the same gravity as live fire. Verify an unloaded weapon in a controlled area, establish movement boundaries, and require an audible and visible empty-weapon announcement for each student. Make dry-fire mandatory, logged, and inspected — no excuses.

Anticipation in Shooting: Causes, Mechanics, and Diagnostics

One of the most frustrating pet peeves I encounter as a seasoned firearms instructor surfaces when I assess troubled or failing law enforcement shooters. I start by asking them to pinpoint their issues, and they almost always echo their previous instructor's diagnosis: "I'm anticipating." This vague label irritates me because anticipation does not function as a universal scapegoat for poor marksmanship. In reality, shooting errors stem from a web of interconnected breakdown points, each demanding precise identification and targeted correction. Competent instructors bear the responsibility to scrutinize the shooter's entire structure from behind the gun—observing stance, grip, arm extension, and body alignment in real time—and dissect the true culprits, whether flawed fundamentals, physiological responses, or equipment mismatches, to foster genuine improvement rather than superficial fixes.

To truly expound on this, let's first define anticipation in the context of firearms training. Shooters "anticipate" when they subconsciously brace for recoil before the shot breaks, often causing the muzzle to dip, push, or jerk off target. This manifests as low-left hits for right-handed shooters (or low-right for lefties) on diagnostic targets. Instructors love this term because it sounds insightful and shifts blame to the student's mindset. However, it oversimplifies the problem. True anticipation rarely occurs in isolation; it often signals deeper flaws in technique that trigger the flinch as a symptom, not the root. For instance, a weak or inconsistent grip allows the pistol to rotate excessively during recoil, prompting the shooter to overcompensate on subsequent shots. Similarly, poor stance—such as standing too upright without a forward lean—fails to absorb energy, amplifying perceived recoil and breeding that anticipatory twitch.

Consider the multiple breakdown points that masquerade as mere anticipation. Grip issues top the list: if the shooter fails to achieve a high, firm hold with both hands compressing inward and rearward, the gun shifts unpredictably, eroding confidence and inviting preemptive movements. Stance breakdowns follow closely; a balanced, athletic posture with feet shoulder-width apart and weight forward on the balls of the feet channels recoil straight back into the body, but many students default to a rigid, rear-weighted position that exacerbates muzzle rise. Trigger control represents another frequent offender—jerky pulls or staging the trigger midway disrupt smooth shot breaks, mimicking anticipation's effects. Sight alignment and focus compound these: if the shooter fixates on the target instead of the front sight, or allows parallax errors in red-dot optics, hits scatter wildly, leading instructors to wrongly cry "flinch!" Equipment factors play a role too; ill-fitted holsters, mismatched ammunition, or even vision problems like uncorrected astigmatism can induce compensatory behaviors that resemble anticipation.

As instructors, we must commit to rigorous analysis from behind the gun, a vantage point that reveals truths the shooter themselves often misses. Position yourself directly in line with the muzzle, and watch the entire kinetic chain during live fire. Does the muzzle flip upward excessively? That points to insufficient arm extension or elbow lockout. Observe the slide's cycle: erratic ejection patterns suggest grip inconsistencies. Track the shooter's shoulders and torso—hunching or leaning back indicates fear of recoil, while a forward-aggressive posture promotes control. Use tools like slow-motion video capture or laser training aids to quantify these observations, stripping away subjectivity. This methodical breakdown transforms vague complaints into actionable insights: "Your grip slips because your support hand rotates counterclockwise—let's reinforce it with this drill."

Ultimately, mislabeling errors as anticipation harms students by delaying progress and eroding trust. Law enforcement officers, in particular, cannot afford such shortcuts; their lives depend on split-second accuracy under stress. By embracing a holistic diagnostic approach, instructors empower shooters to address root causes, build resilient fundamentals, and achieve consistent, confident performance. This not only resolves the immediate pet peeve but elevates the craft of instruction itself.

Anticipation is not a single "flinch" but a family of *pre-ignition disturbances*—movements initiated by the shooter *before* the pistol discharges. These movements occur within milliseconds of the shot and are often subconscious, originating from a combination of **neuromuscular reflexes, startle responses, and learned compensation habits**.

Each type of anticipation recruits different muscle groups—from the fine motor control of the distal phalanges (trigger finger) to gross motor bracing of the shoulders, torso, and even the lower body. Understanding which body parts are engaged, and *how*, allows the instructor to rapidly diagnose and correct errors on the range.

Primary Anticipation Types and Involved Body Parts

1. Recoil Management Flinch

Muscles Involved:

- **Forearms & wrists:** Flexor carpi radialis, flexor carpi ulnaris (downward push)
- **Hands:** Thenar eminence (thumb pad) applying forward pressure
- **Upper arms:** Biceps (pull) and triceps (brace)
- **Core:** Rectus abdominis and obliques tighten to stabilize
  Mechanics: Shooter pushes the muzzle forward or down in an attempt to "meet" the recoil before it happens. Often results in low hits.

2. Noise Startle Response

Muscles Involved:

- **Neck:** Sternocleidomastoid contracts, causing slight head recoil

- **Shoulders:** Trapezius tightens, causing a "shrug"
- **Face:** Orbicularis oculi (blinking) and masseter (jaw clench)
  Mechanics: Body reacts to the expected sound with micro-tensing that disrupts the sight picture at the moment of discharge.

3. Visual Blink Anticipation

Muscles Involved:

- **Eyes:** Orbicularis oculi (eyelid closure)
- **Forehead:** Frontalis (raising brows during blink reflex)
  Mechanics: The blink occurs microseconds before the break, eliminating the visual reference needed for precise alignment.

4. Body "Crash" or Collapse

Muscles Involved:

- **Shoulders:** Deltoids and trapezius contract
- **Chest:** Pectoralis major pulls arms inward
- **Spine/Core:** Erector spinae and rectus abdominis flex forward
  Mechanics: The shooter compresses the upper body forward and down to "absorb" recoil before it arrives, shifting the muzzle low or off-target.

5. Trigger Slap or Jerk

Muscles Involved:

- **Trigger Finger:** Flexor digitorum profundus and flexor digitorum superficialis (rapid pull)
- **Forearm:** Flexor carpi radialis stabilizes but can over-engage

- **Hand:** Entire hand may tighten sympathetically
  Mechanics: The shooter "punches" through the trigger instead of pressing straight to the rear, throwing shots laterally or low.

6. Grip Clench Anticipation

Muscles Involved:

- **Hands:** Flexor pollicis longus (thumb) and flexor digitorum (fingers)
- **Forearms:** Pronator teres and wrist flexors
  Mechanics: Both hands suddenly squeeze tighter just before the break, dipping the muzzle or shifting point of impact.

7. Breathing Disruption

Muscles Involved:

- **Diaphragm:** Sudden tightening or release
- **Intercostals:** Rib cage muscles contract
- **Core:** Abdominals tense
  Mechanics: Breath-holding or forceful exhalation shifts upper body stability and moves the sight package.

8. Pre-Ignition Push / Heeling

Muscles Involved:

- **Hands/Wrist:** Thenar muscles push forward
- **Forearm:** Wrist extensors activate
- **Shoulder:** Anterior deltoid engages to drive muzzle upward/forward
  Mechanics: Heel of the hand presses into the backstrap to "control" recoil before it occurs, producing high or diagonal hits.

9. Lower-Body Bracing

Muscles Involved:

- **Legs:** Quadriceps (front knee lock), gastrocnemius (calf tension)
- **Hips:** Gluteus maximus and hip flexors tighten
- **Core:** Lower abdominals brace the pelvis
  Mechanics: Sudden weight shift or knee lock changes upper body alignment, pulling sights off target.

Instructor Note: a firearms instructor's should gain extensive knowledge—honed through years of dedicated study, practical application, and mastery of diagnostic technique that should equip them to dissect anticipation issues beyond mere symptoms, pinpointing root causes like grip flaws or stance imbalances for precise corrections. This expertise imposes a profound responsibility to students: to provide thorough, individualized guidance that builds trust, enhances safety, and fosters lasting proficiency, ensuring no shooter endures superficial fixes that could compromise performance in critical moment

Professional Diagnostic Table: Anticipation Patterns

Anticipation Type	Primary Body Parts Engaged	Observable Target Signature	Likely Cause	Corrective Drill
Recoil Management Flinch	Forearms, wrists, core	Tight low grouping, often centered	Bracing for recoil	Ball-and-dummy drill, surprise break training
Noise Startle Response	Neck, shoulders, facial muscles	Random miss pattern, inconsistent	Reaction to sound	Dry fire with hearing protection layering
Visual Blink Anticipation	Eyelids, forehead	Poor follow-through, shots wander	Flinch to muzzle flash	Flash acclimatization dry fire
Body Crash/Collapse	Shoulders, chest, core	Low-left (RH shooter), body tension visible	Over-bracing	Video slow-mo feedback, wall drill
Trigger Slap/Jerk	Trigger finger, forearm	Lateral spread, often low	Timing the shot	Trigger reset drills, cadence shooting
Grip Clench Anticipation	Hands, forearms	Low-center grouping	Sympathetic hand squeeze	Grip isolation drills, coin-on-sight dry fire
Breathing Disruption	Diaphragm, intercostals	Slight vertical stringing	Breath-hold under stress	Controlled breathing cadence drills
Pre-Ignition Push / Heeling	Hands, wrist, shoulder	High/diagonal impacts	Overcompensation	Support-hand-only fire for recoil isolation
Lower-Body Bracing	Legs, hips, core	Erratic vertical displacement	Whole-body bracing	Dynamic stance drills, balance board shooting

A law enforcement officer must always recognize that every bullet fired in a lethal or potentially kinetic encounter carries not only life-and-death consequences but also the weight of potential legal scrutiny. Each round discharged will be tied to an investigation, and possibly to civil or criminal litigation. This reality underscores the critical importance of disciplined marksmanship, adherence to use-of-force policy, and a clear understanding of necessity and proportionality in the moment of engagement.

Equally important is the recognition that, statistically, the majority of rounds fired by law enforcement officers in actual confrontations fail to strike their intended target. This is not simply a reflection of training, but of the realities of human performance under extreme stress: physiological responses such as elevated heart rate, tunnel vision, loss of fine motor control, and the unpredictable dynamics of armed resistance. Each missed shot introduces additional risk—to bystanders, fellow officers, and the officer's own legal and professional standing.

For these reasons, law enforcement professionals must train with the mindset that every trigger press carries both tactical and legal consequences. The duty is not only to stop the threat but also to do so with precision, control, and accountability.

Every Round Counts: Legal and Tactical Realities of Law Enforcement Firearms Use

Legal Liability

For the law enforcement professional, every bullet fired in a lethal or potentially kinetic encounter is more than a ballistic event—it is a legal act. Each round discharged will be linked to a report, an investigation, and, potentially, to civil litigation or criminal review. Whether the round strikes the intended threat, misses entirely, or causes unintended

damage, the officer will be held accountable. This reality reinforces the necessity of not only acting within policy and law but also maintaining a level of professional firearms proficiency that reflects the weight of the responsibility.

Every bullet fired carries responsibility. If a shot is discharged in a lethal or potentially kinetic encounter, it will be investigated, and the officer may face civil or criminal scrutiny. Even when a shooting is justified, missed rounds or collateral damage can create serious consequences. Every trigger pull must be viewed as both a tactical and a legal act.

Firearms instructors and law enforcement leaders must ensure that officers understand that every bullet fired is a potential legal event. The vast majority of rounds fired do not strike the intended target, which underscores the importance of rigorous, scenario-based training and clear understanding of policy and use-of-force laws. Leadership must emphasize that every round carries both operational and legal consequences.

Performance Under Stress

Statistics consistently show that the majority of rounds fired by law enforcement officers in actual confrontations do not strike their intended target. This outcome is not simply a matter of inadequate training but is heavily influenced by human performance under extreme stress. High-stakes encounters trigger the body's sympathetic nervous system, producing elevated heart rate, tunnel vision, auditory exclusion, and reduced fine motor control. Officers must fight not only the threat in front of them but also their own physiological responses, which can degrade accuracy and decision-making in fractions of a second.

Most rounds fired in real-world encounters fail to hit the intended target. This is due to natural human responses under stress: elevated heart rate, tunnel vision, auditory exclusion, and reduced fine motor control. Recognizing these limitations allows officers to train deliberately to overcome them, ensuring shots are both effective and safe.

Human Performance Considerations

Stress-induced physiological responses—heart rate elevation, tunnel vision, auditory exclusion, and loss of fine motor control—reduce accuracy and decision-making in high-pressure encounters. Instructors must design training programs that replicate these stressors to prepare officers for real-world conditions.

The Cost of a Missed Round

Every missed shot carries consequences beyond tactical failure. A round that fails to hit its intended target becomes an uncontrolled risk, potentially endangering innocent bystanders, striking unintended property, or escalating the chaos of the engagement. Missed rounds also carry legal repercussions: even when a shooting is deemed justified, stray rounds can result in lawsuits, departmental scrutiny, and long-term career implications. The officer must therefore view each trigger press as both a tactical necessity and a legal commitment.

Missed rounds are more than tactical failures—they introduce risk to bystanders, fellow officers, and the shooter themselves. Each missed shot can have legal repercussions, complicating justifications and accountability. Officers must treat every trigger press as a measured decision.

Minimizing Risk and Liability

Missed shots increase risk to bystanders and department liability. Training must focus on precision, controlled aggression, and decision-making under pressure. By instilling discipline and accountability, leaders ensure officers are capable of defending both themselves and the organization when firearms are discharged.

Training Implications

Understanding these realities compels a shift in the way law enforcement professionals view firearms training. Accuracy under stress cannot be treated as optional or secondary; it must be considered an ethical obligation. Training must go beyond static qualification to incorporate realistic stress inoculation, decision-making under pressure, and dynamic engagement drills that mirror the unpredictability of real-world encounters. Officers should develop the mindset that every shot must be defensible—legally, ethically, and tactically.

Accuracy under stress is not optional. Training should replicate real-world stress and decision-making scenarios. By developing proficiency under pressure, officers reduce risk, enhance survivability, and ensure their actions remain defensible both tactically and legally.

Training Recommendations

- **Stress Inoculation:** Incorporate drills that mimic high-pressure environments.
- **Decision-Making Under Fire:** Teach officers to identify threats accurately before shooting.
- **Dynamic Engagement:** Encourage scenario-based exercises with movement and multiple targets.
- **After-Action Review:** Analyze misses and hits for tactical and legal lessons.

By reinforcing these principles, instructors and leadership create a culture where every round fired is intentional, defensible, and as safe as possible for all parties.

Conclusion

In the profession of law enforcement, every round fired is an extension of both the officer's authority and accountability. The intersection of tactical necessity and legal liability means that proficiency with a firearm is not simply a skill—it is a duty. Officers must train, prepare, and operate with the understanding that every shot counts, both on the street and in the courtroom.

Calling Your Shot

"Calling your shot" is one of the highest benchmarks of true marksmanship skill. It is the ability to know, without looking at the target, exactly where the round impacted based on the visual information you had at the moment the shot broke.

I think that the only true "Advanced" Pistol skill is the ability to call your shot! One this skill is understood and the ability to apply it is learned your shooting skills will take off. Once the skill is mastered and you can teach others, you know you have a very firm grip on the diagnostics needed to make your shooters better.

This is not a parlor trick—it's the product of disciplined fundamentals, visual processing, and self-awareness. When a shooter can call shots accurately, they transition from reactive shooting (checking the target after every string) to **proactive shooting** (trusting their process and correcting in real time).

What Calling Your Shot Really Means

- **Definition:** The mental confirmation of where the round should impact based on sight alignment, sight picture, and trigger break at the moment of firing.
- **Key Insight:** The bullet goes where the sights were aligned when the trigger broke—*not* where you wish it went.

Why It Matters

1. **Self-Correction:** If you know where the round went, you don't need to look at the target. Instead, you adjust grip, trigger control, or sight focus immediately.
2. **Efficiency:** Eliminates wasted time checking targets every shot. Essential for both defensive and competitive shooting.

3. **Diagnostics:** If your "call" doesn't match your hit, you immediately know something external is wrong (ammo, sights, lighting, etc.).
4. **Confidence:** Builds trust in your fundamentals, which is critical when stress, speed, and distance are added.

How to Train Calling Your Shot

1. Slow Fire at Distance

- Start at **15–25 yards** on a B8 bull.
- Fire one round at a time. After each shot, say (or think) exactly where the sights were at the break: *"9 ring at 3 o'clock."*
- Only then, confirm on the target. Over time, your mental "call" should match reality within 1–2 inches.

2. Ball & Dummy

- Mix live rounds and dummy rounds.
- Watch what your sights do when the trigger breaks on a dummy. This trains awareness of visual disruption and refines your ability to predict outcomes.

3. Dot Drills

- Shoot 2–3" dots at 7–10 yards.
- Call every shot, then verify.
- Small targets magnify errors and sharpen visual processing.

4. Speed Integration

- Run short strings (Bill Drill, 5x5, controlled pairs).
- At the end, before checking, mentally walk through each shot: *"First two in A-zone, third broke high left, last three in center."*
- Confirm accuracy only afterward.

Instructor Layer

- **Beginner Level:** Teach students to pause after each shot, describe sight picture at break, then verify.
- **Intermediate Level:** Call shots during short strings, then confirm.
- **Advanced Level:** Run longer strings or movement drills, then debrief each shot placement before checking.
- **Instructor Tip:** Do not let students rush to the target—train them to trust their eyes and sights.

When a shooter can **accurately call every shot**—from precision bullseye to high-speed drills—they have reached a professional-level understanding of applied marksmanship.

Would you like me to **integrate "calling your shot" into the 25-yard Speed Bull progression** we laid out earlier, so it becomes part of that layered curriculum?

Let's integrate **"calling your shot"** into the full **25-yard Speed Bull progression** so that it becomes a built-in habit, not an afterthought. This way, shooters are developing both technical execution *and* the mental discipline of predictive accuracy at every stage.

Progression with Shot Calling Integration

Phase 1 – Foundation at Close Range (3–7 yards)

- **Focus:** Grip, trigger press, visual patience.
- **Shot Calling Integration:**
    - After each shot, shooter states (or records mentally) where the sights were when the trigger broke.
    - Example: *"Center of the dot, front sight slightly high."* Then confirm.
- **Drills:**

1. **Dot Torture (3 yards)** – Call every shot before looking.
2. **1-Shot Drill (3–5 yards)** – From the draw, call where the shot landed before confirming.
3. **3" Circle, 5 Shots (5 yards)** – Call each impact in sequence before checking.

Phase 2 – Mid-Range Control (7–15 yards)

- **Focus:** Consistency under light time pressure.
- **Shot Calling Integration:**
    - During 5-round strings, call the *last shot* before checking.
    - Progress to calling *every* shot in a string.
- **Drills:**

1. **5x5 Drill (10 yards)** – Call each shot into the 5" circle.
2. **Bill Drill (10 yards)** – Fire 6 rounds, then verbally reconstruct the string: *"First two center, third pushed left, last three in A-zone."*
3. **Strong/Support Hand Only (10 yards)** – Call every shot; isolates grip effect.

Phase 3 – Precision Expansion (15–20 yards)

- **Focus:** Long-range accuracy, patient sight use.
- **Shot Calling Integration:**

- o Require shooters to *verbalize exact ring/clock position* on B8 target before confirming.
- o Example: *"That broke at 9 ring, 4 o'clock."*
* **Drills:**

1. **10-Shot B8 Slow Fire (15 yards)** – Call all 10 shots, confirm only after string is complete.
2. **Half & Half Drill (20 yards)** – Call last 3 shots in each distance phase.
3. **Walk-Back Drill** – Call every round at each distance. If call ≠ impact, stop and address fundamentals.

Phase 4 – Mastery Challenge (25 yards)

* **Focus:** Speed + precision under stress.
* **Shot Calling Integration:**
  - o Before checking target, shooter must recall and report:
    - Where each shot broke.
    - Which fundamentals they controlled well / poorly.
* **Drills:**

1. **B8 Slow Fire (25 yards)** – Call each shot by ring and clock. Verify only after string.
2. **Controlled Pairs (25 yards)** – Call both shots before checking.
3. **Speed Bull Standard (25 yards)** – 10 rounds in 10 seconds on a B8. Shooter must "mentally score" and describe group placement before walking forward.

Instructor Notes on Calling Shots

* **Beginners** tend to call based on *feel* (how the recoil felt). Correct this: they must base the call on *what the sights showed at break*.

- **Intermediates** start getting it right ~70% of the time. Encourage them by having them track calls in a notebook.
- **Advanced shooters** should be 90%+ accurate in calls at 25 yards. If not, there's a gap in visual discipline or trigger control.
- **Instructor trick:** Cover the target between strings (don't let them peek). Forces reliance on shot calling.

Calling your shot is the shooter's ability to know—without looking at the target—where the bullet impacted based solely on sight picture, sight movement, and trigger press at the moment of the shot breaking.

At its core, it's a feedback skill. Instead of waiting for the target to tell you where the round landed, you're *reading your sights in real time* and instantly evaluating:

- **Did the sights stay stable during the trigger press?**
- **Where were they aligned the moment the shot broke?**
- **Did the dot/front sight lift in the direction of proper recoil, or did it jump from anticipation, flinch, or grip collapse?**

Why It Matters

- **Immediate feedback:** You don't need to walk downrange or wait for a spotter—you already know.
- **Efficiency in training:** Lets you self-correct during strings of fire, tightening groups faster.
- **Performance under stress:** In defensive or competitive shooting, knowing where rounds are going allows for faster, more confident follow-up shots.

How to Develop It

1. **Slow Fire with Accountability**
   Shoot bullseyes or small dots. After each shot, call where it landed before looking. Check against the target.
2. **Dry Fire Discipline**
   Watch the sights through the trigger press. Note if they dip, jump, or drift.
3. **Ball & Dummy Drills**
   When a dummy round chambers, call the shot and watch what actually happened.
4. **Red Dot Advantage**
   With RDS pistols, the dot's lift pattern gives clear feedback. With irons, it takes more discipline to register front sight movement.
5. **Target Progression**
   Start with large, clean bullseyes to establish awareness, then shift to smaller dots at distance. This forces precision in calling your shots.

Advanced Layer

At a mastery level, "calling your shot" evolves into **tracking your shot**—not just knowing where the round hit, but instantly processing it and making the micro-adjustments necessary for the next round, without conscious thought.

The Speed Bullseye — 10 rounds in 10 seconds from 25 yards — is my definitive diagnostic tool. Distance exposes limitations; the seven-yard line flatters no one, but 25 yards does not lie. At that distance every technical fault becomes visible, and when speed is added those faults are revealed without excuse. The Speed Bull was the Special Operations standard for a reason: it quickly separates capability from illusion and gives instructors concrete data to analyze. Failure in training is not only acceptable — it is essential. When a student fails the drill, do not criticize; observe, diagnose, and correct. The Speed Bull lets you do that with clarity.

Expanded instructor notes (use as a checklist)

- Purpose: Use the drill to reveal hidden flaws in grip, sight alignment, trigger press, follow-through, and recoil management that shorter-range work can mask.
- What to watch for: repeated horizontal or vertical stringing, flaring between shots, inconsistent sight picture at break, anticipating the recoil, or poor re-indexing of the sights.
- Analysis, not blame: Treat each miss as data. Ask "what pattern does this form?" rather than "who's at fault?" That turns a failure into an actionable lesson.
- Coaching sequence: 1) Slow it down and re-establish fundamentals (sight picture, grip, trigger), 2) isolate the fault with a focused drill (single-shot, double-tap, or stress-pause), 3) rebuild speed progressively back toward the 10/10 standard.
- Progressions & regressions: If the shooter cannot produce acceptable groups at 25 yards, regress to deliberate fire at the same distance, or move to 15–18 yards for transitional work before returning. Conversely, for advanced students, add movement or target transitions while keeping the 10/10 cadence.
- Measurement: Record times and groupings. Use the data to track trends — are misses narrowing, shifting, or random? Trends tell the story, not the one-off outcome.

How distance exposes limitations in pistol shooting

Distance is the microscope that shows what's really working (and what's not) in a shooter's technique, equipment, and tactics. Below I'll break down *why* distance magnifies problems, *what* usually breaks first, and *how* to diagnose and train to remove those limits.

Why distance matters (the physics + human factors)

- **Angular error grows with range.** A small angular error at the wrist, elbow, or sight alignment translates to a much larger linear miss at longer ranges. Tiny inconsistencies that are irrelevant at 3–5 yards become critical at 15–25 yards.
- **Time and motion increase.** To be accurate at distance you need slower, more repeatable motion and better follow-through. Speed introduces variability that distance punishes.
- **Recoil and recovery matter more.** The effect of recoil on sight alignment and the time to recover to the sights affects precision more as range increases.
- **External factors show up.** Wind, light, and subtle sight parallax have negligible effects at point-blank but become measurable at longer ranges.
- **Target presentation grows smaller.** The sight picture is reduced, making precise alignment and trigger timing harder to judge.

Most common limitations revealed by distance

1. **Poor sight alignment / inconsistent cheek & head position** — tiny sight errors become big misses.
2. **Unsteady support / weak grip** — muzzle flip and lateral movement add up over longer sight radius.
3. **Flawed trigger technique** — jerking, anticipating, or varying press speed breaks groups more at range.

4. **Indexing and draw inconsistencies** — inconsistent grip/hand placement changes point-of-impact.
5. **Inadequate follow-through** — stopping the shot or immediately moving the muzzle ruins precision.
6. **Wrong equipment or zero** — sights not properly zeroed or optic parallax magnify misses.
7. **Poor ammunition consistency** — more noticeable at precision distances.

How to diagnose what's failing (practical checks)

- **Start close and move back.** If you can put 5 rounds into an inch at 3–5 yards but open up at 15 yards, the problem isn't fundamentals of aim — it's stability, trigger control, or follow-through.
- **One-change tests.** Change only one variable (grip, trigger press, stance) and see whether groups tighten at distance.
- **Slow-fire precision first.** Work slow, controlled shots at distance to isolate mechanical errors before adding speed.
- **Use slow-motion video.** Record draws and shots to see muzzle movement and grip changes not felt during the shot.

Training drills that expose and fix distance problems

(Use progressive steps — only advance once you meet the accuracy standard at the previous distance.)

1. **Foundation check — 3–5 yards slow fire**
    - Purpose: confirm zero, grip, and sight picture.
    - Goal: consistent, centered impacts.
2. **Stability drill — 7 yards 5×5 slow**
    - 5 shots slow, 5 times. Watch group size and vertical dispersion.

- Focus: grip pressure symmetry, minimal muzzle rise.
3. **Trigger isolation — ball & dummy / single-load drill at 7–10 yards**
    - Purpose: reveal anticipation and flinch that grows at distance.
4. **Precision at pace — 15 yards slow-controlled**
    - Take 2–3 deliberate shots with full recovery between shots.
    - Focus: follow-through and sight realignment after recoil.
5. **Timed precision — 15–25 yards**
    - Two-shot strings within a controlled time (e.g., 3–4s) to blend speed and accuracy.
    - Measure: group size and horizontal dispersion; wind and lighting notes.
6. **Long-range confirmation — 25 yards+**
    - Use slower strings and analyze group centering. If groups are consistent but off center, adjust zero. If groups open, work fundamentals back at shorter ranges.

Equipment and ballistic considerations

- **Sights/optics:** Small sight radius on pistols makes distance accuracy sensitive to tiny sight errors. Red dot parallax and height-of-sight must be understood and zeroed at intended engagement distances.
- **Barrel length & ammo:** Short barrels and light defensive ammo reduce inherent accuracy; expect decreasing precision at longer ranges.
- **Ergonomics:** Grip design, trigger reach, and sight picture that work up close may reveal flaws when you push range.

Measurable progress markers (use these to gauge improvement)

- Can you hold a consistent, repeatable group size at 7, then 15, then 25 yards under the same drill conditions?
- Do you see *pattern* changes (e.g., consistent vertical stringing = trigger issue; lateral spread = grip/torque)?
- Do your follow-through and sight recovery times shorten while group size remains tight?

Coaching cues that help at distance

- "Press the trigger to the rear — don't move the gun."
- "Find the front sight and hold it there until the recoil completes."
- "Grip like you mean it — firm, consistent, and steady into your body."
- "Breathe, settle, and press — speed without stability is just noise."

Practical final advice

Distance doesn't create problems — it *reveals* them. Use progressively longer ranges as a diagnostic tool: start where you can succeed and only push the range when fundamentals are reliably repeatable. Train deliberately: isolate variables, measure results, and correct one thing at a time. Over time the same tiny inconsistencies that once blew up groups at 25 yards will stop showing up — because you fixed them at 3, 7, and 15.

Cycle of Operations of a Semi-Automatic Pistol

The **cycle of operations** is the series of mechanical actions that a semi-automatic pistol performs to **fire, extract, eject, reload, and prepare** for the next shot. Understanding this cycle is essential for diagnosing malfunctions, performing maintenance, and teaching others how the system works.

There are typically **8 steps** in the cycle of operations for a semi-automatic pistol:

1. Feeding

Definition:
The process of moving a live round from the magazine into alignment with the chamber.

How it Works:

- When the slide moves rearward and then forward (due to recoil or manual manipulation), it strips the top cartridge from the magazine.
- The round is pushed forward along the feed ramp toward the chamber.

Key Components Involved:

- Magazine spring and follower
- Slide
- Feed lips
- Feed ramp

Instructional Note:
If the feed ramp is dirty or the magazine spring is weak, feeding can fail—resulting in a **failure to feed (FTF)** malfunction.

2. Chambering

Definition:
The process of seating the cartridge fully into the chamber.

How it Works:

- As the slide drives the cartridge forward, the base of the round moves into position under the extractor claw.
- The round is pressed into the chamber, ready for locking.

Key Components:

- Barrel chamber
- Slide
- Extractor

Instructional Note:
A failure to fully chamber may result in a "press check" discrepancy or a malfunction where the slide is slightly out of battery.

3. Locking (Battery)

Definition:
The barrel and slide lock together, ensuring the pistol is safe to fire and can manage chamber pressure.

How it Works:

- In Browning-style tilting-barrel designs (common in modern pistols), the barrel rises and locks into the slide via lugs or cam surfaces.

- The pistol is now **"in battery"**—meaning the action is locked and ready to fire.

Key Components:

- Barrel locking lugs
- Slide lugs
- Barrel cam or link

Instructional Note:

If the pistol is out of battery (not fully locked), most designs will **prevent the trigger from releasing the firing pin** as a safety measure.

4. Firing

Definition:

The action of igniting the primer and firing the cartridge.

How it Works:

- When the trigger is pressed, the firing mechanism (striker or hammer) releases.
- The firing pin or striker hits the primer, igniting the powder charge.
- Expanding gases push the bullet down the barrel and cause recoil.

Key Components:

- Trigger
- Hammer or striker
- Firing pin
- Primer

Instructional Note:

Teach students proper **trigger control** to ensure clean ignition and minimize movement that could affect shot placement.

5. Unlocking

Definition:

The process of disengaging the barrel from the slide after firing, allowing the slide to move independently.

How it Works:

- Recoil forces the slide and barrel to move rearward together briefly.
- After a short distance, the barrel drops or cams downward, disengaging from the slide.

Key Components:

- Barrel link or cam
- Slide rails
- Recoil energy

Instructional Note:

This step is part of **short recoil operation**, typical in most modern semi-automatic pistols.

6. Extracting

Definition:
The process of removing the spent casing from the chamber.

How it Works:

- As the slide continues rearward, the extractor (a hook-shaped part) grips the rim of the spent casing.
- It pulls the casing out of the chamber.

Key Components:

- Extractor
- Cartridge case rim

Instructional Note:
If the extractor is broken, dirty, or weak, it may cause a **failure to extract (FTE)** malfunction.

7. Ejecting

Definition:
The act of expelling the spent casing from the ejection port.

How it Works:

- The casing hits the ejector (a fixed or spring-loaded part in the frame).
- This causes the casing to pivot out and away from the pistol through the ejection port.

Key Components:

- Ejector
- Slide
- Spent casing

Instructional Note:

An obstructed ejection port or improper grip (e.g., "limp-wristing") can cause the casing to stovepipe or fail to eject properly.

8. Cocking and Resetting

Definition:

The process of preparing the firing mechanism for the next shot.

How it Works:

- During the slide's rearward movement, it resets the trigger mechanism and re-cocks the hammer or striker.
- As the slide moves forward under spring pressure, it completes the cycle, and the pistol is ready to fire again.

Key Components:

- Striker/firing pin or hammer
- Trigger bar
- Disconnector

Instructional Note:

This is a critical phase for **trigger reset**. Teaching shooters how to feel and use the reset improves speed and accuracy.

Cycle Summary (Flow)

1. Feeding →

2. Chambering →

3. Locking →

4. Firing →

5. Unlocking →

6. Extracting →

7. Ejecting →

8. Cocking & Resetting

Instructor-Level Teaching Tips

- **Layered instruction:**
    - *Beginner:* Focus on the basic cycle and malfunctions (e.g., feed, fire, eject).
    - *Intermediate:* Dive into timing, recoil behavior, and reset.
    - *Advanced:* Discuss tolerance stacking, mechanical delays, and shooter input effects on function.

Professional Ballistics Reference Guide for modern semi-automatic pistol calibers. It includes commonly used bullet weights, average muzzle velocities, energies, penetration depth, and intended applications—formatted for use as a **training handout or quick-reference sheet**.

Modern Pistol Caliber Ballistics Reference Guide

For Law Enforcement, Instructors, Defensive Shooters, and Competitors

Caliber	Common Bullet Weights (gr)	Average Muzzle Velocity (fps)	Average Muzzle Energy (ft-lbs)	Typical Penetration (Gel, JHP)	Expansion (JHP)	Typical Use Case
9mm Luger (9x19)	115, 124, 147	1,000–1,300	350–400	12–18"	0.60–0.70"	Duty, CCW, Competition
.45 ACP	185, 200, 230	800–950	350–450	13–16"	0.70–0.80"	Tactical, Suppressed, Home Defense
.40 S&W	155, 165, 180	950–1,200	400–500	13–16"	0.60–0.75"	LE Use, Vehicle Defense
.380 ACP	90, 95, 100	900–1,000	180–220	10–12"	0.50–0.60"	Pocket Carry, Deep Concealment
.357 SIG	125	1,350–1,450	500–600	13–15"	0.60–0.70"	Vehicle Interdiction, Duty
10mm Auto	155, 180, 200	1,100–1,300	550–700	16–20"+	0.70–0.80"	Bear Defense, Hunting, Backcountry
.22 LR	36, 40	1,000–1,200	100–150	8–10"	Minimal	Training, Low-Noise Shooting

Key Terms

- **gr (grain):** Unit of bullet weight (437.5 grains = 1 ounce).
- **fps:** Feet per second—how fast the bullet travels.
- **ft-lbs:** Foot-pounds of energy—impact power at the muzzle.
- **Gel Penetration:** Based on calibrated 10% ballistic gelatin (FBI standard).
- **Expansion:** The increased diameter of a hollow-point bullet upon impact.

Instructor Notes

- **FBI Ideal Penetration:** 12–18 inches in 10% ballistic gel.
- **Acceptable Expansion:** ≥0.60" is ideal for self-defense calibers.
- **9mm Performance:** Modern bonded JHPs make 9mm highly effective and controllable.
- **.380 ACP Warning:** Many loads **fail to meet FBI minimums**; careful ammo selection is critical.
- **10mm Auto:** Most powerful mainstream semi-auto pistol round—requires recoil training.

Caliber Selection Matrix

Purpose	Recommended Caliber(s)
Concealed Carry (CCW)	9mm, .380 ACP
Duty / Law Enforcement	9mm, .40 S&W, .357 SIG
Home Defense	9mm, .45 ACP
Bear / Woods Defense	10mm Auto
Low Recoil / Training	.22 LR, 9mm (low recoil loads)
Vehicle / Barrier Use	.40 S&W, .357 SIG

Quick Reference for Federal HST JHP Loads (Standard Pressure)

Caliber	Bullet Weight	Velocity (fps)	Energy (ft-lbs)	Penetration	Expansion
9mm	124gr	1,150	364	14–16"	0.65"
.45 ACP	230gr	890	404	14–16"	0.72"
.40 S&W	180gr	1,010	408	14–15"	0.70"
.380 ACP	99gr	1,030	233	10–12"	0.58"

The Mathematics of Designing a Shooting Drill

A well-designed shooting drill must have a measurable standard. That standard comes from knowing what a competent shooter **should be able to accomplish within a specific time frame**. Drill design is not arbitrary—time and task must be calculated, evaluated, and tied directly to the desired training outcome.

Take the example of a **draw and fire drill**. A competent shooter should be able to:

- Draw from the holster, acquire the proper visual confirmation, and break the first shot in **1.5 seconds**.
- Fire follow-up shots at **0.5-second splits**, maintaining grip, managing recoil, resetting the trigger, and reacquiring the sight package.

This means that firing **three controlled rounds** (1.5s to first shot + 0.5s + 0.5s) can realistically be done in **2.5 seconds**. To set a fair standard, allow **3.0 seconds** as the drill time. This accounts for minor variances while keeping performance expectations high.

Another example is the **"Failure Drill" (two to the body, one to the head) at 7 yards**:

1. Draw and fire first body shot: **1.5 seconds**
2. Fire second body shot: **+0.5 seconds** (total 2.0s)
3. Transition eyes to head, move gun accordingly: **+1.5 seconds**
4. Fire final head shot: **+0.5 seconds** (total 4.0s)

So the mathematical standard is **4.0 seconds**. Compare this to institutional benchmarks: the U.S. Marshals allow **5.0 seconds** for a novice, while FLETC's Special Police Course allows **7.0 seconds**. By setting a professional-level standard at 4.0s, instructors ensure the drill has meaning and progression without inflating time limits to the point of losing training value.

Building Standards by Math and End-state

The process of drill design is straightforward:

1. **Define the End-state** – What specific skill must the shooter demonstrate?
2. **Calculate the Task** – Break down the sequence (draw, sights, trigger, recoil management, transitions).
3. **Set the Standard Time** – Add the component times, then establish the maximum time allowed for competent execution.
4. **Adjust for Novices** – Add approximately **20% more time** to allow learning while maintaining pressure.
5. **Refine for Progression** – Once the shooter meets the baseline, reduce time or increase accuracy demand to raise the standard.

Why Standards Matter

If too much time is allowed, the drill loses purpose and fails to measure competency. If too little time is allowed, the drill becomes a setup for failure. By using **mathematics as the backbone of drill design**, instructors can justify standards, explain expectations to students, and measure real progress.

A firearms instructor who understands this process is not just running shooters through drills—he is **developing performance through standards that are fair, challenging, and achievable**.

Core formula

Base Par (s)

Draw_to_First + (Shots_Total − 1)×Split + Transitions_Count×Transition_Time + Reloads_Count×Reload_Time + Movement_Time + Malfunction_Time

Tier multipliers

- Competent Par = Base Par × Accuracy_Factor
- Novice Par ≈ Competent × **1.20**
- Advanced Par ≈ Competent × **0.85**
- Expert Par ≈ Competent × **0.75**

Accuracy Factor (guide):

1.00 (A-zone / 8" at 3–7 yd) · 1.10 (B-8 9/10-ring) · 1.15 (3×5 head box/partials) · 1.25 (low light or SHO/WHO)

Two worked examples (using the formula)

- **Draw-3 @ 3/5/7**: Draw_to_First=1.5s, Shots_Total=3, Split=0.5s, no transitions → Base=**2.5s**. With Accuracy_Factor **1.20**, Competent Par=**3.0s**.
- **Failure Drill @ 7**: Draw_to_First=1.5s, Shots_Total=3, Split=0.5s, one transition=1.5s → Base=**4.0s**. Accuracy_Factor **1.00** → Competent Par=**4.0s**.

From the Team Room Wall-PLAXCO'S Shooting Standards

- ***Accuracy takes precedence over speed**. "The most important thing is to hit what you are shooting at. No matter what else happens, you must hit your target."
-
- ***Learn to apply your skills on demand**. "Consistent top performers in any sport have a thorough understanding of the basics and have learned to apply the principles at all times. Don't be distracted from the shooting."
-
- ***You must compete at your natural body speed**. "Don't attempt to speed up or slow down. You must learn to allow it to happen."
-
- ***Speed is economy of motion**. "Every move is directed toward gaining something. There is no wasted motion or effort."
-
- ***Speed will increase through practice; it is a byproduct of proper training and technique**. "You don't have to try to be fast. As your skill increases and you are able to execute at the subconscious level, speed increases naturally."
-
- ***Let the sights dictate your cadence of fire**. "Sight alignment is your speedometer– it shows you how fast you can or cannot go. If the sights are acceptably aligned, fire the shot. If the sights are not acceptably aligned, don't fire the shot until they are– whether it takes a quarter-second, half-second or two seconds."
-
- ***Learn what an acceptable sight picture is, and trigger squeeze for the required shot**. "Quality of sight alignment for a 15-yard shot is not as exact as for a 50-yard shot. You'd like to always see perfect sight alignment, but you must learn to accept less if it will still allow you to hit your target."
-
- ***Shoot one shot at a time. The next shot you are about to fire is the most important one of your life**. "Don't fall into the trap of thinking of strings of fire. A match [or a fight] is won shooting one shot at a time."
-
- ***When all else fails, align the sights and squeeze the prepped trigger**. No matter what else happens, if you align the sights and squeeze the prepped trigger, you will hit the target."

There is no such thing as an advanced gunfight…just gunfights in which the fundamentals were performed really well."

I leave you with this finial reflection,

Ecclesiastes 3:8
"A time to love and a time to hate, a time for war and a time for peace."

To live in peace, I must be prepared for war.
To protect love, I must be willing to confront hate.
The beast within me is disciplined, restrained, and under command—
released only when necessity calls.

Peace without strength is fragile.
Love without the will to defend it is fleeting.
I will not falter when danger comes.

I choose to be dangerous—
not reckless, but controlled;
not cruel, but resolute.
A dangerous man is a good man,
able to protect what he loves,
able to stand firm when others cannot.

Be that man.
Be dangerous.

www.ingramcontent.com/pod-product-compliance
Lightning Source LLC
Chambersburg PA
CBHW081327230426
43667CB00018B/2855